Seoul

Robert Storey

L ONELY PLANET PUBLICATIONS
M elbourne • Oakland • London • Paris

Seoul
3rd edition – October 1999
First published – May 1993

Published by
Lonely Planet Publications Pty Ltd ABN 36 005 607 983
90 Maribyrnong St, Footscray, Victoria 3011, Australia

Lonely Planet Offices
Australia Locked Bag 1, Footscray, Victoria 3011
USA 150 Linden St, Oakland, CA 94607
UK 10a Spring Place, London NW5 3BH
France 1 rue du Dahomey, 75011 Paris

Photographs
Many of the images in this guide are available for licensing from
Lonely Planet Images.
email: lpi@lonelyplanet.com.au

Front cover photograph
Traditional dance performance at Korea House, Seoul
(John Borthwick, Lonely Planet Images)

ISBN 0 86442 779 4

text & maps © Lonely Planet 1999
photos © photographers as indicated 1999

Printed by Colorcraft Ltd, Hong Kong

Contents – Text

Contents – Maps

The Author

Robert Storey

Robert has had a number of distinguished careers, including mon-keykeeper at a zoo and slot-machine repairman in a Las Vegas casino. It was during this era that he produced his first book, *How to Do Your Own Divorce in Nevada*, which sold nearly 200 copies. Since this wasn't enough to cover costs, Robert decided to skip the country and sought his fortune in Taiwan as an English teacher. But writing was in his blood, and he was soon flooding the Taiwanese market with various books.

Robert's *Taiwan On Your Own* attracted the attention of Lonely Planet, and was rehashed to become *Taiwan*. Since then, Robert has been involved in over a dozen LP projects, all to do with East Asian countries. His latest scheme – still a work in progress – is his first novel, *Life in the Fast Lane*.

FROM THE AUTHOR

I'd like to express my gratitude to a number of travellers, expats and Korean locals including Mark Tuttle, Patty (Jung Eun-an), Lee In-suk, Gary Rector, James Russell, Yune Sangjine, Helen Kim, Casey J Lartigue Jr, Rob Housley, David Ellis and Ken Kaliher.

This Book

The first edition of *Seoul* was written by Chris Tayor. Robert Storey undertook a major update for the second edition.

This third edition had Robert back on the Seoul trail, dodging traffic as he tracked down new hole-in-the-wall pubs, selected the best *bulgogi* restaurants and headed off to seldom-visited offshore islands.

FROM THE PUBLISHER

This edition was edited by Russ Kerr and proofed by Sally O'Brien, Chris Wyness and Justin Flynn. Jack Gavran was in charge of mapping, design and layout, with cartographic assistance from Chris Thomas.

Quentin Frayne overhauled the Language chapter, the climate chart was created by Tim Fitzgerald, Mick Weldon supplied the cartoons and Guillaume Roux designed the cover.

THANKS
Many thanks to the travellers who used the last edition and wrote to us with helpful hints, advice and interesting anecdotes. Your names appear in the back of this book.

Foreword

ABOUT LONELY PLANET GUIDEBOOKS

The story begins with a classic travel adventure: Tony and Maureen Wheeler's 1972 journey across Europe and Asia to Australia. Useful information about the overland trail did not exist at that time, so Tony and Maureen published the first Lonely Planet guidebook to meet a growing need.

From a kitchen table, then from a tiny office in Melbourne (Australia), Lonely Planet has become the largest independent travel publisher in the world, an international company with offices in Melbourne, Oakland (USA), London (UK) and Paris (France).

Today Lonely Planet guidebooks cover the globe. There is an ever-growing list of books and there's information in a variety of forms and media. Some things haven't changed. The main aim is still to help make it possible for adventurous travellers to get out there – to explore and better understand the world.

At Lonely Planet we believe travellers can make a positive contribution to the countries they visit – if they respect their host communities and spend their money wisely. Since 1986 a percentage of the income from each book has been donated to aid projects and human rights campaigns.

Updates Lonely Planet thoroughly updates each guidebook as often as possible. This usually means there are around two years between editions, although for more unusual or more stable destinations the gap can be longer. Check the imprint page (following the colour map at the beginning of the book) for publication dates.

Between editions up-to-date information is available in two free newsletters – the paper *Planet Talk* and email *Comet* (to subscribe, contact any Lonely Planet office) – and on our Web site at www.lonelyplanet.com. The *Upgrades* section of the Web site covers a number of important and volatile destinations and is regularly updated by Lonely Planet authors. *Scoop* covers news and current affairs relevant to travellers. And, lastly, the *Thorn Tree* bulletin board and *Postcards* section of the site carry unverified, but fascinating, reports from travellers.

Correspondence The process of creating new editions begins with the letters, postcards and emails received from travellers. This correspondence often includes suggestions, criticisms and comments about the current editions. Interesting excerpts are immediately passed on via newsletters and the Web site, and everything goes to our authors to be verified when they're researching on the road. We're keen to get more feedback from organisations or individuals who represent communities visited by travellers.

Lonely Planet gathers information for everyone who's curious about the planet – and especially for those who explore it first-hand. Through guidebooks, phrasebooks, activity guides, maps, literature, newsletters, image library, TV series and Web site we act as an information exchange for a worldwide community of travellers.

Research Authors aim to gather sufficient practical information to enable travellers to make informed choices and to make the mechanics of a journey run smoothly. They also research historical and cultural background to help enrich the travel experience and allow travellers to understand and respond appropriately to cultural and environmental issues.

Authors don't stay in every hotel because that would mean spending a couple of months in each medium-sized city and, no, they don't eat at every restaurant because that would mean stretching belts beyond capacity. They do visit hotels and restaurants to check standards and prices, but feedback based on readers' direct experiences can be very helpful.

Many of our authors work undercover, others aren't so secretive. None of them accept freebies in exchange for positive write-ups. And none of our guidebooks contains any advertising.

Production Authors submit their raw manuscripts and maps to offices in Australia, USA, UK or France. Editors and cartographers – all experienced travellers themselves – then begin the process of assembling the pieces. When the book finally hits the shops, some things are already out of date, we start getting feedback from readers and the process begins again …

WARNING & REQUEST

Things change – prices go up, schedules change, good places go bad and bad places go bankrupt – nothing stays the same. So, if you find things better or worse, recently opened or long since closed, please tell us and help make the next edition even more accurate and useful. We genuinely value all the feedback we receive. Julie Young coordinates a well travelled team that reads and acknowledges every letter, postcard and email and ensures that every morsel of information finds its way to the appropriate authors, editors and cartographers for verification.

Everyone who writes to us will find their name in the next edition of the appropriate guidebook. They will also receive the latest issue of *Planet Talk*, our quarterly printed newsletter, or *Comet*, our monthly email newsletter. Subscriptions to both newsletters are free. The very best contributions will be rewarded with a free guidebook.

Excerpts from your correspondence may appear in new editions of Lonely Planet guidebooks, the Lonely Planet Web site, *Planet Talk* or *Comet*, so please let us know if you *don't* want your letter published or your name acknowledged.

Send all correspondence to the Lonely Planet office closest to you:

Australia: Locked Bag 1, Footscray, Victoria 3011
USA: 150 Linden St, Oakland, CA 94607
UK: 10A Spring Place, London NW5 3BH
France: 1 rue du Dahomey, 75011 Paris

Or email us at: talk2us@lonelyplanet.com.au

For news, views and updates see our Web site: www.lonelyplanet.com

HOW TO USE A LONELY PLANET GUIDEBOOK

The best way to use a Lonely Planet guidebook is any way you choose. At Lonely Planet we believe the most memorable travel experiences are often those that are unexpected, and the finest discoveries are those you make yourself. Guidebooks are not intended to be used as if they provide a detailed set of infallible instructions!

Contents All Lonely Planet guidebooks follow roughly the same format. The Facts about the Destination chapters or sections give background information ranging from history to weather. Facts for the Visitor gives practical information on issues like visas and health. Getting There & Away gives a brief starting point for researching travel to and from the destination. Getting Around gives an overview of the transport options when you arrive.

The peculiar demands of each destination determine how subsequent chapters are broken up, but some things remain constant. We always start with background, then proceed to sights, places to stay, places to eat, entertainment, getting there and away, and getting around information – in that order.

Heading Hierarchy Lonely Planet headings are used in a strict hierarchical structure that can be visualised as a set of Russian dolls. Each heading (and its following text) is encompassed by any preceding heading that is higher on the hierarchical ladder.

Entry Points We do not assume guidebooks will be read from beginning to end, but that people will dip into them. The traditional entry points are the list of contents and the index. In addition, however, some books have a complete list of maps and an index map illustrating map coverage.

There may also be a colour map that shows highlights. These highlights are dealt with in greater detail in the Facts for the Visitor chapter, along with planning questions and suggested itineraries. Each chapter covering a geographical region usually begins with a locator map and another list of highlights. Once you find something of interest in a list of highlights, turn to the index.

Maps Maps play a crucial role in Lonely Planet guidebooks and include a huge amount of information. A legend is printed on the back page. We seek to have complete consistency between maps and text, and to have every important place in the text captured on a map. Map key numbers usually start in the top left corner.

Although inclusion in a guidebook usually implies a recommendation we cannot list every good place. Exclusion does not necessarily imply criticism. In fact there are a number of reasons why we might exclude a place – sometimes it is simply inappropriate to encourage an influx of travellers.

Introduction

Seoul is an intriguing city bent on transforming itself from the Yi Dynasty capital of the Hermit Kingdom to a major mover and shaker in the international world of trade and commerce. And sports too – the city hosted the Asian Games in 1986, the Summer Olympics in 1988 and hosts soccer's World Cup in 2002.

No other Korean city approaches the size and importance of Seoul, and it shows. The city has poured money into infrastructure, resulting in excellent transport and communication systems. Yet despite its tall buildings, neon lights and other modern intrusions, Seoul offers the visitor a wealth of cultural sights. The central city area is ringed with ancient royal palaces. Around the old eastern and southern city gates are enormous bustling markets stocked with everything from dried squid and ginseng to cellular phones and hiking supplies. Ten minutes from the high-rise buildings of the city centre, the back-streets of Insa-dong form a maze of traditional-style Korean houses and inns. On the other side of Namsan, the small peak that rises from the southern periphery of central Seoul, is the foreigner-oriented shopping and nightlife area of It'aewon.

Despite being one of the world's largest cities, Korea's capital is a remarkably safe and friendly place. Lost-looking foreigners wandering the streets are almost invariably approached by locals and asked if they need any help. Despite the nation's often unhappy dealings with foreign countries, the Koreans are almost without exception excellent hosts. The graciousness of Seoulites is often the warmest memory that foreign visitors have of the city.

Finally, perhaps the thing that strikes the first-time visitor most is Seoul's uncompromising Korean-ness. Don't be fooled by the ubiquitous fast-food barns, luxury department stores and the skyline: Seoul is a kimch'i-crunching, rough-at-the-edges, go-get-it Korean city, where the business-suited workers of commerce slurp back bowls of silkworm soup on the footpath. For the Koreans, Seoul is the centre of all things, and for the visitor it is *the* place to witness and experience the Korean drive to come to terms with a turbulent and fractured past.

Facts about Seoul

HISTORY

Neolithic sites have been discovered in the Seoul area, proving that it was inhabited as long ago as 4000 BC. However, Korea only starts to feature in Chinese records in the 1st century BC. At this time a renegade general fled from China and set up a kingdom called Chosŏn (literally 'Morning Freshness'), near present-day P'yŏngyang, capital of North Korea. Chosŏn was soon overpowered by the Chinese, and Chinese influence percolated into the peninsula.

What followed was called the Three Kingdoms Period (57 BC to 668 AD). Of the three kingdoms – Koguryŏ, Shilla and Paekche – the largest and probably earliest was Koguryŏ. Its borders extended far north of the present Chinese-Korean border and south as far as the Han River, which runs through modern Seoul. The south was dominated by the kingdoms of Shilla and Paekche. It is at this point that

Seoul starts to figure in Korean history, although it was to be a very long time before it came to pass under the name we know it by today.

The Paekche kingdom established its capital city at Wiryesong, present-day Sŏngnam, a town on the outskirts of contemporary Seoul. For some time, the Shilla kingdom in the south came to dominate Korea. Seoul lost its pre-eminence and was renamed Hanyang.

In 918 Wang Kŏn, a soldier from the Koguryŏ kingdom, clambered to the apex of political power and founded the Koryŏ Dynasty (918-1392), from which Korea takes its name. In 1231 the Mongols swept into Korea, but they permitted the Koryŏ king to retain his position.

Royal Seoul

In 1392, Yi Sŏng-gye, a Korean general sent to campaign against militant Ming Chinese in northern Korea, decided to throw in his luck with

Picasso's Quixote is long predated by this Three Kingdoms warrior figure.

the enemy. He turned his forces back on the Koryŏ capital and deposed the Korean king.

Yi Sŏng-gye, in keeping with his promoted status, changed his name to Yi T'ae-jo. Yi named his new dynasty Chosŏn, after the ancient kingdom, and in 1394 he moved his capital to Hanyang. The city became known unofficially as Seoul, a native Korean word meaning 'capital'. By 1404 the population of the new capital had already reached 100,000.

Yi T'ae-jo initiated great public works in Seoul, carried out land reforms and broke the back of the old gentry class. The neo-Confucianism of Ming Dynasty China was stressed at the expense of Buddhism, and Yi T'ae-jo established a Confucian examination system and civil service.

The embrace of Confucianism as a state ethic was also part of an attack on the power and wealth that Buddhist temples and monasteries had accumulated. Yi T'ae-jo drove the Buddhist monasteries out of the capital. It was only in 1895 that a state edict forbidding the presence of Buddhist monks in Seoul was relaxed.

Japanese & Manchu Invasions

Why do Koreans profess to hate the Japanese today? Japanese pirates *(waegu* in Korean*)* had been the scourge of eastern and southern Korea for centuries, but things really got hot when Hideyoshi Toyotomi attacked Korea in 1592. His forces met little resistance and quickly captured Seoul. Much of the city was destroyed and the royal family fled north. But a Korean admiral, Yi Sun-shin, used the new innovations of cannons and cladding his 'turtle ships' *(kŏbuksŏn)* in iron plates to achieve a stunning naval victory over the numerically stronger Japanese.

In the north, the Japanese forces met with a combined Chinese-Korean force that proved formidable. The Japanese retreated but, in the first of many acts that the Koreans consider unforgivable, they looted much of Korea's cultural heritage and forcibly took many of the country's best artisans back to Japan.

In 1636, eight years before they dealt China the same fate, the Manchus invaded

Korea. The Korean king quickly sent his family to Kanghwado, while he retreated to Namhansansŏng fortress, to the south of Seoul. Once again Seoul was ransacked. The Korean King Injo signed Korea over to the Manchus and made military contributions to the wars that brought the Manchus to power in China as the Qing Dynasty.

Japanese Return

Shaken by the turmoil of the early 17th century, Korea withdrew into itself and became known as the Hermit Kingdom (a term still appropriate for North Korea).

An alliance between the Korean king and the Chinese gave the Japanese an excuse to strike. In 1894 the Japanese attacked the Chinese fleet, achieving rapid victory. The Japanese gained wide-ranging influence over Korea. Anti-Japanese feeling continued to grow, and in 1897 King Kojong proclaimed himself the emperor of an independent Korea. The new Korean Empire was short-lived. In 1904 the Japanese embarked on the Russo-Japanese War over Tsarist Russia's occupation of Manchuria. Despite Korean declarations of neutrality, Japanese forces landed at Inch'ŏn and moved into Seoul. The Japan-Korea Protection Treaty was signed in 1905, effectively giving Japan control over much of Korea's affairs. On 29 August 1910 a Korean royal ordinance announced the annexation of Korea by the Japanese. The Japanese completely took over and spent the next 35 years trying to erase Korean culture.

Korean War

Japanese rule of Korea ended when Japan lost WWII. Rather than being granted full independence as expected by the Koreans, they were subjected to a period of trusteeship, with the US forces in control of the South and the Russians running the show north of the 38th parallel. The plan was for a joint US-USSR commission to work with local political parties to set up a government for the peninsula. In reality, the increasing frostiness of US-USSR relations led to an institutionalisation of the North-South split.

The Soviet dictator, Joseph Stalin, installed a young Korean officer named Kim Il-sung to take charge of rapidly communising the north. It had been the plan of the United Nations that nationwide democratic elections be held. In 1948 the South went ahead with UN-sponsored elections when the North refused to let UN personnel enter their territory. Negotiations failed to resolve the problem, and the temporary division became permanent as neither side was willing to yield.

Both the USA and USSR pulled most of their troops out of Korea by the end of 1948. On 25 June 1950, approximately 100,000 North Korean troops invaded the South.

It only took the North Korean army three days to capture Seoul, and South Korean troops were forced back into a tiny enclave around Pusan. A United Nations' command with the USA as executive agent moved to the assistance of the South. US General Douglas MacArthur executed a masterful amphibious landing at Inch'ŏn, cutting off the North Korean supply lines. Seoul was quickly recaptured and the retreating North Korean army was pursued into China.

Celebrations of this quick victory proved premature. Chairman Mao Zedong of China sent a force of 'volunteers' to the aid of North Korea, and UN forces were once again pushed back south of Seoul. Negotiations over a truce dragged on for two years, and when the truce finally came, Korea lay in ruins and was once again divided at the 38th parallel.

Postwar Years
Economic recovery in the South was slow, hampered largely by the economic ineptitude of President Syngman Rhee and his associates. Despite widespread unpopularity and political opposition, Rhee managed to hang onto the reins of power through to 1961. Protests finally forced the resignation of the cabinet, and Rhee went into exile.

Despite the fact that the government had been toppled from power by a popular movement, democracy was to be denied to South Koreans. In 1961, a group of army officers led by Park Chung-hee wrested power from the government in a bloodless coup. Park retired from the army two years later and stood successfully for election.

If there is anyone who can be called 'the father' of modern Korea, it is Park. Educated in Japan and more fluent in the Japanese language than Korean, he set about moulding Korean society in Japan's image. Hostile to foreign investors and imported goods, Park's military-style government borrowed cash and technology from abroad, and turned Korea into an export machine.

Park survived the 1967 elections creditably, but in 1971 his narrowly defeated opponent, Kim Dae-jung, cried foul and protests resulted. Park's response was to declare martial law, shut down the universities and enforce complete press censorship. Park became increasingly reclusive after a failed assassination attempt took the life of his wife. Park was assassinated in 1979 by Kim Chae-kyu, the head of his own secret police.

1980s to the Present
On 17 May 1980 General Chun Doo-hwan effected another military coup. The coup sparked nationwide protests (with repression to match), but in the southern city of Kwangju things got particularly out of hand when protesters seized an armoury. Chun's troops responded with bullets, and the result was the 'Kwangju Massacre', later to be Chun's undoing.

Chun's dictatorship was more benign than Park's, though dissenters were dealt with harshly. The opposition – principally the three Kims: Kim Dae-jung, Kim Young-sam and Kim Jong-pil (a prime minister under Park) – were arrested.

Against rising protests, Chun remained steadfast in seeing through his term of office until 1988, when he promised a peaceful transfer of power would be effected. In early 1987, with the Seoul 1988 Olympics just around the corner, widespread rioting began to convince the rest of the world that perhaps a Seoul Olympics really wasn't such a good idea. Chun sidestepped the problem by resigning. His chosen successor, Roh Tae-woo, came up with a package of reforms that included direct presidential elections.

Kim Dae-jung and Kim Young-sam formed a new opposition party, promising to field a single presidential candidate. As it happened, neither of the two could bear to see the honours go to the other and both ran. The split in the opposition allowed Roh Tae-woo to win the presidency with only 35% of the vote.

Kim Young-sam merged his opposition party with the ruling Democratic Liberal Party (DLP) to form the Grand National Party (GNP) and won the presidency in December 1992. The election was considered the cleanest in Korean history. With little left to protest, much of the radical student movement dissolved. But Hanchongnyon – a hardcore leftist student organisation with links to North Korea – has remained committed to the overthrow of capitalism and the South Korean government.

After evidence surfaced in 1995 that former presidents Chun and Roh had pocketed millions of dollars in elicit 'campaign contributions', there was a massive public outcry to prosecute both men for bribery and their role in the 1980 Kwangju Massacre. Although he resisted at first, President Kim finally supported the necessary legislation to extend the statute of limitations. In August 1996 Chun was given the death sentence and Roh was sentenced to 22 years. Another 14 military officers were prosecuted for their roles at Kwangju, and nine business tycoons were convicted on bribery charges. Chun's death sentence was not carried out, and none of the nine tycoons were imprisoned. In December 1997 President Kim Young-sam granted a presidential pardon to Chun and Roh, and the two were released from prison.

The year 1997 started out in chaos when half a million unionised workers went on strike and took to the streets in protest against a new labour law. The new law made it legal for companies to lay-off workers – previously, South Korean labourers could expect lifetime employment by whatever company hired them. In the end, the government had to water down the law and the lay-off clause was postponed for two years.

With the strike settled, Kim Young-sam's government hoped for a peaceful year, but it was not to be. A series of corporate bankruptcies and the beginning of the great Asian economic crisis kept the country in a state of havoc. Major corruption scandals swept the president's friends, and even his son, into jail.

On 18 December 1997 a presidential election swept Kim Dae-jung into office, the first time in Korea's history that an opposition candidate won the presidency. Almost immediately he found himself beleaguered by the country's economic problems and resistance to his necessary reforms.

Economic issues have also determined President Kim's reunification policy towards North Korea. With recession, earlier confidence that the South could simply absorb the North in a Germany-style union has been replaced by Kim's so-called 'sunshine policy' of fostering a warm climate of mutual trust, mostly through symbolic (and cost-free) gestures. The South Korean government seems to remain less trustful of its own citizens, however – the dreaded National Security Law, used by successive dictatorships to silence opposition (including Kim's, not so long ago) in the name of 'anti-communism', was still in force at the time of this writing.

GEOGRAPHY

Seoul is in the north-west corner of South Korea, 37° 30' north of the equator. The city covers an area of 605 sq km and is 32km from Inch'ŏn, its port on the Yellow Sea – called Sŏ-hae (West Sea) in Korean. Large mountains dominate the horizon both to the north and south of the centre, but most of the city is below 100m elevation.

CLIMATE

Korea has four seasons, and a notable feature is the summer and winter monsoons (seasonal winds). Seoul enjoys its best weather from September through November.

The autumn period is a time of little rain and mild temperatures. The winter monsoon is characterised by an icy Siberian

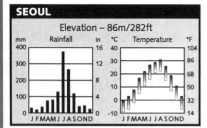

SEOUL

Elevation – 86m/282ft

wind blowing from the north. Winter is very cold but at least it's dry. Temperatures in January average -5°C. The worst of the cold is usually over by mid-March.

Spring temperatures are as mild as in autumn, but the springtime is more prone to rain. Summer is not a particularly great time to be in Seoul. The summer monsoon brings hot and muggy weather, with lots of rain. Occasionally destructive typhoons are also a possibility from late June through September.

ECOLOGY & ENVIRONMENT

South Korea has taken some praiseworthy steps in recent years to clean up the environment. The Han River was at one time little more than an open-air sewer. Nowadays, the Han-gang is suitable for swimming and boating. Korea's streets and parks were at one time noted for their bright decorations of plastic bags and discarded bottles, but a public education campaign has produced excellent results.

On the downside, the rapid increase in motor vehicles has led to serious air pollution which the locals insist on calling 'fog'. Foreign residents have some less polite words for it.

FLORA

Seoul didn't get to be the capital for nothing. Korea's best agricultural soils are alluvial and are found in river valleys and coastal plains. It was for this reason that Seoul was able to support such a large population.

The upper slopes of surrounding mountains are covered with coniferous forests, including pine, fir, larch and spruce trees. Deciduous trees include aspen, elm and maple trees. Unfortunately, urban development has wiped out most of the natural forest within the city limits.

FAUNA

The Seoul area was once home to such wild animals as deer, lynx, wolves, bears, leopards and tigers. These creatures now exist only in the city zoo. The creatures you are most likely to see are birds and squirrels in the parks.

NATIONAL PARKS

Just in the northern suburbs of Seoul is Puk'ansan National Park, a stunning area of steep granite peaks and cliffs which also includes an ancient fortress and several temples.

In addition, there is Namhansansŏng Provincial Park to the south-east of Seoul.

A number of other attractive mountain areas surrounding Seoul are worth visiting even if they lack official national park status. This would include Suraksan (Mt Surak) and Kwanaksan (Mt Kwanak).

GOVERNMENT & POLITICS

Every district of Seoul (Chung-gu, Chongno-gu etc) has its own elected mayor, thus giving the city a total of 22 mayors. It all sounds very democratic, but local governments only have limited power. Crucially, the central government still controls the purse strings – even education is nationally controlled.

ECONOMY

South Korea in general, and Seoul in particular, has witnessed an amazing rags-to-riches story over the past four decades. Rising from the debris of the Korean War, South Korea has gone on to join Hong Kong, Taiwan and Singapore as one of Asia's 'economic tigers'. Or at least that was the case until 1997, when the tigers all suffered a serious setback known as the 'Asian Economic Crisis'. Currencies and stock markets crashed all around the region, as panicked foreign speculators suddenly got wind of the fact that they had been pouring money into dodgy 'bubble' investments, such as real estate, that were ridiculously overvalued.

Korea was forced to go hat in hand to the International Monetary Fund (IMF) for a bail-out loan. The loan came with a number of stringent conditions attached, including a requirement to raise interest rates to 'protect' the value of the Korean currency. The same conditions were applied to other countries in the region, and the results have been mixed. Many economists now say that the higher interest rates did more damage than good, and the IMF has been put on the defensive. Happy to have foreigners to blame, almost all Koreans refer to their current economic difficulties as 'the IMF crisis'. Indeed, you can see signs all around Seoul advertising 'IMF sales', 'IMF lunch specials' and the Koreans have even produced a music CD entitled *IMF Power Hits*.

Unlike the other tigers, the South Korean economy is engineered by a bloated bureaucracy that controls everything from the flavour of ice cream to the price of ginseng. Another key feature of Korea's economy are the *chaebŏl*, huge family-run conglomerates which are close cousins to Japan's notorious *zaibatsu*. Officially there are 30 chaebŏl. The top five, Hyundai, Samsung, Daewoo, LG (Lucky Goldstar) and SK (Sunkyong), account for more than a third of the total sales of all South Korean companies and 50% of the country's exports.

The chaebŏl have traditionally depended on cheap government-backed loans and subsidies for their survival. Yet ironically, the chaebŏl have become so gigantic that they are now 'too large to fail' – the government simply cannot let them go under despite the monstrous debts that these companies have run up. Furthermore, the chaebŏl have gained so much political influence that it's difficult to tell whether the country is being run by the government or big business. Thus, the cynical term 'Korea Inc' is not a joke.

Given the structural impediments to recovery from the 'Asian economic flu', by early 1999 some chaebŏl were giving lip service to reforms aimed at encouraging small and medium-sized firms. Small wonder: reform proposals include the threat to workers of widespread layoffs (Korea's unemployment rate by April 1999 was already a record 8.7%), and further reduction in the power of unions. In other words, IMF-style reforms may be less of a threat to the way Koreans have done business than many ardent nationalists suppose.

While some signs of modest economic 'positive growth' have begun to appear, President Kim's biggest challenge probably remains to work out how palatable reforms might co-exist with Korea's dependence on the big-family cartels.

POPULATION & PEOPLE

Especially since the end of the Korean War, Seoul has been a magnet for people and the city has grown exponentially. In 1936 the population was 600,000. Now it's officially 10.6 million, but the figure rises to about 18 million when you throw in the urbanised areas just beyond the city limits. By some estimates, this makes Seoul the fifth largest city in the world.

Considering that South Korea has a population of 45 million, this means that about 24% of the nation's population lives in Seoul proper, or around 40% if you include Seoul's environs.

The population is very homogeneous. Seoul does have a small Chinese community. The number of foreign residents in Seoul (both legal and illegal) is around 200,000, but many of them are ethnic-Koreans.

Far more significant than the non-Korean population is the growing imbalance between the sexes. Using modern ultrasound techniques, many Korean parents are detecting the sex of their unborn children and terminating female foetuses. On average, elementary schools now report that only 48% of their students are female, and the shortage of females is increasing. The whole problem boils down to the fact that Korean couples want to have sons, not daughters. The growing gender discrepancy could have serious social implications in the future.

EDUCATION

Han'gŭl (as distinct from *hanja*, the old system of writing in Chinese characters) has been a boon to literacy in Korea. The literacy rate in South Korea has now reached 96%. For most Koreans, 12 years of education is the norm (from age 6 to 18 years).

Gaining entrance to a university is a formidable task and students are badgered for years by their parents to prepare for the much-feared entrance exams. Preparation begins at an early age, so getting into a good elementary school is important. One reason why virtually all Koreans want to live in Seoul is because the best schools are there. The 'examination hell' has profound effects on Korean society. Pity the poor middle school students who must spend all evening, weekends and holidays studying. The final irony is that those students who don't commit suicide and successfully pass the entrance exams can then look forward to a four year study-free holiday – university students are practically guaranteed to graduate.

Foreign Schools

There are several schools in Seoul catering to the children of expat workers, the Seoul Foreign School being the largest. You can contact these schools as follows:

Centennial Christian School
  (☎ 773 8460) 2-22 Namsan-dong, Chung-gu
French School
  (☎ 535 1158) San 85-24 Panp'o-dong,
  Soch'o-gu
Hanyong School of Foreign Language
  (☎ 429 0360) 166 Sang-il-dong, Kangdong-gu
Samyuk Foreigners' School
  (☎ 248 8682) San 6-2 Hwigyong-dong,
  Tongdaemun-gu
Seoul Academy
  (☎ 554 1690) 988-5 Taech'i-dong,
  Kangnam-gu
Seoul Foreign School
  (☎ 335 5101) 55 Yonhui-dong, Sodaemun-gu
Seoul German School
  (☎ 792 0797) 4-13 Hannam-dong, Yongsan-gu
Seoul International School
  (☎ 233 4551/2) San 32-16 Pokchong-dong,
  Chung-gu
Seoul Liberty Foreigners' School
  (☎ 792 4116/7) 260-7 Pogwang-dong,
  Yongsan-gu

ARTS
Music & Dance

The traditional music of Korea can be broadly divided into court, religious and folk music. All three have associated dance forms. Court music employs an orchestra whose members remain seated on the ground throughout the performance. For the most part, court music was an accompaniment to Confucian ceremonies. The music tends to be slow and sombre, and relies heavily on wind and string instruments.

The two principal forms of religious music and dance are very different. Buddhist chanting is repetitious, soothing and somewhat eerie. On the other hand, music performed as

A Modern Tradition

Samulnori falls into the broad category of 'folk dance and music'. It is considered the definitive traditional Korean 'farmer's dance', yet it has a short history.

'Samulnori' was the name adopted by four musicians who formed a band in 1978. *Sa* means 'four', *mul* means 'musical instruments' and *nori* means 'playing'. The four musicians – Kim Young-bae, Choi Tae-hyun, Kim Duk-su and Lee Chong-dae – played four traditional Korean percussion instruments. Their instruments were, respectively, the *kkwaenggwari* (a small gong), *ching* (large gong), *changgu* (hourglass drum) and *puk* (large barrel drum).

Samulnori was an attempt to recreate an old tradition of folk music and dance, in which wandering entertainers went from village to village to perform for local audiences (who were mostly farmers).

While the original Samulnori group no longer exists (Kim Young-bae died in 1985 and the other performers have gone their separate ways), the term 'Samulnori' has been adopted by other bands who continue to play the same traditional instruments. Thus, in a remarkably short time, Samulnori has been embraced as one of Korea's folk arts, and is hugely popular.

Piwon (Secret Garden) at the rear of Ch'angdŏkkung is perhaps Korea's finest garden.

Tiled roofs complement the country's four seasons and once helped uphold the cosmic order.

You can leave your hat on – a clean and well kept hat traditionally indicated that a Korean man was a Confucian gentleman who did not involve himself in rowdy behaviour.

an accompaniment to Shamanistic rituals is very much of the boom-crash variety. There has been a good deal of cross-pollination between religious and folk dances, with folk dance absorbing the postures and movements of shamanistic rituals. Certain Buddhist dance forms have also been secularised so that they are now performed by young women in bright, traditional attire.

Film

Korean films are seldom subtitled in English, which definitely limits their appeal to foreign audiences.

Foreign films (English dialogue, Korean subtitles) dominate the market to such an extent that the government has felt compelled to 'encourage' the production of Korean films. Cinemas are forced to limit foreign films to 60% of the total shown. The problem is that even the 40% of the movies which must be Korean fail to attract sufficient customers. Indeed, the cinemas have on occasions had to subsidise the Korean film industry with box office revenues gained from showing foreign films.

However, things are starting to look up for the Korean movie industry. In the past, one reason why Korean-produced films weren't successful was that they are carefully censored for political content. True, foreign films also have to get past the censors, but this is less of a problem with political content since foreign films are rarely about Korea. The good news is that Korea has lightened up considerably in recent years, and censorship is no longer the bugaboo it once was.

Starting from the early 1990s, South Korean cinema has experienced something of a renaissance. Some of the country's better-known directors include Hong Sang-soo, Jang Sun-woo and Im Kwon-taek. Unfortunately, Seoul does not as yet have an international film festival, but the southern port of Pusan (South Korea's second largest city) holds one every October.

Theatre

While modern drama (western and western-inspired plays etc) is very popular in Seoul's many small, student-oriented theatres, traditional folk forms remain the core of Korean theatre.

P'ansori is a folk narrative form that often gets its laughs at the expense of the ruling elite, snubbing a nose at the values that keep social hierarchies intact.

Sandaenori (mask dance) has enjoyed a very long history in Korea. It has been an art form at least since the 12th century (under the Koryŏ Dynasty), but it may have existed earlier. The masks are made from the wood of the alder tree, and are meant to convey emotion (anger, sorrow, joy, laughter) as well as social status.

Masks usually represent humans, but sometimes animals and supernatural beings. There are many designs – some masks have nostrils, others have mouths that open and close. Troupes of mask dancers once went from village to village to entertain locals, most of whom were poor farmers. The performances often parodied the cruel ironies of life, making it a popular rebellion of sorts against the privileged classes. Buddhist and Shamanist ritual was often incorporated into the show. Audience participation was common, and performances typically lasted for hours (sometimes almost all night).

Sandaenori is still a popular art form, though one has to wonder why there aren't more parodies of Korea's current crop of politicians.

Ceramics & Pottery

Examples of pottery dating back to the Paekche period have been discovered, but Korean pottery was not to truly come of age until the Koryŏ period. From the 16th century Korean pottery was especially admired by Japanese schools of *chanoyu* (tea ceremony in Japanese; the Korean word is *tado*).

Celadon pottery is perhaps the best known of all Koryŏ cultural achievements. It owes its origins to China, but Korean glazing techniques won the admiration of the Chinese themselves. In the later Chosŏn Dynasty, potters turned to the production of blue and white porcelains and a form of white celadon ware.

Painting

The earliest examples of Korean painting are to be found mainly in Japanese collections. The Paekche and Shilla kingdoms are thought to have produced a great wealth of Buddhist-inspired art, but very little of it remains. Korean techniques of the time, such as painting against a gold background, were particularly influential in Japan, and Korean originals were highly valued there. The full extent of Korean Buddhist art, however, will probably never be known. The vast majority of it fell prey to Korea's turbulent history, and with the founding of the Chosŏn Dynasty, Buddhist influences were eschewed in the official embrace of neo-Confucianism.

The Chosŏn Dynasty saw a dramatic shift in the visual arts towards secular themes much influenced by Chinese forms. Chinese landscapes were the most prevalent, but court scenes and portraits were also common. As in China, painters were also expected to be calligraphers.

SOCIETY & CONDUCT
Traditional Culture

South Korea is probably the most Confucian nation in Asia, even more so than China, where Confucianism originated. At the heart of Confucian doctrine are the Five Relations. These prescribe behaviour between ruler and subject, father and son, husband and wife, old and young and between friends. This structuring of relationships is very important in making sense of Korean society.

All relationships require a placement of some kind in order for one party to determine how to behave with respect towards the other. Bear in mind the Korean concept of 'face' – the term *kibun* is often heard in this context. Efforts are made to smooth over potential problems, such as remarks that could lead to political disagreements. If someone says something silly, there will be at most an embarrassed laugh before someone steers the topic on to safer ground. Arguments, or any situation that is going to lead to one party having to back down, will involve 'a loss of face' for both parties, a disruption of harmonious kibun, and this is a big no-no.

Until fairly recently, Korean marriages were always arranged. In modern Korea, couples generally marry for romantic reasons, but this should not obscure the fact that family approval remains of paramount importance. All women are expected to be virgins when they marry, and those who have already lost their virginity often secretly have it surgically 'restored'.

Until quite recently, one traditional complication for young couples was the Confucian stricture that forbade marriage within a clan. The definition of 'clan' is somewhat vague – to strict Confucianists anyone with the same surname should not marry. As there are only a few hundred surnames in Korea, this had tended to limit marriage prospects (about 20% of Koreans are surnamed 'Kim'!).

Fortunately, the law was never that strict, but all people with the same surname from the same community (such as all the Kangnŭng Kims, for example) could not marry – to do so would be to commit incest. The legal restrictions against intra-clan marriages were lifted in 1988, much to the consternation of Confucianists. The new law permits marriage to anyone not related as a second cousin or closer. However, there is still strong family pressure not the marry anyone who is considered part of the 'clan'.

Dos & Don'ts

Shoes Off In places where the floors are polished wood or covered with *tatami*-style mats (and this includes many restaurants and hotels), shoes must be removed before entering the room. In some cases you remove your shoes at the front entrance and exchange them for a pair of flip-flops (thongs) or slippers. If this is the case, you will see a big pile of shoes at the entrance.

It's not unknown for shoes to go missing in Seoul, especially at the budget hotels where some destitute backpackers rip off their fellow travellers. You may want to take your shoes into your room and put them in the shoe rack (often provided) or on top of some newspapers.

No Red Ink It's generally not a good idea to write a note to somebody in red ink. In the not-too-distant past, this would be regarded as a serious insult as it conveys a message of unfriendliness. The younger generation is not too concerned about this, but it's best to be safe and use blue or black ink.

Unlucky Number It probably won't be long before you notice that most Korean hotels do not have a 4th floor. That's because the word meaning 'four' *(sa)* sounds just like the Korean pronunciation of the *hanja* (Chinese character) for 'death' (the native Korean word for death is *chugŭm*).

Also, Koreans see nothing funny about the 'gallows humour' that some western writers employ. In general, anything to do with death (funerals, ghosts etc) are topics to be avoided in conversation.

Gift Giving It's a custom to bring along a small gift when visiting somebody at their home. It can be almost anything – flowers, chocolates, fruit, a book, a bottle of liquor, tea etc. It's also appropriate to have your offering giftwrapped.

When presented with a gift, your host may at first refuse it. This doesn't necessarily mean he or she doesn't want the gift, but the idea is to not look greedy. You should insist that they take it, and they should do so 'reluctantly'. For the same reason, the recipient of a gift is not supposed to open the package immediately, but rather put it aside and open it later.

If you are invited to a Korean wedding, you should not take gifts but rather money. Approximately W30,000 to W50,000 is now customary. The money should be put in a white envelope. Write your name on the envelope, along with a few upbeat words like 'Congratulations!' or 'Happiness!'

Body Language Making a circle with your forefinger and thumb (the western symbol for OK) signifies 'money' to Koreans. The thumb sticking out between the forefinger and middle finger in a fist is an obscene gesture.

Food Etiquette

Like the Japanese, Koreans have a social taboo against eating while walking down a street or riding on a bus or subway. This might lead you to wonder what you are supposed to do when you purchase snacks from a vendor's pushcart. The answer is you stand next to the pushcart and eat it there. You are not expected to walk down the street while munching away. True, young people tend to break this taboo, especially when it comes to munching ice cream cones and hot dogs, and eating on long-distance bus and train rides is perfectly acceptable (but not on the subway). The principle to remember is that Koreans regard eating as a social occasion, and it's rude to eat in places where people normally do not take meals together.

Rice is normally eaten with a spoon and the rice bowl is left on the table as you eat. This is exactly the opposite of Chinese etiquette, where the rice bowl is held near the face and the rice shovelled into the mouth with chopsticks.

Leaving your chopsticks or spoon stuck upright in your bowl of rice is a definite no-no. This is a gesture of symbolic significance when making offerings of food to the dead.

When handing something to somebody, always use both hands. It's also polite to accept something with two hands rather than just one.

Head bowing is a common way to show respect. It's especially important to give a big bow to elderly people on special days, such as New Years day.

The western hand signal for motioning somebody to come to you (with the palm facing up and fluttering the fingers) is very rude to Koreans. The palm should face down (fingers pointed to the ground) and then flutter. If in doubt, ask a Korean friend to show you.

If a Korean commits some obvious blunder (the waiter spills coffee on you etc), he or she may give you a big grin or even laugh nervously. The smile is offered as an apology, an attempt to smooth things over. It does not mean that you are being ridiculed and you should not get angry.

RELIGION
Counting souls in Korea is hardly an exact science – many people see nothing contradictory in professing to adhere to several faiths at once. For what it's worth, statistically about half of all South Koreans profess to be religious sceptics. The other half is mostly Buddhist and Christian, with a smattering of Confucianism and Shamanism.

Buddhism
Buddhism entered Korea from China around the 4th century AD. About 25% of the South Korean population regard themselves as practicing Buddhists. There are 18 Buddhist schools in Korea, but the largest by far is the Chogye school, with its headquarters in Seoul's Chogyesa temple. The Chogye school represents around 90% of Korean Buddhists. Next in size is the T'aego school, representing about 7% of the total. Headquarters for the T'aego school is in Seoul at Pongwonsa, a temple close to Ehwa Women's University.

Christianity
Another 25% of South Korea's population are practicing Christians. Nowhere else in Asia, with the exception of the Philippines, have proselytising missionaries been so successful. There are now over 100 Protestant denominations in South Korea, while about one in four of the country's Christians are Catholic.

Confucianism
Confucianism is not a religion but a system of ethics of Chinese origin. You may come across Confucianists in temples or even on the streets of Seoul – generally elderly bearded men wearing a small hat. While these hardcore practitioners represent less than 1% of the population and are dying out, the impact of their ideas is still solidly embedded in South Korean society. Much of the underlying conservatism of Korean culture is essentially Confucianist in nature.

Shamanism
Shamanism originated in central Asia and remains a small but active cultural force in Korea today. Shamanism is not an organised religion. It has no temples, no body of scriptures or written texts. Nonetheless, it is an important part of religious experience in Korea. Central to shamanism is the *mudang*, who is as an intermediary between the living and spirit worlds. The mediating is carried out through a *kut*, a ceremony that includes dance, song and even dramatic narrative. Mudang are almost always female. Official records claim that there are 40,000 registered mudang in South Korea.

Practicing shamanists probably represent less than 1% of Korea's population, but it is not uncommon even for modernised urban elites to call on a mudang when disturbing signs (recurring nightmares etc) appear.

Shamanist wood carvings (used as spirit guardian posts in villages) are found at a number of venues in Seoul, including modern versions which are increasing in popularity (even leftist radicals have adopted them to their cause).

Ch'ondogyo
This is a home-grown Korean religion with a short history. Ch'ondogyo contains Buddhist, Confucian and even Christian elements. It originally grew out of the Tonghak ('Eastern learning') movement that emerged in 1860, embracing the idea of equality between all human beings, a unique concept in the neo-Confucian order of the time. The religion claims around 60,000 followers.

Religious Services
There are prayers in English, Arabic and Korean at the Korean Islam Mosque (Map 8, ☎ 794 7307) on Friday at 1 pm. Other prayer sessions are in Korean and Arabic only. The mosque is in It'aewon.

The Lotus Lantern Buddhist Centre (☎ 735 5347) has Buddhist ceremonies in English every Sunday at 6.30 pm. You can also pursue the topic of Korean Buddhism at Chogyesa temple (☎ 720 1390), but only Korean is spoken here.

Christian churches easily outnumber Buddhist temples in Seoul, but most services are in Korean. Churches with English-language services include the following:

Adventist
  Seoul Adventist Hospital
  (☎ 967 0934) Hwikyong-dong, east of
  Ch'ŏngnyangni station
Anglican
  Anglican Cathedral
  (☎ 730 6611) in front of the British Embassy
  in Chong-dong
Baptist
  Yongsan Baptist Church
  (☎ 796 0284) near the Crown Hotel in
  It'aewon
  Seoul International Baptist Church
  (☎ 785 5970, 780 6268) Yŏŭido

Catholic
  Franciscan Chapel
  (☎ 793 2070) Hannam Village Apartments
  Myŏng-dong Cathedral
  (☎ 774 3891)
First Methodist
  (☎ 753 0001) 34 Chong-dong, Chung-gu,
  near Tŏksugung (Tŏksu Palace)
Hallelujah Christian (Inter-denominational)
  Korea Torch Mission Centre
  (☎ 574 9483) Yangjae-dong, Sŏch'o-gu
Lutheran
  Hannam Village Chapel
  (☎ 7913 7441)
Methodist
  (☎ 546 0151) Shinsa-dong, Kangnam-gu
Mormon
  (☎ 232 3637) Shindang-dong
Presbyterian
  Chunghyun Presbyterian Church
  (☎ 552 8200) Yŏksam-dong, Kangnam-gu
  (same block as the Seoul Renaissance
  Hotel)
  Yŏngnak Presbyterian Church
  (☎ 274 6311) Ch'o-dong, Chung-gu
  Somang Hope Presbyterian Church
  (☎ 546 5971) Apkujŏng-dong, Kangnam-gu.

Facts for the Visitor

WHEN TO GO

When you visit depends on your tastes. Most people like the Korean autumn, when the skies are clear and the forests turn into an astonishing riot of colours. Winter is also a beautiful season if you can tolerate the subarctic cold – the temple roofs draped in snow are particularly photogenic. The onset of spring brings a short-lived but beautiful cherry blossom season. The best that can be said for the rainy summer is that at least you won't need to carry a lot of clothes.

Major public holidays can be a real drag in Seoul. Stores close, buses and trains fill to overflowing, hotels raise their rates and sightseeing places swarm with camera-clicking tourists. In this respect, the worst time to visit is during the Lunar New Year and Ch'usŏk (see the Public Holidays & Special Events section later in this chapter for the exact dates).

ORIENTATION

The most important sightseeing and accommodation part of Seoul is the **central city** area, with **Namsan** mountain forming the southern perimeter of this area. The tourist shopping and entertainment area of **It'ae-won** is on the south side of Namsan. South of It'aewon, the **Han-gang** (Han River) winds its way through the city, effectively severing it in two. The **Kangnam** area (also called Yŏngdong) on the south bank is considered Seoul's ritziest area, where every

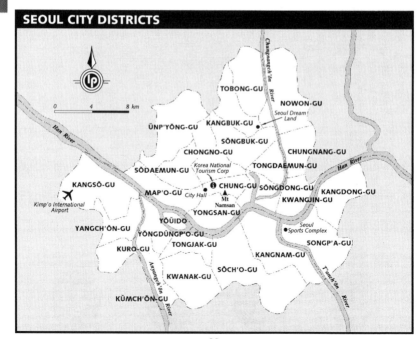

SEOUL CITY DISTRICTS

TOBONG-GU

NOWON-GU

Seoul Dream Land

ÚNP'YŎNG-GU   KANGBUK-GU

SŎNGBUK-GU

CHONGNO-GU   CHUNGNANG-GU

Korea National Tourism Corp

SŎDAEMUN-GU   TONGDAEMUN-GU

KANGSŎ-GU

MAP'O-GU City Hall   CHUNG-GU SŎNGDONG-GU   KANGDONG-GU

Mt Namsan   KWANGJIN-GU

Kimp'o International Airport

YONGSAN-GU

YŎUIDO

YANGCH'ŎN-GU   YŎNGDŬNGP'O-GU

Seoul Sports Complex

TONGJAK-GU   SONGP'A-GU

KURO-GU   KANGNAM-GU

SŎCH'O-GU

KWANAK-GU

KÙMCH'ŎN-GU

Han River

Changnangch'ŏn River

Han River

Tonch'ŏn River

Anyangch'ŏn River

0   4   8 km

Street Savvy

The most maddening thing about Seoul is that written addresses are all but useless. As much as the Koreans seem to detest Japan, they dutifully adhere to the highly dysfunctional Japanese addressing system which was imposed on Korea during the Japanese occupation era.

A written address is useful for receiving mail, but it's nearly impossible to locate a house from its address alone. Addresses are given according to an arbitrarily allocated number within a block of land. Just showing an address to a taxi driver will at best get you to within a few blocks of where you want to go, but then you may have a long and fruitless search on foot. It's not surprising that business name cards usually have maps drawn on the back side.

Still, there is a bare-bones addressing system and it helps to learn it. Seoul is divided into 26 districts known as *gu*, and 527 small neighbourhoods called *dong*. Narrowing an address down this far is not particularly difficult – you just need to look at a map (though you'll never find a map index).

The problem arises when you're looking for, say, the Korean National Tourism Organisation (KNTO) which is at 10 Ta-dong, Chung-gu. All this address tells you is that KNTO is in the Ta-dong area of Chung-gu (Central District). Unfortunately, Ta-dong is a sprawling maze of skyscrapers and narrow alleys. The address gives no clue that KNTO is in fact on a major boulevard called Ch'ŏnggyech'ŏnno. At least we can be grateful that Ch'ŏnggyech'ŏnno has a name (most streets don't), though you still won't find any signs labelling Ch'ŏnggyech'ŏnno (or any other street), nor does the building even have a number written on it.

Without street names or signs – or a hand-drawn map – how does one find an address? Seoulites have a simple way: call and ask the office staff to fax a map to you. This is one reason why fax machines are so prevalent in Seoul. Failing that, find a local police box or tourist information booth and ask them. More than likely you'll be told the name of the building (if any) – not that most buildings have a sign outside indicating its name either.

A few more address terms are worth learning. The word for boulevard or large street is *no* or *ro*. Thus, Chongno means Chong St, Ŭlchiro is Ŭlchi St etc. Some major streets are divided into *ga* (sections), eg Chongno 2-ga, Chongno 3-ga etc. A *gil* is a smaller street – Insadong-gil is one such example.

The word for province is *do*, and Seoul is in Kyŏnggi-do. Provinces are subdivided into counties, or *gun*, and these can be further subdivided into townships, or *myŏn*. A *ni* or *ri* is a small village. Thus, in the countryside we can have an address like this: 130 Yongsan-ni, Toam-myŏn, P'yŏngch'ang-gun, Kangwon-do.

upwardly mobile citizen aspires to live. The small island of **Yŏŭido**, an important administrative area, sits in the river to the west. To the east is **Chamshil**, with its mega-housing and sports complexes.

The sights south of the river have much less historical and cultural interest than those to the north, and generally fall into the category of planned efforts to bring some life and colour to an otherwise arid urban sprawl.

MAPS

The Korean National Tourism Organisation (KNTO) has a number of free maps which have all the information the average visitor needs for getting around town. The municipal government also chips in with a cheap (W1000) street map and a freebie shopping map.

If you need highly detailed topographic maps large enough to wallpaper your room, there are two places that can accommodate you: Chung'ang Atlas Map Service (Map 4, ☎ 730 9191), 125-1 Kongpyŏng-dong, Chongno-gu; and Kangnam Map Centre (Map 7), just south of Shinsa station on subway line 3.

Bookshops are also good sources of maps and atlases. There are several atlases on the market (entirely in Korean script) which show all the major hiking routes in the mountains around Seoul.

TOURIST OFFICES
Local Tourist Offices

KNTO operates a tourist information centre (Map 4, ☎ 757 0086, 080-757 2000 toll-free) in the basement of the KNTO building, 10 Ta-dong, Chung-gu, Seoul. The well stocked display of illustrated booklets and maps should be thoroughly plundered by any visitor. KNTO is open daily from 9 am to 6 pm, except from November to the end of February, when it closes at 5 pm. Travellers with less pressing needs can contact KNTO corporate headquarters (☎ 729 9600, fax 757 5997), which is upstairs in the same building.

KNTO also operates two tourist information counters at Kimp'o airport in terminals No 1 (☎ 665 0088) and No 2 (☎ 665 0986).

In addition, there is a separate municipal Seoul Tourist Information Centre (TIC, ☎ 735 8688) right inside Seoul City Hall (Map 4). The same outfit operates the helpful tourist information booths scattered throughout the city – you can find these in the following locations:

Chongno 5-ga
(Map 3, ☎ 272 0348) opposite the Cheil Bank
It'aewon
(Map 8, ☎ 794 2490) near the Hamilton Hotel
Korea City Air Terminal
(Map 7, ☎ 566 4331) Samsŏng station on subway line 2
Myŏng-dong
(Map 5, ☎ 757 0088) opposite the Hanil Bank
Seoul express bus terminal
(Map 7, ☎ 537 9198)
Tŏksugung
(Map 5, ☎ 756 0045) opposite the palace

There is a Tourist Complaint Centre (☎ 735 0101, fax 777 0102), CPO Box 1879, Seoul 110-618. Alternatively, you could try the municipal government's tourist complaint service (☎ 750 8491). These phone numbers can be used for information if you need help or advice, but also to complain about shops which you think ripped you off (particularly if you were sold counterfeit goods that the vendor claimed were real). You can also write to the Tourist Complaint Centre, CPO Box 1879, Seoul 110-618, South Korea. The It'aewon Merchants' Union (☎ 798 5545) will entertain complaints against any of its members. There is also a Consumer Protection Centre (☎ 778 4233) in the Hoehyŏn Underground Arcade (Map 5) near the Central Post Office (CPO) – look for the sign in English.

KNTO Tourist Offices Abroad

Australia
(☎ 02-9252 4147, fax 9251 2104)
17th floor, Tower Bldg, Australia Square, George St, Sydney 2000
Canada
(☎ 416-348 9056, fax 348 9058, email knto.tt@sympatico.ca)
Suite 406, 480 University Ave, Toronto, Ontario M5G 1V2
China
(☎ 10-6526 0837, fax 6526 0839, email bjknto@info.iuol.cn.net)
Room 408-410, B Tower, COFCO Plaza No 8, Jianguomen Neidajie, Beijing;
(☎ 2523 8065, fax 2845 0765, email kntohk@netvigator.com)
Suite 3203, 32nd floor, Citibank Tower, 3 Garden Rd, Central, Hong Kong
France
(☎ 01-45 38 71 23, fax 45 38 74 71, email knto@club-internet.fr)
Tour Maine Montparnasse, 33 Avenue de Maine, Paris
Germany
(☎ 069-233 226, fax 253 519, email kntoff@msn.com)
Baseler Strasse 48, 60329 Frankfurt
Japan
(☎ 03-3580 3941, fax 3591 4601, email korea@int-acc.or.jp)
Room 124, Sanshin Bldg, 4-1-1 Yurakucho, Chiyoda-ku, Tokyo;
Branch offices:
Fukuoka (☎ 092-471 7174, fax 474 8015)
Osaka (☎ 06-266 0847, fax 266 0803)

Nagoya (☎ 052-933 6550, fax 933 6553)
Sendai (☎ 022-711 5991)
Singapore
　(☎ 533 0441, fax 534 3427, email
　kntosp@singnet.com.sg)
　20-01 Clifford Centre, 24 Raffles Place 7,
　Singapore 048621
Taiwan
　(☎ 02-2720 8049, fax 2757 6514, email
　kntotp@ms5.hinet.net)
　Room 1813, International Trade Centre,
　333 Keelung Rd, Section 1, Taipei 110
Thailand
　(☎ 02-231 3895, fax 231 3897)
　15th floor, Silom Complex Bldg,
　191 Silom Rd, Bangkok 10500
UK
　(☎ 0171-409 2100, fax 491 2302, email
　koreatb@dircon.co.uk)
　20 St George St, London W1R 9RE
USA
　(☎ 213-382 3435, fax 480 0483, email
　kntola@mail.wcis.com)
　Suite 1110, 3435 Wilshire Blvd,
　Los Angeles, CA 90010;
　(☎ 312-819 2560, fax 819 2563, email
　kntocg@idt.net)
　Suite 2212, 205 North Michigan Ave,
　Chicago, IL 60601;
　(☎ 201-585 0909, fax 585 9041, email
　kntony@aol.com)
　Suite 750, 7th floor, 2 Executive Drive,
　Fort Lee, NJ 07024

DOCUMENTS
Visas
Transit Visa With an onward ticket, visitors from almost anywhere – except countries not recognised by South Korea (Cuba, Laos and Cambodia) – will be granted a transit stay of up to 15 days without a visa. Some other countries which don't qualify include the Philippines, Nepal, India, Sri Lanka, the former Soviet republics, and a few other places in Asia and Africa. But be warned, the 15 day stay is not extendible and there are steep fines for overstaying.

Visa Exemptions In addition, South Korea has reciprocal visa-exemption agreements with numerous countries. There are visa exemptions for nationals of all west European nations except Ireland. If you fall into this category you'll be given a 90 day or three

month permit; 60 days in the cases of Italy and Portugal. Canadians get 180 days.

Tourist & Business Visas Nationals of all other countries – including Australia, New Zealand and the USA – require visas for stays over 15 days. If your nationality does not permit you a visa exemption and you need more than 15 days, apply for a visa before you go to South Korea.

South Korean embassies and consulates are notoriously fickle. Many of them require that your visa photos be 6x6cm (a size used nowhere else in the world). And they can be slow in issuing visas – allow at least three working days no matter what they tell you. On the other hand, some of the consulates will accept 3x5cm photos and issue the visa the same day you apply.

Visas are usually issued for a stay of 90 days. Onward tickets and/or proof of 'adequate funds' are not normally required. If you apply for a visa in your own country, you might get a multiple-entry visa – you usually *cannot* get this if you apply at a South Korean embassy in a nearby Asian country.

If you're coming to South Korea on business, then say so on the application. Most countries do not care if you do business on a tourist visa, but the South Koreans do. The immigration authorities are known to fine foreigners who 'violate' the terms of their visa.

Work Visas Applications can be made inside the country and are processed in as little as one week, but you must exit the country to pick up the visa. You can also apply for a work visa before entering Korea, though in this case it may take two to four weeks for the visa to be issued.

Your contract has to be turned in to the Korean authorities by your prospective employer. The employer does all the bureaucratic processing, then just mails you a visa-confirmation paper. The contract is unsigned by the worker at that point (and there might be a penalty if it were!). After getting the visa and entering Korea, the worker signs the contract and takes it with passport to the immigration office to get a residence permit. There are definitely penalties for starting to work *before* getting the visa, or if the starting date on the contract is prior to your visa-obtaining date.

Re-Entry Visas If you don't want to forfeit your working visa, you should apply for a multiple re-entry visa before making any trips out of the country. Again, the local immigration office is where this is accomplished.

Visa Extensions Extensions of tourist visas are generally not granted. If you have good reasons for an extension (eg illness) you should apply at the immigration office at least one day before your visa expires.

The main headquarters of the Seoul Immigration Office (Map 2, ☎ 653 3041) covers both Seoul and the surrounding province of Kyŏnggi-do. The office is inconveniently located in Yangcho'ŏn-gu, out near the airport. You can get there by taking subway line 5 to Omokkyo station, and then walking south-west for about 15 minutes.

Fortunately, there is a much more convenient branch in the city centre (Map 4, ☎ 732 6214) on the 5th floor of the Chŏksŏn Hyŏndae building. This is easily reached by taking subway line 3 to Kyŏngbokkung station. When walking out of the station, take exit 7 (the sign says 'Seoul Metropolitan Police Administration').

Residence Certificates

If you are working or studying in South Korea on a long-term visa, it is necessary to apply for a residence certificate within 90 days of arrival. The Seoul immigration office is where you apply for these certificates; they currently cost W30,000.

You can apply for single entry or multiple entry certificates. Obviously, most foreigners want the latter. In case you are issued with a single-entry certificate, you will need to apply for a re-entry permit every time you make a trip abroad during the life of the residence certificate.

Alien registration must be done at the Immigration Office of the province where you live, so if you live just outside the Seoul city limits, you cannot do this at the Seoul Immigration Office (even if it's closer to where you live).

Travel Insurance

It's very likely that a health insurance policy purchased in your home country will *not* cover you in Korea – if unsure, ask your insurance company.

A travel insurance policy can cover theft, loss and medical problems. The best policies even cover ambulances and an emergency flight home. These policies are usually available from travel agents, including student travel services.

Some policies offer lower and higher medical-expense options; the higher ones are chiefly for countries such as the USA, which have extremely high medical costs. There is a wide variety of policies available, so check the small print.

Some policies specifically exclude 'dangerous activities', which can include scuba diving, motorcycling and even trekking. A locally acquired motorcycle licence is not valid under some policies.

Some policies also pay doctors or hospitals directly rather than you having to pay on the spot and claim later. If you have to claim later, make sure you keep all documentation. This can include medical and police reports, baggage receipts from airlines, receipts of purchase and so on – if possible, try to get these in English. Some policies ask you to call back (reverse charges) to a centre in your home country where an immediate assessment of your problem is made.

Another thing to consider is that if you're planning to become an expat working in Korea, your employer may cover you with local medical insurance. But you'll probably want an insurance policy for when you are taking holidays outside of Korea. This is available from a number of places in Seoul, but check out the United Service Organisation (USO), which sells such policies for a reasonable price (see the Useful Organisations entry later in this chapter for USO contact details).

Driving Licence

If you intend to drive in Korea, you must be at least 21 years old and have one year's driving experience, your own passport and an international driving permit. A national licence from your own country is not acceptable. It is possible to obtain a temporary Korean driving licence valid for three months against your national licence in Seoul, but you'll spend a day doing so.

There are three places in Seoul where you can get this licence if you need one, but you must make sure that the address you are going to give is covered by the office where you apply. Seoul's three offices are:

Kangnam
   (☎ 555 0855) near Samsŏng station on subway line 2
Kangsŏ
   (☎ 664 3610) near Kimp'o airport
Tobong
   (☎ 975 4710) near Nowon station on subway line 4

All the licensing centres have a counter which deals exclusively with temporary licences for foreigners, so you won't have to join endless queues at other counters.

To obtain the licence you will need: your passport plus photocopies of the relevant front pages and your Korean visa page, your national driving licence plus a copy of both sides, six photographs of a size suitable for the Korean licence (about half the size of a normal passport photograph) and money to pay for the licence (the exact cost depends on nationality and visitor status).

Photographs, photocopies and fiscal stamps can all be obtained at the licensing centres. The forms you will be given are entirely in Korean, but the staff can usually help you fill them in. Once you've done this, obtained photographs, photocopies and fiscal stamps, you must take a compulsory eye test (the chart has numbers on it, not Korean letters). Assuming you pass it, you can pick up your licence 24 hours later.

The procedure for getting a permanent driving licence (valid for five years) is much the same, but you'll need a Korean residence permit to qualify. Furthermore, you must surrender your own country's driving licence to the Korean authorities in order to obtain the Korean licence.

Hostel Cards

If you don't already have a Hostelling International (HI or IYH) card, you can obtain one in South Korea, although there is only one hostel in Seoul and it's not cheap or conveniently located. In short, a hostel card is of limited use in South Korea. Hostelling is very big in Japan, however, and you should definitely pick up a hostel card in Korea if Japan is your next stop.

The place to contact is the Korean Youth Hostel Association, or KYHA (Map 4, ☎ 725 3031, fax 725 3113), room 409, Chŏksŏn Hyŏndae building, Chŏksŏn-dong, Chongno-gu, Seoul, 110-052.

Student Cards

Full-time students can often get some good discounts on tickets with the help of an International Student Identity Card (ISIC). This card entitles the holder to a number of discounts on airfares, trains, museums etc. To get this card, inquire at your campus. Cards can be issued in Korea at the Korean International Student Exchange Society (KISES, ☎ 733 9494, fax 732 9568) in room 505 of the YMCA building (Map 4) on Chongno 2-ga (next to Chonggak subway station) in central Seoul. A student ID card or a university letter of acceptance is required.

Photocopies

Prudent travellers keep photocopies of vital documents in a separate place. Also leave a copy of all these things with someone at home.

Useful things to photocopy include your passport (data pages only), credit cards, airline tickets, educational and employment qualifications (if you plan to work) and driving licence (if you plan to drive). Keep a list of travellers cheques serial numbers separate from the cheques themselves, and while you're at it, throw in an emergency stash of about US$100. If you're travelling

FACTS FOR THE VISITOR

with your spouse and/or children, a copy of your marriage certificate/birth certificate(s) could come in handy if you get involved with hospitals, the police or various bureaucratic authorities.

Tax Documents

It's a good idea to save tax documents from every company that you've *legally* worked for in Korea. You should also get a certificate of employment from each place where you've worked. This sort of information can be useful years later – for example, some countries will require such documentation if you marry a local and want to bring your spouse back to your home country.

EMBASSIES & CONSULATES

As a tourist, it's important to realise what your own embassy – the embassy of the country of which you are a citizen – can and can't do.

Generally speaking, embassies won't be much help in emergencies if the trouble you're in is remotely your own fault. Remember that you are bound by the laws of the country you are in. Diplomatic staff will not be sympathetic if you end up in jail after committing a crime locally, even if such actions are legal in your own country.

In genuine emergencies you might get some assistance, but only if other channels have been exhausted. For example, if you need to get home urgently, a free ticket home is exceedingly unlikely – the embassy would expect you to have insurance. If you have all your money and documents stolen, it might assist with getting a new passport, but a loan for onward travel is out of the question.

Embassies used to keep letters for travellers or have a small reading room with home newspapers, but these days the mail holding service has been stopped and even newspapers tend to be out of date.

Some embassies maintain a staff of financial experts who can provide information to businesspeople involved in import and export.

South Korean Embassies & Consulates Abroad

Australia
  Embassy:
  (☎ 02-6273 3044)
  113 Empire Circuit, Yarralumla, ACT 2600;
  Consulate:
  Sydney (☎ 02-9221 3866)
Canada
  Embassy:
  (☎ 613-232 1715)
  150 Boteler St, Ottawa, Ontario K1N 5A6;
  Consulates:
  Toronto (☎ 416-598 4608)
  Vancouver (☎ 604-681 9581)
China
  Embassy:
  (☎ 10-6505 3171)
  3rd & 4th floors, China World Trade Centre,
  1 Jianguomenwai Dajie, Beijing;
  Consulate:
  (☎ 2529 4141)
  5th floor, Far East Finance Centre,
  16 Harcourt Rd, Central, Hong Kong
France
  (☎ 01-47 53 01 01)
  125 Rue de Grenelle, 75007 Paris
Germany
  (☎ 0228-267 960)
  Adenauerallee 124, 53113 Bonn
Ireland
  (☎ 01-608 800)
  20 Clyde Rd, Ballsbridge, Dublin 4
Japan
  Embassy:
  (☎ 03-3452 7611)
  2-5 Minami-Azabu 1-chome, Minato-ku,
  Tokyo 106
  Consulates:
  Fukuoka (☎ 092-771 0461)
  Kobe (☎ 078-221 4853)
  Nagoya (☎ 052-935 4221)
  Niigata (☎ 025-243 4771)
  Osaka (☎ 06-213 1401)
  Sapporo (☎ 011-621 0288)
  Sendai (☎ 022-221 2751)
  Shimonoseki (☎ 0832-665 341)
Netherlands
  (☎ 070-352 0621)
  Verlengde Tolweg 8, 2517 JV, The Hague
New Zealand
  (☎ 04-473 9073)
  11th floor, ASB Bank Tower Bldg,
  2 Hunter St, Wellington
Russia
  (☎ 095-956 1474)
  Ul Spiridonobka Dom 14, Moscow

Singapore
 (☎ 256 1188)
 101 Thomson Rd, United Square 10-03,
 Singapore 113
Taiwan
 Visa Office:
 (☎ 02-2758 8320)
 Room 2214, Korea Trade Centre,
 333 Keelung Rd, Section 1
Thailand
 (☎ 02-247 7537)
 23 Thirmruammit Rd, Ratchadaphisek,
 Huay Kwang, Bangkok 10310
UK
 (☎ 0171-227 5500)
 60 Buckingham Gate, London SW1E 6AJ
USA
 Embassy:
 (☎ 202-939 5600)
 2450 Massachusetts Ave NW,
 Washington DC 20008;
 Consulates:
 Los Angeles (☎ 213-385 9300)
 New York (☎ 212-752 1700)
 San Francisco (☎ 415-921 2251)
 Also in: Anchorage, Atlanta, Boston, Chicago,
 Honolulu, Houston, Miami and Seattle
Vietnam
 (☎ 04-822 6677)
 29 Nguyen Dinh Chieu St, Hanoi

Foreign Embassies in Seoul

Australia
 (Map 4, ☎ 730 6490)
 11th floor, Kyobo Bldg, 1-1 Chongno 1-ga,
 Chongno-gu
Canada
 (Map 4, ☎ 753 2605)
 10th floor, Kolon Bldg, 45 Mugyo-dong,
 Chung-gu
China
 (Map 5, ☎ 319 5101, 771 3726)
 83 Myŏng-dong 2-ga, Chung-gu
France
 (Map 3, ☎ 312 3272)
 30 Hap-dong, Sŏdaemun-gu
Germany
 (Map 5, ☎ 726 7114)
 4th floor, Daehan Fire & Marine Insurance
 Bldg, 51-1 Namch'ang-dong, Chung-gu
Ireland
 (Map 5, ☎ 774 6455)
 Daehan Fire & Marine Insurance Bldg,
 51-1 Namch'ang-dong, Chung-gu

Israel
 (☎ 564 3448)
 823-21 Yŏksam-dong, Kangnam-gu
Japan
 (Map 4, ☎ 733 5626)
 18-11 Chunghak-dong, Chongno-gu
Netherlands
 (Map 4, ☎ 737 9514)
 14th floor, Kyobo Bldg, Chongno 1-ga,
 Chongno-gu
New Zealand
 (Map 4, ☎ 730 7794)
 18th floor, Kyobo Bldg, Chongno 1-ga,
 Chongno-gu
Russia
 (Map 7, ☎ 552 7094)
 1001-13 Taech'i-dong, Kangnam-gu
Singapore
 (☎ 794 3981)
 7th floor, Citicorp Centre Bldg,
 89-29 Shinmunno 2-ga, Chongno-gu
Taiwan (visa office)
 (Map 4, ☎ 399 2767)
 6th floor, Kwanghwamun Bldg
 (above Donghwa Duty-Free Shop)
UK
 (Map 4, ☎ 735 7341)
 4 Chŏng-dong, Chung-gu
USA
 (Map 4, ☎ 397 4114)
 82 Sejongno, Chongno-gu

CUSTOMS

Because of high duties on many imported goods, customs are very thorough with Koreans returning from overseas. For visiting foreigners, customs are generally easy-going, though officially you should declare any gifts worth more than W300,000 (about US$250).

Most seriously, it is required that you declare amounts of over US$10,000 – this *includes* travellers cheques. By not doing so you could risk having the balance confiscated when you try to leave with it. Upon departure, travellers *are* often asked how much money they are taking out – if you say any figure over US$10,000 you will have some explaining to do.

Aside from the usual prohibited items (narcotics, subversive literature, bombs etc), you cannot bring in walkie talkies or other wireless transmitters and receivers.

There is a duty-free allowance of 200 cigarettes (or 50 cigars or 250g of tobacco),

2 oz (59mL) of perfume and one bottle of spirits (not exceeding a total of 1L).

If you have any further queries, there is a Customs Information Service (☎ 665 3100) at Kimp'o airport.

For those leaving the country with antiques purchased in South Korea, take note of the Cultural Properties Preservation Law. The law forbids the export of items deemed 'important cultural properties'. If there is any doubt as to whether one of your purchases might fall into this rather vague category, you should contact the Art & Antiques Assessment Office (☎ 662 0106).

MONEY
Currency
The South Korean unit of currency is the *won* (W), with coins of W1, W5, W10, W50, W100 and W500. The W1 and W5 coins are rarely seen outside of banks, and if you should get your hands on one, you'll have a hard time spending it. Notes come in denominations of W1000, W5000 and W10,000.

Theoretically, you should have your exchange receipts when reconverting *won* back to foreign currency. In practice, you can usually change up to US$2000 worth of *won* at the airport exchange services without showing receipts.

Exchange Rates

Country	Currency		Won
Australia	A$1	=	807
Canada	C$1	=	895
China	RMB1	=	164
Euro	€1	=	1319
France	FF1	=	234
Germany	DM1	=	786
Hong Kong	HK$1	=	175
Japan	¥100	=	1000
New Zealand	NZ$1	=	698
Taiwan	NT$10	=	390
UK	UK£1	=	1968
USA	US$1	=	1226

Exchanging Money
Central Seoul is thick with banks offering foreign exchange services, and these are the best places to change your money. It's also convenient to change money at the airport. There is typically a 1.5% commission on foreign exchange.

Cash Within all US military bases, and including the USO and DMZ, you can use US currency (notes and coins). Occasionally you'll find shops near the bases, particularly in It'aewon, which will accept US currency. Otherwise, you'll have to use Korean money for all transactions.

US dollars (notes) are easiest to exchange at banks, but changing other major currencies, especially Japanese yen, should not prove problematic. Coins, except Korean ones, cannot be exchanged. Also, bills which are visibly dirty, tattered and wrinkled could be difficult to exchange.

Travellers Cheques Aside from the benefit of safety, another advantage of travellers cheques is that the exchange rate is more favourable than for cash. Travellers cheques in US dollar denominations will be easiest to change.

If you are not a resident of Korea but want to buy travellers cheques in Seoul, this can be done at some banks if you use a credit card to purchase the cheques. You could also buy checks if you have money wired to a bank in Korea. The main advantage of doing this is if you are going further into the hinterlands of Asia where credit cards are not easily used. Korea Exchange Bank and Korea First Bank are two places that sell travellers cheques, though there are others.

ATMs You'll find 24-hour 'cash advance' machines all over Seoul, especially in major subway stations. Some of these machines are marked 'Cirrus' and will therefore accept foreign-issued credit and ATM cards. You may need local help to use these, since the instructions are in Korean only.

Credit Cards You will have no problem finding opportunities to put any of your credit cards to use in Seoul. International credit cards such as American Express,

Diners Club, Visa, MasterCard and JCB are widely accepted throughout Seoul. The main offices of credit card companies are:

American Express
(English, ☎ 394 4100) 181-1 Puam-dong, Chongno-gu
Diners Club
(☎ 596 4100) 2-191 Hankongro, Yongsan-gu
Visa
(☎ 524-8000, 752 6523) 50 Sogong-dong, Chung-gu

International Transfers Getting money wired to you in Seoul poses no special difficulty – inquire at any foreign exchange bank for the exact procedure.

Sending money out is somewhat more complicated, and nonresident foreigners will encounter difficulties. However, obtaining a bank draft for an amount under US$1000 is usually not questioned. Telegraphic transfers are also possible, but these cost considerably more than bank drafts and you will be scrutinised more closely. Legal foreign residents are permitted to send out US$10,000 per year.

You need to have your passport available when you wire money out of Korea – the amount you send is stamped into your passport to make sure that you don't exceed the US$10,000 limit.

Black Market There is a black market, used mostly by foreigners working illegally in Korea and thus unable to exchange large amounts of cash at the banks. Most of the action takes place in Namdaemun Market. Obviously you won't find signs saying 'black market' – you mostly have to search for the old women sitting around with black bags (of money) looking like they have nothing to do. If you stare at them for a moment, they will usually motion you to come over. However, just because they look elderly and harmless does not mean that they won't cheat you.

If at all possible, try to avoid the black market. Counterfeit bills are rife, and the quality of the fakes is so good that even an expert would be hard pressed to spot the difference. If you've been ripped off by a black marketeer, there are no refunds and you have no legal recourse.

The black market operates on US dollars, usually US$100 notes. People who do resort to the black market only accept the newer style US$100 notes (which have water marks when held up to the light). Old-style US$100 notes are nearly out of circulation, and most of those in the black market are fakes. Before visiting the black market, some people first obtain a new US$100 bill from a bank or airport moneychanger to thoroughly familiarise themselves with just how it's supposed to look.

Security
Seoul does not have a serious pickpocketing problem, but theft does exist and may get worse due to recent economic difficulties.

Rather than lose your precious cash and travellers cheques (not to mention passport), large amounts of money and other valuables should be kept secure from sticky fingers. Various devices which can usually thwart pickpockets include pockets sewn on the inside of your trousers, velcro tabs to seal pocket openings, a money-belt under your clothes or a pouch under your shirt.

A vest (waistcoat) worn under your outer jacket will do very nicely only during the colder months. Beltpacks are a fairly easy target for pickpockets, though you may be able to close the zippers securely with clips.

A secret stash (maybe inside your backpack frame or lining?) is a good idea for those special emergencies.

Costs
First, the bad news – a survey in 1995 found that Seoul was the world's 10th most expensive city. The good news for travellers is that by 1998, Seoul was only ranked the 130th most expensive city. This remarkable transformation owes much to the fact that the Korean currency has plunged to about half its former value.

There are ways to minimise expenses. For the budget traveller, dormitory accommodation could cost as little as US$7 a night and food perhaps another US$7 a day. So if you do nothing but eat (on the cheap) and sleep, you could theoretically survive on US$14 a day.

In practice, you'd probably better figure on US$25 a day as a more realistic starting figure, but that allows for very few luxuries.

If you're a mid-range traveller with some sightseeing aspirations, you can probably get by comfortably on US$35 to US$50 a day, not counting shopping sprees.

For those for whom money is no object, Seoul is very accommodating. The city's top-end hotels provide international standards of service at international prices.

Tipping & Bargaining

Tipping is generally not necessary or expected in Seoul. However, a 10% service charge is added to the bill at tourist hotels, which could be thought of as a mandatory tip. Not surprisingly, in the big international hotels, international standards apply with regard to tipping.

Seoul's big department stores have fixed prices, and the low-paid employees are in no position to offer you a discount. It's a different story in small street markets and shops where you can talk directly to the shop owner. Asking for a discount in these places is common practice.

Koreans don't take too well to nastiness when bargaining – always remember to be polite and smile. If your bargaining gets too persistent and the shopkeeper starts to get angry, that is a clear sign to end the negotiations swiftly – either pay up and take the goods, or graciously depart from the scene. Whichever way you go, always smile and say *'Kamsa hamnida'* ('Thank you').

Taxes & Refunds

Most items purchased in South Korea are subject to a 10% value added tax (VAT) which is included in the selling price. At upmarket hotels, there is a 10% VAT on top of a 10% service charge, making for a steep 20% surprise surcharge when you go to pay your bill. VAT is not normally charged at the cheaper budget hotels.

POST & COMMUNICATIONS
Post

You'll find the poste restante counter on the 3rd floor of the Seoul CPO (Map 5). All incoming mail is entered into a logbook which you have to sign when you pick up mail – check carefully for your name, as letters are often misfiled. Normally, hotels will hold mail for a limited period, or a longer period if you let them know you are expecting mail.

Domestic postal rates are W170 for up to 50g; postcards cost W140. Domestic parcels are also cheap at W2500 for up to 2kg.

International rates vary according to region. The Korean postal service divides the world into four zones: zone 1 is East Asia; zone 2 is South-East Asia; zone 3 is Australia, New Zealand, the USA, Canada, Middle East, Europe and Oceania; and zone 4 is Africa and Latin America.

International postcards cost W350 regardless of zone, and aerograms are W400. Depending on the zone, letters (up to 10g) cost from W420 to W500; letters up to 20g are W450 to W630; registered letters (up to 10g) cost W1720 to W1800; and printed matter up to 20g costs W300 to W500.

Post offices are open from 9 am to 6 pm Monday to Friday (until 5 pm during winter) and until noon on Saturday. Public mail boxes are always coloured red. Domestic mail can be delivered in about two days if it bears an address in Korean characters – if written in English, figure on a week.

If you're sending parcels or printed matter, you don't have to worry about chasing around for cardboard boxes and the like. Major post offices like the Seoul CPO have excellent, inexpensive packing services.

Sending printed matter is about 40% cheaper than sending letters, but to get this discount you must seal the envelope with string rather than with tape or glue. The postal packing services know just how to prepare printed matter so that you can get this discount, so it's worth your while to let them do it.

If speed is of the utmost importance, you can send documents and small packets by

ROBERT STOREY

CHOE HYUNG PUN

MARTIN MOOS

Koreans love children, and the passages of their lives are carefully watched over by Confucian rituals known as *kwanhonsangje* (birth, coming-of-age, marriage, ancester honouring and death).

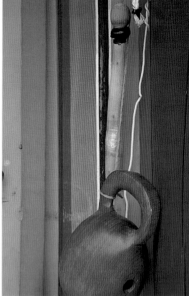

The Land of Morning Calm lives on in the details, as here in a delicate temple ceiling painting, a monk's wooden 'bell' and restored courtyard houses at Namsankol Traditional Korean Village.

Express Mail Service (EMS) Speedpost *(kokje t'ŭkgŭ pop'yŏn).*

If you need to send things too large or valuable to trust to the post office, or simply need more speed, there are a number of foreign private courier services available. The main courier services are Federal Express (☎ 333 8000), DHL (☎ 716 0001), United Parcel Service (☎ 3664 0361) and Airborne Freight (☎ 323 5813); all offer pick-up service.

There are specialised companies for moving international freight (including all your household belongings). Some companies based in Seoul include: Ahjin Transportation (☎ 538 1612, fax 538 1615, email ajtc@ahjin.co.kr); Korea Transport (☎ 358 5411, email ktms@unitel.co.kr), which has a Web site (www.kidb.co.kr/tr/ktms); Cho Yang Transport (☎ 335 2642, fax 335 2644); and Saejin Express (☎ 752 9462, fax 756 5681).

Telephone

There is a 30% discount on calls made before 8 am and after 8 pm Monday to Friday, before 8 am and after 4 pm on Saturday, and for 24 hours on Sunday and public holidays.

Pay phones accept three types of coins: W10, W50 and W100 (but *not* W500). Pay phones can be used for local and long distance calls, and there is no time limit as long as you keep feeding money into the machine. The cost for local calls is W50 for three minutes.

When using local-call phones you will often find that the phone is off the hook and there is still a credit on the phone. The reason for this is that it is not possible to get change from a W100 coin, but you can use the credit from a W50 call to make further calls as long as you don't hang up. To make another call, simply press the green button on the phone (it doesn't always work).

Phone Cards

A wide range of domestic and international phonecards is available. Lonely Planet's eKno Communication Card (see the insert at the back of this book) is aimed specifically at independent travellers and provides cheap international calls, a range of messaging services and free email – for local calls, you're usually better off with a local card. You can join online (www.ekno.lonelyplanet.com).

Locally produced magnetic telephone cards come in denominations of W2000, W3000, W5000 and W10,000, but you get a 10% bonus (for example, a W5000 card is really worth W5500). The phone cards *(chŏnhwa kadŭ)* can be bought from banks, shops near the card phones and 24-hour convenience stores.

The local phone cards are notoriously poor quality – the charge on the cards will often disappear a week or two after you've broken the seal on the plastic packet, but sometimes the card will be defective the first time you use it! If this happens, try flexing the card (not too vigorously) and it *might* work. If it doesn't, take the card to any phone company office and it will be exchanged for free. Needless to say, this is a hassle best avoided, so if you plan to use local cards, try to purchase the minimum denomination (W3000) cards and use them up quickly before they go bad.

A recent innovation are credit-card phones – all major international credit cards are accepted.

International Calls

International Direct Dialling (IDD) calls can be placed through Korea Telecom (☎ 001), Dacom (☎ 002) or Onse (☎ 008). Calls placed through Dacom and Onse are slightly cheaper than Telecom, but you can only access these services from a private phone – Korea Telecom owns the public phones and its phones will not connect to Dacom or Onse.

To make an IDD call, first dial ☎ 001 (or 002, 008), then the country code, area code (minus the initial zero if it has one) and the number you want to reach. You receive a 30% discount on calls made between 9 pm and 8 am (Monday to Saturday) and all day Sunday and public holidays.

To place an international call through an English-speaking operator, dial ☎ 0077. Dial ☎ 0074 for information about international

FACTS FOR THE VISITOR

dialling (country codes, rates, time differences etc). Placing a call through an international operator means that you must pay for a three minute minimum call. There are four types of operator assisted calls: station to station, person to person, reverse charges and credit card calls.

The following are the full daytime IDD rates when dialling the ☎ 001 prefix:

Country	First minute	Per extra minute
Australia	W1320	W996
Canada	W1734	W1302
France	W1572	W1182
Japan	W984	W738
UK	W1320	W990
USA	W840	W630

Another dialling option is called 'home country direct', which allows you to talk directly to an operator in the country you are calling. This system is useful only for collect calls or if you want to charge to a credit card, and it's not available for every country. There are special home country direct telephones at Kimp'o airport and at the KNTO in Central Seoul. You can also access home country direct at any card phone – insert the card, dial ☎ 0090 (or 0091 for the USA) plus the country direct number.

Here's a list of common destinations and their access numbers:

Australia	0090+610
Brazil	0090+055
Canada	0090+015
Chile	0090+560
Denmark	0090+450
Finland	0090+358
France	0090+330
Germany	0090+049
Guam	0090+671
Hawaii	0090+012
Hong Kong	0090+852
Hungary	0090+036
Indonesia	0090+620
Italy	0090+390
Japan	0090+081
Macau	0090+853
Malaysia	0090+060
Netherlands	0090+310
New Zealand	0090+640
Philippines (Philcom)	0090+631
Philippines (PLDT)	0090+630
Portugal	0090+351
Singapore	0090+650
Spain	0090+034
Taiwan	0090+886
Thailand	0090+660
UK (BT)	0090+440
UK (Mercury)	0090+441
USA (AT&T)	0091+1
USA (MCI)	0091+4
USA (Sprint)	0091+6

If you will be staying in Korea for more than a few months and make frequent calls abroad, it's worth signing up for call-back services. These companies are almost entirely based in the USA (because of the low phone rates), though you can use their services to call elsewhere. US-based call-back companies include:

Kallback
(☎ 206-599 1992, fax 599 1982) Web site: www.kallback.com
Justice
(☎ 310-526 2200; fax 526 2100) Web site: www.justicecorp.com
NewWorld
(☎ 201-287 8400, fax 287 8434); UK office (☎ 0171-360 5037, fax 360 5036) Web site: www.newworldtele.com

Area Codes

South Korea's country code is (82). Area codes for major cities (do not dial the first zero if calling from outside Korea) include:

Seoul	(02)
Inch'ŏn	(032)
Kwangju	(062)
Pusan	(051)
Taegu	(053)
Taejŏn	(042)

Cellular Phones There's bad news if you want to bring your digital GSM phone to Korea – it won't work. Korea uses the controversial CDMA technology, which is compatible with the USA but incompatible with the GSM system that is common in Europe and elsewhere.

There is lots of competition in the Korean cellular market, and some companies will give you a free cellular phone if you sign up for two years of service. The downside is that there have been many complaints about the quality of cellular service and the charges for air-time, so be careful about signing a contract. Before making a commitment, it's best to first talk to friends and colleagues to find out how satisfied they are with their cellular service.

For those trying to keep expenses down, there is a service in Seoul called 'city phone'. City phones are cheaper than standard cellular service. The difference is that you can only dial out – you cannot receive calls. So if you go this route, you might need a pager too.

Short-term visitors can rent cellular phones for about W8000 per day from Rent-a-Cell (☎ 3444 0733); the Korean Yellow Pages (☎ 725 0411), which has a Web site (www.yellowpages.co.kr); or from Samsung (☎ 516 5877). Making international calls on these phones using special prepaid phone cards can be quite economical.

Pagers Everyone seems to have a pager these days in Korea, including many short-term expat English teachers. The cost of buying a pager and setting up an account varies from W45,000 to W110,000. The cheaper pagers can only be used in the Seoul metropolitan area, while the more pricey models work throughout South Korea. Maintaining your account costs about W11,000 per month for the Seoul area only, or W16,000 to W21,000 per month for Korea-wide service.

Even if you don't have your own pager, it's still useful to know how to contact somebody by this method. The system is fully automated – you don't speak to an operator at

Emergency Numbers	
Ambulance	☎ 119
Fire	☎ 119
Police	☎ 112
Report A Spy	☎ 113

all. All Korean pager numbers start with ☎ 012 or 015 followed by at least seven digits. Simply dial this number (no area code necessary) and you will hear either a beep or a recorded voice message followed by a beep. At this point you have two options – you can punch in your phone number or leave a voice message. For the first option, after the beep press '1', dial your phone number, finish by pressing the asterisk (or pound sign) and wait a couple of seconds before hanging up. To leave a voice message, after the beep press '2', start talking (maximum 25 seconds), and press a '*' or '#' sign before hanging up. If you forget to press the asterisk or pound sign, it still seems to work, despite the fact that the paging companies say it won't!

The worst thing about pagers is that you can never be sure if the person you want to contact received the page. Sometimes the recipient doesn't get the message because the pager is turned off, the batteries are low or they are in the subway.

Useful Phone Numbers The very useful *Korean Yellow Pages* is published annually in English, and is available from major bookshops in Seoul. If you can't find a copy, contact the publisher directly (☎ 725 0411).

There are no 'white pages' available in English, so you will have to manage with *han'gŭl*. You'll also need the ability to speak Korean to get any information from directory assistance, or to communicate with the police, fire and ambulance emergency services.

With that caveat in mind, the following list contains some of the more common telephone numbers you may require.

Directory Assistance	
(toll-free)	☎ 080-211 0114
English Operator	☎ 080-211 0114
International Dialling	
Assistance	☎ 0074
International Operator	☎ 0077
Local Directory Assistance	☎ 114
Long-distance Directory	
Assistance	☎ area code + 114
Phone Repairs	☎ 110
Telegrams (Domestic)	☎ 115
Telegrams (International)	☎ 005
Time	☎ 116
Weather (local)	☎ 131
Weather (long-distance)	☎ area code + 131

Fax

Major post offices offer a fax service. Aside from business centres in tourist hotels, there are also many small shops offering photo-copying and fax service – these are most numerous around university areas.

Email & Internet Access

Electronic mail *(chonja meil)* and Internet surfing have both become very chic in Korea. There are several ways to get online whether you are a permanent resident or just a short-term visitor to Seoul.

If you don't have your own computer, you can still go online at a cybercafe. Cyber-cafes in Seoul are cheap, typically charging W3000 for 30 minutes of use. A few super-deluxe hotels also have business centres equipped with computers and modems, but fees for using these can add up fast.

If you're a member of CompuServe and you've brought your own portable com-puter, plug a phone line into your modem and dial up EQT (☎ 775 6647) or INW (☎ 795 1002, 795 1005) in Seoul.

If you take up residence in Korea, you can establish a local Internet account and do your email on the cheap. Korea's most popular Internet service providers (ISPs), more or less in descending order, are:

Chollian
  (☎ 220 7275) which belongs to Dacom;
  Web site: www.chollian.net
Kornet
  (☎ 080-014 1414) run by Korea Telecom;
  Web site: www.kornet.net

Unitel
  (☎ 528 0114) run by Samsung;
  Web site: www.unitel.co.kr
Hitel
  run by Korea PC Telecom;
  Web site: www.hitel.net
Nownuri
  (☎ 590 3800) Web site: www.nownuri.co.kr
ELIMnet
  (☎ 3149 4800) Web site: www.elim.co.kr

These networks are mostly in han'gŭl, but Chollian, Kornet and Unitel provide an English option on their home pages (Hitel, Nownuri and ELIMnet do not). Costs are very reasonable – about W15,000 for a basic account with unlimited usage.

Cybercafes You can cruise cyberspace at the Net Cyber Cafe (Map 4, ☎ 733 7973, fax 738 5794). This was the first cybercafe in Seoul to cater to foreigners, and it's still the favourite hang-out for backpackers in the central area. The cafe features a notice board, a fax machine for customer use and special discounts for members. Operating hours are Monday to Friday from 9.30 am to 11 pm, Saturday 11 am to 11 pm and Sunday from noon to 10 pm. The cafe is on the 2nd floor of a small building in an alley adjacent to Kyobo Book Centre. Naturally, it has a Web site (www.net.co.kr).

Another option is Net House (Map 4, ☎ 725 4417, fax 725 4419). This cybercafe (Web site www.korea-travel.com) is more Koreanised, but has a quiet setting (much like a library coffee shop) and the staff speak English. The nearest subway stations are Kwanghwamun on line 5 (exit 2) or Anguk on line 3. Look for the building with a large Coca-Cola and Fanta sign on top – Net House is on the ground floor.

Over in the Taehangno area is the Forest Cyber Cafe (Map 6, ☎ 765 4588, 745 6281). It's on the 3rd floor of the Uchŏng building. It's open daily from 10 am until midnight.

In It'aewon, there is Cyberia (Map 8, ☎ 3785 3860), which also has a Web site (www.cyberia.co.kr).

Net Plaza (Map 7, ☎ 501 3007, email abraham63@hanmail.net), on the south side of the Han River, is open daily. It's on the 3rd floor above Ponse Coffee Shop, in an alley on the north-east corner from Kangnam subway station on line 2.

Also on the south side is La Puta Internet Cafe (Map 7, ☎ 508 8261), south of Kangnam subway station. It has a Web site (www.laputa.co.kr).

INTERNET RESOURCES

The World Wide Web is a rich resource for travellers. You can research your trip, hunt down bargain air fares, book hotels, check on weather conditions or chat with locals and other travellers about the best places to visit (or avoid!).

Unfortunately, the Internet changes so fast that almost anything one can say about it is liable to be out of date tomorrow. You could try going online and searching on the words 'Korea', 'Korean' or 'Seoul', but this will likely turn up many thousands of hits, most of them worthless.

There's no better place to start your Web explorations than the Lonely Planet Web site (www.lonelyplanet.com). Here you'll find succinct summaries on travelling to most places on earth, postcards from other travellers and the Thorn Tree bulletin board, where you can ask questions before you go or dispense advice when you get back. You can also find travel news and updates to many of our most popular guidebooks. Finally, the subWWWay section links you to the most useful travel resources elsewhere on the Web.

Some other useful sites are:

www.knto.or.kr The enterprising Korean National Tourism Organisation runs a site with plenty of useful data of interest to travellers. However, pages on this site are overburdened with graphics and consequently load very slowly. Alternatively, you can telnet to the KNTO IP address (203.236.107.10), which has no graphics.

www.metro.seoul.kr/eng/index.html Seoul Focus is run by the Seoul Metropolitan Government and provides lots of useful information. However, the site follows the Korean tradition of being overloaded with graphics and you'll be able to finish off a plate of *kimch'i* and *kimbap* while waiting for a page to load.

www.yellowpages.co.kr The *Korean Yellow Pages* (in English) is more than a phone directory. At this site you can make hotel reservations, rent a cellular phone, contact a courier service, find out what the local cinemas are showing and much more.

www.login.co.kr Log-In Seoul is an electronic bulletin board. The 'guestbook' and discussion forum serve as places to exchange messages.

www.koreaherald.co.kr The *Korea Herald* is one of the two daily English newspapers in Seoul, and its site is worth a peek.

www.koreatimes.co.kr The *Korea Times* is the other daily English-language newspaper in Seoul, and its news site is brilliant (better than the printed edition).

www.arirang.co.kr This is the site of the Korea World Network, which introduces Korean culture to the world.

www.kimsoft.com This is the *Web Weekly* published by the Korean Nationalists Association, a US-based site for flag-waving Korean nationals and other Koreaphiles. Some of the stuff posted here is decidedly xenophobic and occasionally pro-North Korean, so don't tread here if you're easily offended.

www.kcna.co.jp The Korea Central News Agency is the official mouthpiece for North Korea. You'll find plenty of laughable (but deadly serious) propaganda posted here. Do *not* try to access this site from South Korea.

www.amchamkorea.org & www.eucck.org These two Web sites are, respectively, the Korean branches of the American Chamber of Commerce and European Union Chamber of Commerce.

Aside from Web sites, there are mailing lists, which are basically electronic bulletin boards which anyone can participate in. One of the most popular mailing lists with foreign residents of Korea is Kexpat ('Korean expats'). To subscribe, send a message to: kexpat-d-request@uriel.net.

Place the words 'subscribe kexpat' in the subject line. To post a message, email it to: kexpat@uriel.net.

The Web site at www.liszt.com is the place to find out about other mailing lists (not only Korean ones).

BOOKS

Books about Korea are scarce, and books dealing exclusively with Seoul are even scarcer. Most people with an interest in this part of the world want to read about China and Japan. Still, with some perseverance you can come up with some interesting titles.

Most of the following books can be found in Korea or ordered through western bookshops. Another possibility is to order through the Internet (try www.amazon.com).

Lonely Planet

For travel further afield on the Korean peninsula, Lonely Planet guides include *Korea* and the *Korean phrasebook*.

Guidebooks

Discovering Seoul (1986) by James Grayson & Donald Clark is strong on historical Seoul, for those who want to identify every nook and cranny of the palaces. The book is getting dated, as much renovation work has been performed over the past decade.

A somewhat abbreviated version of the foregoing is *Seoul Cultural Properties* (1997). This book has the advantage of being more up to date, and also has colour photos.

Introducing Seoul (1993) by John Holstein & Yoon Myung-sook is a coffee-table book, but it's also informative. The text was written by a long-term expat who knows the city well.

Korea Guide – A Glimpse of Korea's Cultural Legacy (1995) by Edward B Adams is a classic. The author is an expat born in Korea and has written authoritatively about the country for most of his life.

Culture Shock – Korea (1992) by Sonja Vegdahl Hur gives a good overview of Korean etiquette, social customs and taboos.

To Dream of Pigs – Travels in South & North Korea (1994) by Clive Letherdale is an entertaining and unusual book that serves as an interesting guide to the whole Korean peninsula.

History & Politics

Mark Clifford's *Troubled Tiger – Businessmen, Bureaucrats and Generals in South Korea* (1984) is a highly recommended 'unauthorised biography' of Korea Inc's early days.

Korean Cultural Heritage by the Korea Foundation is a multi-volume set of highly detailed reference books. This monumental work covers a number of broad topics, including Korean religion and philosophy.

Korea Between the Wars – A Soldier's Story by Fred Ottoboni is one of the most recent books and provides an interesting perspective of Korea and Seoul in the era leading up to the Korean War.

Seoul – The Making of a Metropolis (1997) by Joochul Kim *et al* is part of the World Cities Series. The book gives a thorough treatment of the city including history, government, business, social and even demographic issues. The steep US$85 price tag may put off some readers.

General

In the Shadow of the Moons (1998) by Hong Nan-sook is a controversial bestseller. The author is the ex-wife of Moon Sun-myung's oldest son (Moon Sun-myung, best known as the leader of the 'Moonies', is the founder of the Unification Church). Ms Hong was married to Moon's son for 14 years, and the book portrays a harrowing tale of abuse.

Also in the blockbuster category is *The Chaebol* by Steers, Shin & Ungson (1989). It gives a not-too-flattering look into the workings of Korea's big corporate conglomerates.

The Comfort Women (1995) deals with the explosive topic of how Korean (and other) women were used as sex slaves by Japanese soldiers during WWII.

Business

How to Achieve Business Success in Korea – Where Confucius Wears a Three Piece Suit (1994) by Nigel & Choi Chong Ju has a title that says it all.

Business Korea – A Practical Guide to Understanding South Korean Business Culture (1994) by Peggy Kenna & Sondra Lacy is informative on the rules of etiquette, culture and ethics in the Korean business world.

Korean Dynasty – Hyundai and Chung Ju Yung (1994) by Donald Kirk is the story of Korea's largest chaebŏl.

FACTS FOR THE VISITOR

NEWSPAPERS & MAGAZINES

Two locally produced English-language newspapers are available: the *Korea Times* and the *Korea Herald*. These papers are published Monday through Saturday – Sunday is everyone's day off. Both seem to glean their news from Korea's official Yonhap news agency, which is why both papers report identical news. The *Herald* has a better TV listing and seems to be more popular with expats than the *Times*, but the difference is not huge.

Seoul Scope is a monthly arts, events and entertainment magazine in English which costs W2000 per issue and is sold at most major bookshops in Seoul. You can order a subscription for W20,000 per year if you live in Korea (W30,000 to W38,000 for overseas subscriptions). For details, ring the Seoul Scope office in Seoul (☎ 743 7784, fax 743 7078) or write to: 102-1 Hyehwa-dong, Chongno-gu, Seoul 110-530.

Be on the lookout for any of the various counter-culture periodicals that occasionally appear and disappear depending on who is willing to devote time to publishing them. These publications are usually free, and try to support themselves through advertising. One of these is *Log-In Seoul* (email login@elim.net), a weekly freebie geared towards cyber-punks. Another is *Bokonon*, which covers the music scene. In Seoul, look for copies at various cybercafes, trendy pubs, bookshops or even the KNTO tourist office.

Koreana magazine is the best source on arts and culture. It's published quarterly by the Korea Foundation and costs W4500 per issue or W18,000 per year by subscription. There are great photos, essays, story and poem translations, plus feature issues on topics such as temples, music, novels, painting, sports, songs and pottery.

The *Korea Economic Report*, *Korea Post* and *Business Korea* are locally published monthly magazines which are mostly of interest to Koreans learning to speak English.

If you want to check up on your horoscope, *USA Today* is on sale at various venues around town.

RADIO & TV

There are five Korean-language TV networks: KBS1, KBS2, MBC, SBS and EBS. AFKN is an English-language station run by the US military and features typical US shows, but in most areas you can only get it on cable. AFKN radio broadcasts in English on AM (549kHz) and FM (102.7mHz).

Arirang is a government subsidised station that broadcasts programs about Korean culture, fine arts, politics, economics and history. Programs are broadcast in both Korean and English. Arirang is only available on cable. For the latest program listings, check Arirang's Web site (www.arirang.co.kr).

Seoul has a number of cable TV companies, but most only operate in a specified district – you need to find out which company serves your area, and also what stations they carry. The Yongsan area (near the US military base) caters to foreign customers, so if you live in its service area you might want to try Yongsan Cable Company (☎ 318 1800, 318 2700). If you don't live in its district, this company should at least be able to tell you the number of your local cable supplier. Failing that, just ask your Korean neighbours – somebody should know. Typically, there are installation costs running from W50,000 to W100,000, plus a monthly charge of W20,000 to W30,000 depending on your neighbourhood. At this price, you should receive all the local stations (including AFKN), all the freebie satellite services (EBS-wisong, KBS-wisong, CNN International, Star World, Star Sports and some Japanese programs) plus all the local pay cable stations (eg K-MTV, Arirang, Doosan Super Network). If you don't need Arirang and the movie channels, you can get a cheap cable service that costs only W4000 per month and supplies everything except the pay cable stations (you still get CNN-I, Star and AFKN). The phone number for one such basic cable supplier (and this is supposed to be good for all of Seoul) is (☎ 719 6400).

Satellite TV is also available if you want to purchase your own dish antenna. There are number of companies which sell these systems, but you could try Kana Satellite (☎ 3424 6303), office C-098, 6th floor; or Techno Mart (Map 2, take subway line 2 to Kangbyŏn station). Another possibility is Sky-Master (☎ 701 6363) at Electroland Main No 212 in the Yongsan Electronics Arcade (Map 2).

A complete TV and radio program schedule is listed in the daily English-language newspapers. The *Korean Yellow Pages* Web site (www.yellowpages.co.kr) also has program listings (click the 'Entertainment' link to find them).

VIDEO SYSTEMS

South Korea has adopted the NTSC video standard. This is the same standard used in the USA, Canada, Japan and Taiwan, but is incompatible with both the PAL standard (used in Australia, Hong Kong, China, New Zealand, UK and most of continental Europe) and SECAM (France, Germany and Luxembourg). The NTSC, PAL and SECAM standards war is an issue when you purchase or rent video tapes, as well as movies stored on laser disks (both VCDs and DVDs).

If you like to buy movies on the new DVD format, be aware that there is a deliberately built-in incompatibility between the different 'zones' of the world. That is to say, DVD disks are encoded to indicate the country of origin, and Asian DVD movies will not play in a standard American or European DVD player (and vice versa). The movie industry claims that this will discourage pirating, though it's hard to imagine why it would. Indeed, many suspect that the real motive behind the 'zone system' is to force users to buy more than one copy of the same movie. However, in Korea and many other Asian countries, one can buy 'all-zone' DVD players which have been modified (illegally?) to play DVD disks from anywhere. For DVDs played on computers, there are now some 'unauthorised' software patches to circumvent the zone system. Many people have suggested that until the movie industry sorts out this zone-encoding mess, it would be safest to avoid

buying DVD disks and players. The zone-encoding problem is not an issue for movies stored on VCDs.

Video rental shops are abundant in Seoul, and many foreign movies are available on video in English with Korean subtitles.

PHOTOGRAPHY & VIDEO
Film & Equipment
Unless you're a professional, there's no need to worry about your film needs in Seoul. All the big-name brands of print film are readily available at reasonable prices. Also, photo-processing facilities are of an international standard and are not too expensive.

On the other hand, Seoul is not a particularly good place to buy photographic equipment or video cameras, due to prohibitive import taxes. If you're going further afield to Hong Kong, Singapore or even Tokyo, you should wait. There are, however, a couple of areas with hole-in-the-wall second-hand camera shops. See the Shopping chapter for details.

Technical Tips
If visiting Seoul in winter, it's useful to note that the Korean underfloor heating system *(ondol)* can bake your film if you leave it or your camera on the floor.

Restrictions
Photography of military facilities can be a sensitive matter – it's best not to risk having your film confiscated. Photographs can be taken around airports but do not try to photograph the airport security procedures.

Photographing People
Koreans are not particularly camera shy, but it's still polite to ask first before shoving a camera in somebody's face. Be careful about taking liberties photographing monks. Student rioters are not particularly fond of being photographed.

Airport Security
There have been recent reports of a new type of x-ray machine called CTX-5000, designed to inspect checked baggage (not

hand-carried baggage). The CTX-5000 makes a double scan – a first scan which is harmless to film, and a second focused scan on any suspicious items. If the second scan hits unprocessed film, it will be ruined. It is not yet certain if or when Korea will be using these new machines, but it would be prudent to avoid the problem entirely by carrying all film in your hand luggage.

TIME

The time in South Korea is GMT/UTC plus nine hours. When it is noon in South Korea, it is 7 pm the previous day in Los Angeles or San Francisco and 10 pm the previous day in New York; and 3 am the same day in London and 1 pm the same day in Sydney.

ELECTRICITY
Voltages & Cycles

Officially, South Korea is on the 220V standard at 60Hz, but some older buildings are still wired for 110V.

Plugs & Sockets

Fortunately, the design of the electrical outlets gives you a clue about voltages. Two flat pins is 110V and two round pins is 220V. There is no third wire for ground (earth).

WEIGHTS & MEASURES

In former times, Korea used the traditional Chinese system of weights and measures. Nowadays, the international metric system is used for everything except the measurement of real estate. If you are buying or renting a flat, area is measured in *p'yŏng*, with 1 p'yŏng being equal to 3.3 sq metres.

Length can be measured in *ja* (1 ja is 0.3m). A p'yŏng is 6x6 ja.

LAUNDRY

Most hotels in Seoul, including the cheap *yŏgwan* (small family-run hotels), have a laundry service and charges are usually quite reasonable.

Searching for laundromats in Seoul is a dead loss, though there are plenty of places that handle dry cleaning.

TOILETS

Koreans deserve infinite praise for the fine job they've done installing public toilets at convenient locations all around Seoul and in other cities throughout the country. Many toilets are of the Asian 'squat' variety, and this can take some getting used to.

Public toilets are generally clean and free of charge, though you'd be wise to bring a small stash of toilet paper, since it is not always available. You'll find public toilets most readily in subway stations, parks, bus stations, museums and almost any other logical location.

LEFT LUGGAGE

Kimp'o airport has bonded baggage facilities which cost about US$2 per day. However, there is no left-luggage room after you've passed through customs. If you do place something into bonded baggage, you will not be able to gain access to it until you depart the country.

Left-luggage rooms are exceedingly rare in Seoul. A few tourist hotels might have private left-luggage rooms for guests only, but finding these are hit or miss. Fortunately, there are lockers at most major train, subway and bus stations. These can be used for a maximum of three days – don't go over the limit or your goods could be confiscated and you'll have to pay a fine to get them back. The price for renting a locker is typically W700, and the machines accept W100 coins only. You feed money into the coin slot for the first day, but if you leave things overnight, you must put in more coins to get them out again. A digital display meter tells you how many coins you must feed in.

HEALTH

Seoul is a very healthy city with standards of sanitation and medical care on a par with most any western country.

No vaccinations are normally required to enter South Korea, but if you're arriving from a place currently experiencing a cholera or yellow fever epidemic, you may be asked for proof of vaccination.

Opinions are divided as to whether you should drink the tap water – some South Koreans do, some don't. Seoul's tap water is chlorinated but gets slightly contaminated in the water mains (at least in the older parts of town). Independent tests have shown that some brands of bottled water are no cleaner than the tap water. However, if you do drink unboiled water, it's unlikely you'll suffer any illness more serious than diarrhoea. All in all, it might be best to drink only boiled water until your body adjusts to the local microbes, but there is little chance of contracting serious intestinal infections.

Emergency medical care in hospitals is excellent and reasonably cheap, but normal outpatient care leaves much to be desired. Westerners are liable to become very frustrated with most Korean doctors because they will not answer questions from patients regarding illness, laboratory tests or the treatment being given. Questions are regarded as insults to the doctor's competence, thus causing a loss of face. Doctors who have studied and worked abroad may be more accustomed to western ways.

Adventist Hospital
(Map 2, ☎ 210 3241) 29-1 Hwaegi 2-dong, Tongdaemun-gu. There are English-speaking foreign-trained doctors here and the facilities are very good.
Asan Medical Centre, International Clinic
(Map 2, ☎ 224 5001) 388-1, P'ungnap-dong, Songp'a-gu. This is open from 8.30 am to 5.30 pm on Monday, Wednesday and Friday.
International Clinic
(Map 8, ☎ 790 0857) 737-37 Hannam-dong, Yongsan-gu. This is It'aewon's main health facility for foreigners.
Samsung Medical Centre, International Clinic
(☎ 3410 0200) 50 Irwon-dong, Kangnam-gu
Seoul National University Hospital
(Map 6, ☎ 762 5171). In Hyehwa-dong, this is Korea's largest and most advanced medical facility. Some English is spoken here, but this hospital is horribly crowded.
Severance Hospital, International Clinic
(Map 9, ☎ 392 3404) 134 Shinch'on-dong, Sŏdaemun-gu. This is not far from the Seoul Foreign School. The clinic is open from 8.30 to 11.30 am and 1.30 to 3.30 pm Monday to Friday, and until 11.30 am on Saturday.

Medical Kit Check List

Since you can buy almost anything you need from local pharmacies in Seoul without a perscription, a medical kit for travel to the city is not essential. However, having one can be convenient when you've suddenly got a dire need at 3 am and the pharmacies are closed. A small, straightforward medical kit could include:

☐ **Aspirin** or **paracetamol** (acetaminophen in the USA) – for pain or fever
☐ **Antihistamine** – useful for allergies, eg hay fever; to ease the itch from insect bites or stings; and to prevent motion sickness
☐ **Loperamide** or **diphenoxylate** – these are 'blockers' for diarrhoea; **prochlorperazine** or **metaclopramide** are for nausea and vomiting
☐ **Rehydration mixture** – to prevent dehydration, eg due to severe diarrhoea; particularly important when travelling with children

Other practical items include a thermometer, scissors, tweezers, insect repellent, sunscreen and lip balm.

If you are in need of urgent medical attention, Asia Emergency Assistance (AEA, ☎ 790 7561) is an organisation that operates 24 hours a day, and will act as an intermediary between foreigners and Korean hospitals. AEA charges for its services but offers a health plan for resident foreigners.

Pharmacies

Self-treatment poses some risks, but Korean pharmacists are willing to sell you all sorts of dangerous drugs over the counter without a prescription. Korean pharmacists know the English names of most drugs but can't pronounce them. However, they can generally read English well, so try writing down what you want to avoid misunderstandings. Many of the pharmacies in

It'aewon have English-speaking staff. Pharmacies seem to be everywhere – to find one look for the character:

약

You can only buy condoms (same word in Korean) from a pharmacy and you have to ask for them. They are kept discretely hidden under the counter, unlike in Hong Kong or Taiwan where they are openly displayed in convenience stores.

If you wear glasses, take a spare pair and your prescription. Losing your glasses can be a nuisance, although in Seoul you can get new spectacles made up quickly, competently and extremely cheaply (W25,000 to W40,000 is the typical charge). However, contact lenses are expensive in Korea.

If you require particular medication, take an adequate supply, as it may not be available in a pinch. Take the prescription or, better still, part of the packaging showing the generic rather than the brand name (which may not be available locally), as it will make getting replacements easier.

WOMEN TRAVELLERS

Seoul is not a particularly dangerous place for women travellers, but it's not the safest either. There is no revolution in sexual roles looming on the horizon, and South Korea remains very much a male-dominated society. The men also tend to have firm ideas of how women should look, dress and behave. Women are expected to be picture perfect – beautiful, quiet, well dressed and respectfully subservient. Korean men don't like to see women smoking in public, or wearing flip-flops (thongs) or halter tops.

Walking alone late at night is probably not a good idea in any big city, and you shouldn't make an exception for Seoul. Some Koreans tend to be big drinkers, and you may encounter some fairly aggressive drunks. It's common from about 10 pm onwards for the streets to be crowded with swaying packs of drunken office workers. The consensus is that western women are safer than Korean women, but foreign women have indeed been raped in Seoul.

Korean women complain of furtive groping on crowded trains and buses. Some carry pins and sharpened umbrellas to deter such behaviour.

GAY & LESBIAN TRAVELLERS

Koreans are somewhat schizophrenic when it comes to gay and lesbian issues. On the one hand, the country has never passed any laws that overtly discriminate against homosexuals. Gay and lesbian sexual acts are not illegal, and homosexuality has not been used as a legal argument in cases involving divorce, child custody, adoption or job dismissal.

On the other hand, one should not mistake this superficially non-hostile legal environment as being a sign of tolerance. Korean law does not mention homosexuality simply because it's considered so bizarre that it's unmentionable in public. When uncomfortably confronted with the issue, most Koreans will insist that there are no gays and lesbians in Korea – it's a 'foreign problem'.

As long as the 'problem' remains invisible, Koreans are content to ignore it. However, recent attempts by gays and lesbians to come out of the closet have been met with hostility from the general public and the legal authorities. Film-makers dealing with gay issues have seen their movies banned. In 1997, students at Yonsei University organised the first Seoul Queer Film and Video Festival, but it had to be cancelled when the prosecutor's office threatened the organisers with a three year prison sentence and a fine of more than US$20,000. Bars, discos and saunas catering to a gay clientele exist in Seoul, but they must remain very low key.

Probably the best source for gay and lesbian activities in Korea is the Internet (try the link at www.utopia-asia.com).

There are numerous gay bars in the Nagwon-dong neighbourhood north and east of T'apkol Park in central Seoul. Cruising takes place in the park in the evening (just before closing time), and moves just outside the park after the gates close.

The other neighbourhood that has a significant gay clientele is I'taewon in the area close to the Hamilton Hotel.

DISABLED TRAVELLERS

Unfortunately, Seoul is geared heavily towards the physically fit. A particular nightmare exists for those who have difficulty ascending and descending stairs. Many of Seoul's major intersections can only be crossed by descending stairs into the subway system.

To make matters worse, it's easy to get confused in this underground labyrinth and emerge from the subway at the wrong exit, which forces you to descend again and seek another route.

A minor compensation is that the pedestrian footpaths in Seoul are generally wide and unobstructed, at least along major boulevards. Unfortunately, there are no wheelchair cut-outs – the high kerbs can be a serious obstacle. Also, the back alleys have no footpaths and are often blocked by illegally parked cars.

SENIOR TRAVELLERS

Ascending and descending stairs is a fact of everyday life in Seoul, especially when crossing major streets, which use underpasses rather than crosswalks. Seniors in good physical shape may enjoy these frequent ups and downs, but many others find the stairs to be a formidable obstacle.

Some of the palaces and museums offer discounts or even free admission to seniors age 65 and over, but you'll need some identification (ie passport) to take advantage of these offers. Senior's discounts on the city's subway and bus system are more problematic – a special senior citizen's ID card is required, and you can only obtain this if you are a resident of Seoul.

SEOUL FOR CHILDREN

Most tourist sites (museums, amusement parks etc) offer substantial discounts for children and students.

Seoul is not over-endowed with family attractions, but kids will love Children's Grand Park, Seoul Grand Park, Lotte World and Seoul Dream Land. For details of these attractions, see the Things to See & Do and Excursions chapters.

USEFUL ORGANISATIONS
Lost & Found

The Lost & Found (☎ 299 1282, fax 298 1282) is operated by the Seoul Metropolitan Police Bureau at 102 Hongik-dong, Sŏngdong-gu; but don't count on an English-speaker answering the phone. If you leave something valuable in a taxi, there is some modest hope of recovering it here.

There are several subway 'lost and found' offices:

Lines 1 and 2
(☎ 753 2408) City Hall station
Lines 3 and 4
(☎ 271 1170) Ch'ungmuro station
Line 5
(☎ 298 6767) Wangshimni station
Line 7
(☎ 949 6767) Taerung station
Line 8
(☎ 418 6768) Chamshil station
Suburban trains
(☎ 869 0089) Kuro station on line 1

There is also a 'lost and found' at Kimp'o airport terminal No 1 (☎ 660 2664) and terminal No 2 (☎ 660 2673).

Foreigners Services

The Foreigners Community Service, also called FOCUS (☎ 798 7529), does a number of things, from social get-togethers to medical referrals.

The USO (Map 2, ☎ 795 3028, 795 3063) is at 104 Galwol-dong, Yongsan-gu, just opposite Gate 21 of the Yongsan US army base. The USO is an entertainment and cultural centre that serves the US military, though it's open to all. Office hours are Monday through Saturday from 8 am to 8 pm. Take subway line 1 to Namyŏng station (one stop south of Seoul station) and walk south for five minutes.

Business Groups

The IBB is a forum for CEOs and top executives of foreign companies present in Korea or doing business with Korea. The country's leading politicians, businesspeople, financial experts and public figures are invited as speakers.

The forum is held on the first Friday of every month at the Westin Chosun Hotel (Map 5), in the Grand Ballroom. Call in advance for an invitation.

There are various foreign chambers of commerce. The more notable ones include:

American Chamber of Commerce
  (☎ 753-6471, fax 755 6579)
  2nd floor, Westin Chosun Hotel (Map 5),
  87 Sogong-dong, Chung-gu
Australian Trade Commission
  (☎ 737 8800, fax 734 5085)
  11th floor, Kyobo Bldg (Map 4),
  1 Chongno 1-ga, Chongno-gu
British Chamber of Commerce
  (☎ 720 9406, fax 720 9411)
  Room 201, Anglican Church Bldg (Map 4),
  3-7 Chong-dong, Chung-gu
European Union Chamber of Commerce
  (☎ 543-9301, fax 543-9304)
  6th floor, Hoechst Bldg,
  84-7 Chungdam-dong, Kangnam-gu
French Chamber of Commerce and Industry
  (☎ 749-3451, fax 749-3454)
  3rd floor, Dongbang Bldg,
  5-3 Hannam-dong, Yongsan-gu
Korean-German Chamber of Commerce
  and Industry
  (☎ 3780-4600, fax 3780-4637)
  8th floor, Shinwon Plaza Bldg,
  28-2 Hannam-dong, Yongsan-gu

LIBRARIES

The USIS Library (☎ 732 2601) is run by the United States Information Service and has the best English-language library in Seoul. The USIS is on the US army's Yongsan military base, but civilians of all nationalities may use the facilities. When entering expect a quick frisk by military personnel, and leave your passport with the guards. Non-military visitors cannot check out books. The library is directly opposite the USO (Map 2). The nearest subway station is Namyŏng on line 1.

The US Business Centre (☎ 397 4178), 1406 Leema building, 146-1 Susong-dong, Chongno-gu, is dedicated mostly to assisting American firms doing business in Korea. However, the Commercial Library here is open to everyone, though again its primary mission is to be a source of information for companies wishing to identify supply sources in the USA.

The National Central Library (Map 7) has mostly Korean books, but there are some English titles. It's inconveniently located south-west of the Seoul express bus terminal. The nearest subway station is Sŏch'o on line 2.

More central is Namsan Public Library in the Botanical Gardens (Map 5). The closest subway station is Hoehyŏn on line 4. The library stocks mostly Korean books.

All major universities have libraries. Again, the stacks are mostly Korean, but there are English books and a few in other languages as well.

UNIVERSITIES

Seoul is by far the nation's educational capital, with more than 50 institutions which grant higher degrees. The government has attempted on several occasions to move some of the universities to more far-flung cities, but has always backed down in the face of fierce opposition from students, parents, teachers and bureaucrats. Seoul is where everyone wants to be.

Seoul National University (Map 2) is Korea's largest. The school got its start as Keijo Imperial University in 1924, during the Japanese era. Indeed, it was the only university in Korea when the Japanese ran the country. It was renamed Seoul National University in 1946 and the main campus was moved to Kwanak-gu, a dull part of the city. About the only good reason to visit here might be to climb nearby Kwanaksan. The nearest subway stop to the campus is Seoul National University station on line 2.

The Shinch'on area (Map 9) contains several high-status universities. Hongik University is the premier art school in Korea, and the area just outside the campus gates has the liveliest nightlife in Seoul. You can reach the school by taking subway line 2 to Hongik University station.

Not far from Hongik, Yonsei University and nearby Ewha Women's University are chiefly notable for the good nightlife around the campus entrances. Yonsei has also distinguished itself by being the main scene of numerous student riots. Sŏgang University (perhaps the most academically respectable of the lot) is a short walk south of Shinch'on subway station on line 2.

Sungkyunkwan University (Map 2) is of special historical interest because it was originally the National Confucian Academy. In fact, virtually every large town in Korea had a Confucian Academy which taught the Chinese classics until the government examination system was abolished in 1894. Although a Confucian education is now a thing of the past, Sungkyunkwan University is still home to Munmyo, the Confucian Shrine, and a Confucian ceremony is staged here twice annually. The closest subway station is Hyehwa on line 4.

CULTURAL CENTRES

For anyone with an interest in Korean culture who is planning on basing themselves in Seoul for an extended period, it would be worth looking into the activities offered by the Royal Asiatic Society (Map 3, ☎ 765 9483, fax 766 3796).

The RAS has been going strong since 1900, and features regular meetings, guest speakers and weekend tours. Membership in the organisation is not required, but costs W25,000 per year and brings a few benefits including a subscription to the society's academic journal *Transactions*, a twice-monthly announcement of activities and news, an invitation to the RAS annual party, and a 10% discount on all of the society's books and tours.

One-hour academic lectures are given on the 2nd and 4th Tuesday of every month (except July and August) at 7.30 pm. The venue for the lectures could change, but it's currently at the British embassy (Map 4), on the north side of Tŏksugung – you must call the RAS in advance to put your name on the guest list (otherwise the security guards won't let you inside the embassy).

You can write to the RAS at: CPO Box 255, Seoul; or visit at room 611, Korean Christian building off Taehangno (take subway line 1 to Chongno 5-ga station and walk north). It's open Monday to Friday from 10 am to noon, and 2 to 5 pm.

For non-Korean cultural centres in Seoul, see Foreign Cultural Centres in the Entertainment chapter.

DANGERS & ANNOYANCES

Seoul is one of the safest cities in Asia but it's not utopia. South Korea has very strict gun control laws, and almost no drug addicts – both of these factors undoubtedly keep crime rates down; however, South Korea is no longer the crime-free country it once was. In Seoul, burglaries have become common, while muggings and rapes are on the rise. The back alleys of It'aewon should especially be avoided late at night, but you can walk major streets after dark without fear. Pickpocketing is not unknown.

Riots

Student rioting is a seasonal sport most common in late spring or early summer. The actual number of student rioters has declined sharply since the democratic elections of 1993, but those who continue to throw firebombs and rocks still maintain the old enthusiasm. Although fatalities are rare, injuries are common. Some foreigners like to get close to the action for that 'special photo' to impress the loved ones at home. This carries certain risks, to say the least.

Macho Posturing

More an annoyance than a risk for the most part, males who head out for a night on the town should watch out for aggressive locals (this particularly applies to It'aewon). Some Korean men (like their western counterparts) can get very cocky after a few beers, and some of the bumps you get on the street late at night may not be accidental. The thing to do is to stay cool and keep walking. If you try to fight your way out of a situation, the chances are that you'll get pounced upon by incensed passers-by. If things get violent, the foreigner is usually seen to be in the wrong.

A foreign man accompanied by a Korean woman (or a woman who looks Korean) runs a particularly high risk of being the recipient of Korean male belligerence. A Korean man may paw his girlfriend in public, but woe to the western man who tries this. The woman will also be given a hard time (typically she'll be called a 'Yankee's whore'). If you are male and with a Korean female friend, at least take the precaution of not holding hands or showing any other intimacy in public.

Asphyxiation

In winter, Koreans use a unique form of heating known as *ondol* in which the floor is heated. In former times, the heat was supplied by burning coal briquettes in an oven built just under the floor. This kept the floor toasty warm, and since Koreans have traditionally slept on the floor, it's easy to see how this would be very comfortable in winter. Unfortunately, sleeping on top of an oven presents a real danger of carbon monoxide poisoning if the floor develops any cracks. The fact that traditional homes had floors made of stone and clay meant that such cracks often developed, and many people did indeed die of asphyxiation.

Fortunately, the technology has improved, and in modern Seoul the danger of carbon monoxide poisoning is almost nil. In order to control air pollution, natural gas – rather than coal briquettes – are now used. Furthermore, the oven has been eliminated and replaced with a boiler – hot water is pumped through pipes in the floor to heat the room. So rather than sleeping on top of an oven, it's more like sleeping on top of a giant radiator.

In the countryside, you can still find some traditional houses using the old system. In the rare event that you get to spend the night in one of these ancient buildings, it would be prudent to leave a window partially open.

War Games

Air-raid drills are held about twice annually – when you hear the sirens you must get off the streets and keep away from doors and windows. If you're on a bus during an air raid, the bus will stop and you'll have to get off and seek shelter. After the all-clear signal is given, you are permitted to get back on the bus without paying an additional fare

– some people take advantage of this to get a free ride.

Pride & Prejudice

Koreans are a proud people who are very much aware of their 5000 year cultural heritage and ethnic uniqueness. This 'being proud' is often a source of irritation to foreigners – the Koreans like to toot their own horn. You may be told that Korea has the world's greatest culture, the best scenery, that han'gŭl is the most perfect writing system in the world, that Koreans created many of the world's most important inventions (the printing press etc), that Koreans are a 'pure race' (unpolluted by ethnic minorities) and that there is no such thing as homosexuality in Korea. There is not much point arguing about these kinds of issues.

This formidable pride is in part a reaction to Korea's turbulent recent history: the Japanese occupation, the carving up of the country by foreign powers and the presence of US armed forces personnel. This means that you should tread carefully when dealing with Koreans – they are very sensitive to any slights of their culture and society, and will not like it one bit if they perceive that you are acting superior. For the sake of smooth relations, politely accept that many Koreans will tell you that their country is the greatest in the world, but you dare not say the same about your country.

Mosquitoes

While not a major threat, mosquitoes can haunt your room at night from May through October. The Korean solution to this problem is 'electric mosquito incense' *(chŏnja mogihyang)*. It consists of a small cardboard pad (soaked in insecticide) and an electric heater. This ingenious device is sold in pharmacies and will keep the demons away when you're trying to sleep.

LEGAL MATTERS

While the Korean police tend to be easygoing with foreigners, you shouldn't think of yourself as being above the law. Most legal problems involving foreigners involve two categories of crimes – visa violations and drugs. In the case of visa transgressions, the penalty is normally a fine and possible expulsion from the country (depending on the seriousness of the offence). As for using or selling narcotics, you could spend a few years researching the living conditions in South Korean prisons.

The police are also strict about jaywalking, littering and motor vehicle violations.

BUSINESS HOURS

For most government offices, business hours are from 9 am to 6 pm Monday to Friday, and until 1 pm Saturday. From November to February, government offices close at 5 pm. Private businesses normally operate from 8.30 am until 6 pm or later on Monday to Friday, and until 1 pm (or later) on Saturday.

Department stores are open from 10.30 am to 7.30 pm daily, though they may be closed for two to four days a month (the off days are staggered between stores so that one is always open). Most small shops stay open from dawn until late at night.

Banking hours are from 9.30 am to 4.30 pm Monday to Friday, and until 1.30 pm on Saturday. As elsewhere in the world, banks are closed on Sunday and public holidays.

As elsewhere in the world, staff at foreign embassies have a plum job. They work from 9 am to 5 pm, Monday to Friday, usually with a long lunch break, plus the embassy closes for every Korean and foreign holiday.

PUBLIC HOLIDAYS & SPECIAL EVENTS

There are two types of public holidays – those that are set according to the solar calendar and those that follow the lunar calendar.

Solar Holidays

Public holidays which follow the familiar solar calender include:

New Year's Day
  1-2 January
Independence Movement Day
  1 March (anniversary of the 1919 Independence movement against the Japanese)

Arbour Day
  5 April (trees are planted across the nation as part of Korea's reafforestation program)
Children's Day
  5 May
Memorial Day
  6 June
Constitution Day
  17 July
Liberation Day
  15 August (marks the Japanese acceptance of the allied terms of surrender in 1945)
National Foundation Day
  3 October (also called Tan'gun Day, marking the mythical founding of the Korean nation in 2333 BC by the god-king Tan'gun)
Christmas Day
  25 December

Lunar Holidays

Lunar holidays fall on different dates each year. There are three lunar festivals which are designated public holidays:

January/February
Sŏllal

Lunar New Year: it falls on the first day of the first moon. Expect Korea to grind to a halt at this time. The schedule for the next four years is: 5 February 2000, 24 January 2001, 12 February 2002 and 1 February 2003.

April/May
Puch'ŏnim Oshilnal

Buddha's Birthday, or Feast of the Lanterns: the eighth day of the fourth moon. In Seoul, there is an evening lantern parade from Yŏuido Park to Chogyesa temple on the Sunday prior to the actual holiday. Buddha's Birthday falls on the following dates: 11 May 2000, 30 April 2001, 19 May 2002 and 8 May 2003.

September/October
Ch'usŏk

Korean Thanksgiving, also known as the 'Harvest Moon Festival' (Hangawi) and Mid-Autumn Festival (Chungch'u-jŏl). It falls on the 15th day of the eighth moon, and is South Korea's biggest holiday. At this time Seoul becomes almost deserted as most city dwellers return to their family homes and prepare offerings for their ancestral tombs. Virtually everybody is busy going to, coming from, bowing in front of, and/or picnicking in front of their ancestors' graves, and if the weather is favourable the evening is spent moon gazing.

This holiday falls on the following dates: 12 September 2000, 1 October 2001, 21 September 2002 and 11 September 2003.

Festivals

Holiday periods such as Lunar New Year and Ch'usŏk are good times to head off to the Korean Folk Village near Suwon (see the Excursions chapter) or Seoul Nori Madang (see the Entertainment chapter), as special performances of traditional dances or wedding services are held at these times of the year. Festivals in Seoul include:

February/March
Sŏkchŏnje

This fascinating ceremony is held twice a year according to the lunar calendar (first day of the second and eighth moons). The ceremony is only staged in the courtyard of the Confucius Shrine at Sungkyunkwan University (Map 2) in the north of Seoul. Performances are done by a traditional court orchestra, and full costume rituals are enacted. To get to the university, take the subway to Hyehwa station. The schedule for the next four years is: 6 March and 29 August 2000; 23 February and 17 September 2001; 14 March and 7 September 2002; 3 March and 28 August 2003.

May
International Labour Day

Held on 1 May, this is *not* an official public holiday, in part because of its Marxist connotations (communist states celebrate 1 May as a major public holiday). Despite the official frown, banks and many other businesses close at this time.

Chyongmyo T'aeje

Called the 'Royal Shrine Rites' in English, this is a homage to the kings and queens of the Chosŏn Dynasty. Full-costume parades are held along with court music. It takes place at Seoul's Chongmyo shrine (Map 3) on the first Sunday of May.

June
Tano Festival

This is held throughout South Korea on the fifth day of the fifth lunar month. The festival features processions of shamans and mask dance dramas. The schedule for the next four years is: 6 June 2000, 25 June 2001, 15 June 2002 and 4 June 2003.

August/September
National Folk Arts Festival

The date and the venue for the National Folk Arts Festival changes from year to year, but falls around September. It is an excellent opportunity to see traditional Korean festival activities. There are some real crowd pleasers, like the wagon battle and torch-hurling events (a tradition carried on by Korean university students every spring). Check with KNTO to find out when it's scheduled.

Sŏkchŏnje

See the March entry for details of this semi-annual ceremony.

October
Armed Forces' Day

This is 'in your face' day for North Korea. This festival is marked with big military parades, warplane acrobatics and honour guard ceremonies on Yŏŭido. The festival is held on 1 October.

Han'gŭl Day

In commemoration of the establishment of the Korean han'gŭl writing system in the 15th century, Han'gŭl Day is held on 9 October.

DOING BUSINESS
Business Organisations

The Korea World Trade Centre, or KWTC, (Map 7) is a huge business complex which opened in 1988 to meet the needs of both foreign and domestic traders. The KWTC consists of the Trade Tower, Korea Exhibition Center (KOEX), Korea City Air Terminal (KCAT), the Inter-Continental Hotel and Hyundai department store.

About 20 import and export-related organisations, including the Korea Foreign Trade Association, and 250 or more trading companies and financial establishments such as banks and insurance companies, have offices in the 55 storey Trade Tower.

Business travellers may want to make contact with the Korea Foreign Trade Association (☎ 551 5268, fax 551 5161); the postal address is 159-1 Samsŏng-dong, Kangnam-gu, Seoul.

KOEX (☎ 551 0114, 551 1201) consists of a four storey main building and a three storey annexe. The exhibition center has three exhibition halls and many permanent display halls.

To visit the KWTC, take subway line 2 to Samsŏng station. There are also direct buses from Kimp'o airport.

The full gamut of bureaucratic offices is too numerous to list, but some of the more notable ones include:

Chamber of Commerce & Industry
 (☎ 316 3114) 45 Namdaemunno 4-ga, Chung-gu
Customs Service
 (☎ 544 3711) 71 Nonhyŏn-dong, Kangnam-gu
Korea Trade Promotion Corporation (KOTRA)
 (☎ 551 4181) 159 Samsŏng-dong,
 Kangnam-gu; Web site: www.kotra.co.kr
Seoul Metropolitan Government
 (☎ 750 8488) 31 T'aep'yŏngno 1-ga, Chung-gu

Business Offices

For the time being at least, Korea's economic troubles have brought office rental rates way down, and it's currently possible to rent executive suites even for the short term with a bilingual secretary included. The English-language newspapers are full of ads for such services.

One service to consider is the Unico World Business Centre (☎ 551 2771) in the Korea World Trade Centre (see the previous entry). Another posibility is IBK Business Centre (☎ 780 5801) in the DLI 63 Building (Map 7). Unico has a home page on the Internet (www.uniconet.com), as does IBK (www.63ibk.co.kr). There are sure to be even cheaper alternatives if you look around with the help of Korean friends.

Translation Services

All of the following translation services are privately run:

Alpnet
 (☎ 3453 2051, fax 3453-2053)
 2nd floor, Samsung Bldg,
 170-8 Samsŏng-dong, Kangnam-gu
Chonha Language
 (☎ 786 0457, fax 769 1859)
 842 Daeyong Bldg,
 44-1 Yŏŭido-dong, Yŏngdŭngp'o-gu
Dagam Communications
 (☎ 267 7181, fax 267 7182)
 Room 601, Nexus Tower,
 206-3 Ojang-dong, Chung-gu

Global Language
 (☎ 420 5505, fax 425 0228)
 183-16 Songp'a-dong, Songp'a-gu
JYS Worldwide
 (☎ 777 1021, fax 777 1022)
 7th floor, Samkoo Bldg,
 70 Sogong-dong, Chung-gu
Koreascope
 (☎ 926 6666, fax 923 0529, email
 gary@koreascope.com)
 Room 303, Samson Bldg,
 346 Samson 4-ga, Sŏngbuk-gu 136-085
Sky International
 (☎ 703 0588, fax 703 0517)
 1002 Jeil Bldg, 256-13 Gongdŏk-dong,
 Map'o-gu

WORK

One unusual method of fund raising is to turn in a North Korean spy – the government pays from W1,000,000 to W5,000,000 for each one you report.

Failing that, you just might need to get a job. South Korea in general, and Seoul in particular, are hot spots to look for work, mainly English teaching at one of the many private language schools *(hagwon)*. Although it is illegal to work on a tourist visa, many people still do. This brings with it certain risks: you might get caught up in the government's endless crackdown campaigns and be deported.

Many well-to-do families would love to hire private tutors to teach their children. However, this is totally illegal, and the government expends an incredible amount of police power trying to catch violators. Indeed, police actually visit the public schools and interrogate young students to find out if they are receiving home tutoring. If a student confesses, both parents and the tutor are then prosecuted. The reason for all this vigilance is that hagwon owners do not like competition from private tutors, and the hagwons are big businesses with good government connections.

Of course, if you are suitably qualified *(ie you've graduated with a degree in something)*, there is no need to run the risks of working illegally. Many schools in Korea are willing to sponsor English teachers on one-year contracts, but don't sign any contracts until *after* you receive the work visa.

Remuneration for English teaching runs in the vicinity of US$1000 to US$2000 per month, but there are pitfalls. The first is that many contracts include ways to keep you until the end of your contract (a fine of two months wages for early resignation is common, and schools usually only pay once monthly so this is easily enforced). The second problem is that some schools simply cheat on wages. If you are being paid less than your contract stipulates, there isn't a whole lot you can do other than quit. Unfortunately, you will lose your work visa within just a few days of quitting, which means you must leave the country. A work visa is valid for one job only – if you quit and want to seek other employment, you must apply for a new work visa. In theory, if you've been cheated by an employer, you can take the case to court, though in practice, this seldom works.

So how do you find teaching work in Korea? The obvious place to look is the classified sections of the two daily English-language newspapers, though some people maintain that the best jobs are never advertised, and that it is only the schools that consistently lose staff that need to advertise.

One other way to find work is to look at the rare travellers' noticeboards that can be found in Seoul. You can find one at the Net Cyber Cafe (see the earlier Email & Internet Access entry) and at the Inn Daewon (see the Central section in the Places to Stay chapter).

Getting There & Away

AIR
Departure Tax
All departure taxes must be paid in Korean *won*. Airport departure tax on international flights is W9000. Children under age two and military personnel stationed in Korea are exempt from paying. There is also a W2000 airport tax on domestic flights, but this is included in the ticket price. For children aged 12 and under, the departure tax on domestic flights is W1000.

Other Parts of Korea
Domestic air service is offered by two companies, Asiana Airlines and Korean Air (KAL). Fares are the same on either airline, and both offer 10% discounts to students. Children under two years of age travel free, and those between two and 13 years of age travel at 50% of the adult fare. Military personnel get a 30% discount. There is no financial penalty for cancellation if you do so at least three hours before departure time.

You must have your passport handy before boarding a domestic flight – you won't be allowed to board the plane unless you have it. The destinations and fares *(in won)* from Seoul are as follows:

Destination	Fare (W)	Airline
Cheju City	59,100	A, K
Chinju	51,300	A, K
Kangnŭng	19,900	A, K
Kunsan	27,300	A, K
Kwangju	37,000	A, K
Mokp'o	43,900	A, K
P'ohang	41,700	A, K
Pusan	44,300	A, K
Sokch'o	32,100	K
Taegu	34,800	A, K
Ulsan	47,400	A, K
Yech'ŏn	25,700	A, K
Yŏsu	48,900	A, K

A = Asiana Airlines
K = KAL

Other Countries
The Asian economic crisis has brought a sharp drop in demand for international flights, which in turn has led to lower prices. Tickets purchased in Korea are particularly cheap, but only if you travel at off-peak times. Furthermore, just how long these great discounts will continue to be available remains uncertain. Another factor to consider is that one-way fares are almost the same price as a return ticket.

All this begs the question – can you purchase a 'back-to-front' ticket? These are best explained by example – if you want to fly from Australia (where tickets are relatively expensive) to Seoul (where tickets are much cheaper), you can pay by cheque or credit card and have a friend or travel agent in Seoul mail the ticket to you. The problem is that the airlines have computers and will know that the ticket was issued in Seoul rather than Australia, and they will refuse to honour it. Consumer groups have filed lawsuits over this practice with mixed results, but in most countries the law protects the airlines, not consumers. In short, the ticket is only valid starting from the country where it was issued. The only exception to this general rule is if you purchase a full-fare (non-discounted) ticket, but of course that robs you of the advantage you gain by purchasing a back-to-front ticket.

At least before the economic collapse, international flights were always heavily booked during certain peak times, especially the Lunar New Year, Ch'usŏk and Christmas. It can also be difficult to get economy trans-Pacific tickets on short notice during the summer school holidays, though you can always get a seat if you're willing to pay for a business or 1st class ticket.

Free baggage allowance for economy class is 20kg, but travellers flying between Korea and North or South America get a 32kg allowance. There are other concessions for 1st class and business-class travellers – check with the airline to be sure.

Korea is a particularly good place to purchase a 'round-the-world' ticket. At the time of this writing, such tickets could be bought in Seoul for US$700. These tickets let you take your time (six months to a year) moving from point to point until you've circumnavigated the globe. The main restriction is that you have to keep moving in the same direction; a drawback is that because you are usually booking individual flights as you go, and can't switch carriers, you can get caught out by flight availabilities, and have to spend more, or less, time in a place than you would like.

The USA There are some very good open tickets which remain valid for six months or one year (opt for the latter unless you're sure) but don't lock you into any fixed dates of departure. For example, there are cheap tickets between the US west coast and Hong Kong, with stopovers in Japan, Korea or Taiwan, and for very little extra money the departure dates can be changed and you have one year to complete the journey.

However, be careful during the high season (summer and Chinese/Korean Lunar New Year), because seats will be hard to come by unless reserved months in advance.

Discounters in the USA are known as 'consolidators' (though you won't see a sign on the door saying 'Consolidator').

It's not advisable to send money (even cheques) through the post unless the agent involved is very well established – some travellers have reported being ripped off by fly-by-night mail-order ticket agents.

Council Travel (☎ 800-226 8624) is America's largest student travel organisation, but you don't have to be a student to use it. Council Travel has an extensive network in all major US cities – look in the phone book or check out its Web site (www.ciee.org).

One of the cheapest and most reliable travel agents on the US west coast is Overseas Tours (☎ 415-692 4892), in Millbrae, California; Overseas Tours also has a good Web site (www.overseastours.com). Another good

agent is Gateway Travel (☎ 214-960 2000, 800-441 1183), based in Dallas, Texas, but with branches in many major US cities.

Some quotes for one-way/return tickets are: Honolulu-Seoul US$450/700; Los Angeles-Seoul US$400/582; San Francisco-Seoul US$800/743; and New York-Seoul US$870/1050. For return tickets purchased in Korea, fares are Honolulu US$450, San Francisco US$550 and New York US$700.

Canada As in the USA, Canadian discount air ticket sellers are known as 'consolidators'. Airfares from Canada tend to be at least 10% higher than from the USA.

Travel Cuts is Canada's national student travel agency and has offices in all major cities. You don't have to be a student to use its services. You can find it in the phone directory, or ring up the Toronto office (☎ 416-977 5228), or visit its Web site (www.travelcuts.com).

Other agencies that have received good reviews are Avia (☎ 514-284 5040) in Montreal and Mar Tours (☎ 416-536 5458) in Toronto.

One-way/return Vancouver-Seoul discount tickets are available for US$582/850. From Toronto, the lowest quoted rates are US$726/1069. For tickets purchased in Seoul, a return ticket to Vancouver can be had for US$450.

Australia The high season for most flights from Australia to Asia is from 22 November to 31 January; if you fly out during this period expect to pay more for your ticket.

Generally speaking, buying a return air ticket works out cheaper than paying for separate one-way tickets for each stage of your journey, although return tickets are more expensive the longer their validity. Most return tickets to Asia have 28 day, 90 day or 12 month validity.

Quite a few travel offices specialise in discount air tickets. Some travel agents, smaller ones particularly, advertise cheap air fares in the travel sections of weekend newspapers, such as the *Age* and the *Sydney Morning Herald*.

Two well known discounters (both with Web sites) are STA Travel and the Flight Centre. STA Travel (www.sta-travel.com) has offices in all major cities and on many university campuses (though you don't have to be a student to use its services). The Flight Centre (www.flightcentre.com.au) has dozens of offices throughout Australia and New Zealand. Both STA Travel and the Flight Centre regularly publish brochures with their latest deals.

Budget one-way/return tickets between Seoul and either Sydney or Melbourne cost US$612/765. A return ticket purchased in Korea can be as low as US$400.

New Zealand Both KAL and Air New Zealand can shuttle you between Auckland and Seoul. Tickets are not especially cheap. Rock-bottom one-way/return fares begin at US$850/1350. In Korea, Seoul-Auckland return tickets cost US$550. At the other end, the Flight Centre has a large central office (☎ 09-309 6171) at 3A National Bank Tower, 205-225 Queen St, Auckland.

The UK Air-ticket discounters are affectionately known as 'bucket shops' in the UK. Despite the somewhat sleazy name, there is nothing under-the-counter about this business. There are a number of magazines in the UK which have good information about flights and agents. These include: *Trailfinder*, free from the Trailfinders Travel Centre in Earl's Court; and *Time Out*, a London weekly entertainment guide widely available in the UK. The best deals are available in London.

When purchasing a ticket from a bucket shop that looks a little unsound, make sure they are bonded, and belong, to the Association of British Travel Agents as well as the Air Travel Organiser's Licensing (ATOL) – the latter is a government agency.

Some recommended London bucket shops include: the aforementioned Trailfinders, Council Travel (☎ 0171-437 7767), Platinum Travel (☎ 0171-937 5122) and STA Travel (☎ 0171-938 4711). Campus Travel (☎ 0171-730 7285) has 44 offices in

the UK and 150 worldwide; it also has a useful Web Site (www.campustravel.co.uk). Flight Bookers (☎ 0171-757 2444) is another big outfit with an online 'office' (www.flight bookers.co.uk).

Internet Travel Services (www.its.net/ta/home.htm) has a very good Web site, with many travel agencies listed. The list includes courier companies in the UK.

Both British Airways and KAL offer service between London and Seoul at competitive prices. The lower end of the market for London-Seoul one-way/return tickets is US$580/970. In Korea, return tickets can be had for US$400.

Continental Europe Fares similar to those from London are available from other western European cities.

The Netherlands, Belgium and Switzerland are good places for buying discount air fares. In Antwerp, WATS has been recommended. In Zurich, you can try SSR (☎ 01-297 1111). In Geneva, there's Stohl Travel. In the Netherlands, NBBS (☎ 071-253 333) is a reputable agency.

In France, OTU is a student organisation with 42 offices around the country. You can contact its Paris office (☎ 01 43 36 80 47). Another recommended agent in Paris is Council Travel (☎ 01 42 66 20 87).

In Germany, there are STA Travel outlets in Berlin (☎ 030-311 0950), Goethestrasse 73; and in Frankfurt (☎ 069-430 191), Berger Strasse 118.

In Sweden, STA Travel (☎ 018-145 404) is at Bangardsgatan 13, 75320 Uppsala.

China Asiana Airlines, KAL and Air China operate routes between Seoul and Beijing. The one way/return fare is US$270/540.

In Beijing, the Asiana Airlines office (☎ 010-506 1118) is in room 134, Jianguo Hotel, 5 Jianguomenwai Dajie. Air China (☎ 010-601 6667) is in the Aviation building, 15 Xichang'an Jie, and there is another branch in the China World Trade Centre.

Asiana and China Eastern Airlines fly Seoul-Shanghai for US$283/566. Seoul-Shenyang costs US$240/480.

There are also flights between Seoul and several other Chinese cities, including Dalian, Guangzhou, Qingdao, Shanghai, Shenyang and Tianjin.

Travel agents cannot give discounts on China-Korea tickets, and return tickets cost exactly double the one way fare.

Hong Kong Buying tickets in Hong Kong requires some caution because there are quite a few tricky travel agents. The most common ploy is a request for a non-refundable deposit on an air ticket. So you pay a deposit for the booking, but when you go to pick up the tickets you are told that the flight is no longer available, though there is another flight at a higher price, sometimes 50% more!

It is best not to pay a deposit, but rather to pay for the ticket in full and get a receipt clearly showing that there is no balance due, and that the full amount is refundable if no ticket is issued. Tickets are normally issued the next day after booking, but for the really cheapie tickets (actually group tickets) you must pick these up yourself at the airport from the 'tour leader' (who you will never see again once you've got the ticket). One caution: when you get the ticket from the tour leader, check it carefully. Occasionally there are errors; for example, you're issued a ticket with the return portion valid for only 60 days when you paid for a ticket valid for one year etc.

Some agents we've found to be cheap and reliable in Hong Kong include the following:

Phoenix Services
 (☎ 852-2722 7378, fax 2369 8884)
 Room B, 6th floor, Milton Mansion, 96 Nathan Rd, Tsimshatsui – scrupulously honest and gets good reviews from travellers
Shoestring Travel
 (☎ 852-2723 2306, fax 2721 2085)
 Flat A, 4th floor, Alpha House, 27-33 Nathan Rd, Tsimshatsui
Traveller Services
 (☎ 852-2375 2222, fax 2375 2233)
 Room 1012, Silvercord Tower 1, 30 Canton Rd, Tsimshatsui

The lowest one-way/return prices on the Hong Kong-Seoul route are US$201/272.

Macau Both KAL and Asiana fly the less travelled Seoul-Macau route. Ticket prices are very similar to Hong Kong. Occasional promotional fares might also include a free Macau-Hong Kong ferry ticket.

Guam & Saipan For jet-setting Koreans, Guam and the nearby island of Saipan have emerged as fashionable overseas honeymoon and vacation spots. Guam is just 4½ hours from Seoul by air. KAL flies into Guam and Asiana flies into Saipan. One-way/return fares begin at US$200/260 if purchased in Korea.

Indonesia Garuda Airlines and KAL fly Jakarta-Seoul direct. Cheap discount air tickets out of Indonesia can be bought from travel agents in Kuta on Bali and Jakarta on Java. There are numerous airline ticket discounters around Kuta, with several on the main strip, Jalan Legian. You can also buy discount tickets in Kuta for departure from Jakarta. In Jakarta, there are a few discounters on Jalan Jaksa. Budget one-way/return prices for Jakarta-Seoul are currently US$555/737. If purchased in Korea, a return ticket to Bali costs US$400.

Japan Japanese tourists comprise the vast majority of foreign visitors to Korea, an odd state of affairs considering how much the Koreans purport to hate their powerful neighbour. As expected, the fares are definitely lower if you purchase your ticket in Korea as opposed to purchasing it in Japan. The following are the cheapest prices you can expect on return tickets if purchased in Seoul: Fukuoka/Hakata US$170, Osaka US$190 and Tokyo US$275.

If you must buy an air ticket in Japan, Tokyo is the best place to look for discounts. You should start by checking the travel ad section of the *Tokyo Journal*. Three long-standing travel agencies where English is spoken and discounted tickets are available are: Across Traveller's Bureau (☎ 03-3374 8721 in Shinjuku, ☎ 03-5391 2871 in Ikebukuro), STA Travel (☎ 03-5269 0751 in Yotsuya, ☎ 03-5485 8380 in

Shibuya, ☎ 03-5391 2922 in Ikebukuro) and Just Travel (☎ 03-3207 8311) in Takadanobaba. There is also an STA Travel office in Osaka (☎ 06-262 7066).

Philippines In Manila, budget one-way/return fares between Seoul and Manila are US$262/452. A return ticket bought in Seoul costs US$275.

Singapore A good place for buying cheap air tickets in Singapore is Airmaster Travel Centre. Also try STA Travel (☎ 065-737 7188), 2-17 Orchard Parade Hotel, 1 Tanglin Rd. Other agents advertise in the *Straits Times* classified columns.

One-way/return Singapore-Seoul tickets start at US$400/673. If purchased in Seoul, a return trip costs US$250.

Taiwan Discount travel agents advertise in Taiwan's three English-language newspapers, the *China News*, *China Post* and *Taipei Times*. Don't believe the advertised rock-bottom fares – most are elusive 'group fares' which are not accessible to the individual traveller. Another thing to be cautious of is sending money through the mail – this never seems to work as well as visiting the travel agent with cash in hand.

A long-running discount travel agent with a good reputation is Jenny Su Travel (☎ 02-594 7733, 596 2263), 10th floor, 27 Chungshan N Rd, Section 3, Taipei. Wing On Travel and South-East Travel have branches all over the island, and both have good reputations and offer reasonable prices.

Budget tickets on the Taipei-Seoul route start at US$180/315.

Thailand Khao San Rd in Bangkok is budget traveller headquarters and the place to look for bargain ticket deals. You could also try STA Travel (☎ 02-233 2582), Wall St Tower, Room 1406, 33 Surawong Rd, Bangrak, Bangkok.

The Bangkok-Seoul run is served by numerous carriers, and it's often possible to get a stopover in Hong Kong for a little

extra. Bangkok-Seoul one-way/return fares start at US$400/550. A return trip ticket purchased in Korea currently costs US$250.

Vietnam Vietnam Airlines, Asiana and KAL all fly Seoul-Ho Chi Minh City (Saigon) for US$350/632. Vietnam Airlines also offers a direct Seoul-Hanoi flight.

Airline Offices

It's essential to reconfirm all onward tickets if you're stopping off in Seoul for more than 72 hours. Even if you're stopping for less than 72 hours, reconfirming your flight as soon as you arrive is advised. Otherwise, it's entirely possible that your reserved seat will be given to someone else. Not all of the airlines listed in this section fly to Korea – some just maintain booking offices so you can book an onward flight with a change of aircraft (eg through Hong Kong or Tokyo).

It's best to call the airlines at their main office in the city, but you can usually also call the airport if the office is closed (see the Airline Details table).

KCAT If you are staying in southern Seoul, and especially if you're in or near the Inter-Continental Hotel – you might want to consider using the services of the Korea City Air Terminal (KCAT, Map 7). Rather than checking in at the airport, you can complete your entire check-in procedure at KCAT. However, only a few airlines offer this service. Furthermore, passengers doing their check-in at KCAT can purchase their airport departure tax ticket at a 50% discount.

The following airlines, with their special KCAT phone numbers, have check-in counters at KCAT:

Air Canada (☎ 551 3321)
All Nippon Airways (☎ 551 0745)
Asiana (☎ 551 0301)
Cathay Pacific Airways (☎ 551 0745)
Delta Airlines (☎ 551 0746)
Korean Air (☎ 551 3321)
Lufthansa (☎ 551 0301)
Northwest Airlines (☎ 551 0977)
Singapore Airlines (☎ 551 0832)

Airline Details

Airline	Code	Office ☎	Airport ☎
Aeroflot	SU	551 0321	665 8672
Air Canada	AC	779 5654	665 8163
Air China	CA	774 6886	665 8766
Air France	AF	3788 0400	663 9575
Air New Zealand	NZ	723 1114	none
Alitalia	AZ	779 1676	660 7114
All Nippon Airways	NH	752 5500	664 3701
Ansett Australia	AN	723 1114	664 4123
Asiana Airlines	OZ	774 4000	664 2626
British Airways	BA	774 5511	664 4123
Cathay Pacific Airways	CX	773 0321	664 0321
China Eastern	MU	518 0330	666 2271
China Northern	CJ	775 9070	666 2741
Continental Airlines	CS	538 4200	662 5422
Delta Air Lines	DL	754 1921	664 3632
El Al Israel Airlines	LY	778 3351	none
Garuda Indonesia	GA	773 2092	664 4643
Japan Air System	JD	752 9090	664 1564
Japan Airlines	JL	757 1711	664 2871
KLM Royal Dutch Airlines	KL	755 7040	664 1850
Korean Air	KE	756 2000	660 7114
Lufthansa Airlines	LH	538 8141	664 9850
Malaysia Airlines	MH	777 7761	662 0285
MIAT-Mongolian Airlines	OM	592 7788	none
Northwest Airlines	NW	666 8700	664 2071
Philippine Airlines	PR	774 3581	666 7407
Qantas Airways	QF	777 6871	666 3282
Singapore Airlines	SQ	755 1226	665 1711
Swissair	SR	757 8901	663 4957
Thai Airways International	TG	3707 0011	664 5491
United Airlines	UA	757 1691	662 0041
Uzbekistan Airways	HY	754 1041	664 7365
VASP Brazilian	VP	511 7304	661 5246
Vietnam Airlines	VN	775 7666	662 7617
Vladivostok Air	XF	323 0011	none

GETTING THERE & AWAY

BUS

There are no international buses to or from Seoul, but there are plenty of long-distance buses that can whisk you across Korea.

Outside Seoul, most Korean cities and even some obscure towns have at least two bus stations, an express bus terminal *(kosok bŏsŭ t'ŏminŏl)* and an inter-city bus terminal *(shi'oe bŏsŭ t'ŏminŏl)*. Logically, you might conclude that express buses are faster and more expensive, while inter-city buses are slower and cheaper. However, this is often not the case. The so-called express buses can be 1st class *(udŭng)* or 2nd class *(chikhaeng)*. The price difference between the two can be substantial. Buses from the inter-city bus terminals are almost always 2nd class, but they are not necessarily any slower than the 'express'.

The 1st class coaches are luxurious, with cushy seats and plenty of legroom. Some of these buses are even equipped with cellular payphones, though none as yet have on-board toilets. Standing passengers are not accepted in 1st class.

Actually, there is a 3rd class consisting of local *(wanheng)* long-distance buses. In most cases, you will not have a chance to use these, as they tend to serve only rural backwaters. These buses operate on set routes and will pick up and drop off anywhere. There are no reserved seats, often as many standing as sitting passengers, and all but the bulkiest of freight may be squeezed on.

It's possible to buy an advance ticket for buses, which will reserve you a particular time and date. Since seat numbers are not assigned even in 1st class, you can sit wherever there is space. If you happen to miss your bus, you can board the next one on a space-available basis.

In most cases, you won't need an advance ticket, but seats are hard to come by on weekends and holidays. At such peak times, you might have to queue for hours to buy a ticket in Seoul. Things are easier in smaller cities and towns, but travel during holidays is synonymous with packed-out buses.

Given the high standard of service, bus fares are certainly reasonable in Korea. The 1st class coaches cost about 50% more than 2nd class buses – you pay a lot for those comfortable seats.

Seoul Express Bus Terminal

The main bus station in town (Map 7) is the Seoul express bus terminal *(Seoul kosok t'ŏminŏl)*, which is also called the Kangnam express bus terminal. It's on the south side of the Han River – take subway line 3 and

Seoul Express Bus Terminal Schedules

Kyŏngbusŏn Building

Destination	First/Last Bus	Frequency	Fare (W)	Travel Time
Ch'ŏnan	6.30 am/9.20 pm	15 min	2600	1 hr
Ch'ŏngju	5.50 am/10 pm	10 min	4000	1¾ hrs
Chinju	6 am/6.30 pm	25 min	12,200	5½ hrs
Kimch'ŏn	7.10 am/6.50 pm	11 daily	7000	3 hrs
Kongju	6 am/11 pm	30 min	4100	2½ hrs
Kumi	6.50 am/7.40 pm	1¼ hrs	7700	3¼ hrs
Kŭmsan	7 am/6.40 pm	11 daily	6200	2¾ hrs
Kyŏngju	6.30 am/6.30 pm	30 min	10,700	4¼ hrs
Masan	6 am/9 pm	15 min	11,200	5 hrs
P'ohang	6 am/6.30 pm	20 min	11,700	5 hrs
Poŭn	7.10 am/6.50 pm	8 daily	6100	2½ hrs
Pugok	8 am/6 pm	2 hrs	10,400	4¾ hrs
Pusan	6 am/8.30 pm	15 min	12,600	5¼ hrs
Taegu	6 am/8.30 pm	5-10 min	8900	4 hrs
Taejŏn	6 am/9.55 pm	5-10 min	4800	2 hrs
Ulsan	6 am/6.30 pm	20 min	11,900	5 hrs
Yŏngdong	7.10 am/7.10 pm	8 daily	6400	2¾ hrs

get off at the Express Bus Terminal subway station. The terminal is very well organised, with signs in English and Korean over all the ticket offices and bus bays. This huge terminal actually consists of two buildings, Kyŏngbusŏn (☎ 782 5552) and Honam-Yŏngdongsŏn (☎ 592 0050). Kyŏngbusŏn is a ten story building with everything useful on the first floor, while Honam-Yŏngdongsŏn building is a two story structure with ticket offices and platforms on the 1st floor and a cafeteria on the second floor. These two buildings are a few hundred metres apart from one another.

In addition to the buses listed in the schedule tables in this section, there are some night buses from Seoul to major cities like Pusan, Taegu and Kwangju. For definition purposes, a 'night bus' is one which runs between 10 pm and midnight. As yet, there are

Seoul Express Bus Terminal Schedules

Honam-Yŏngdongsŏn Building

Destination	First/Last Bus	Frequency	Fare (W)	Travel Time
Ch'ungju	6.20 am/8.30 pm	30 min	4500	2 hrs
Chech'ŏn	5.40 am/8.10 pm	40-50 min	4900	3¾ hrs
Chinan	9.35 am/4.35 pm	4 daily	8200	4 hrs
Chindo	7.35 am/4.20 pm	4 daily	13,400	6¼ hrs
Chŏng-ŭp	6 am/11 pm	30 min	8000	3¼ hrs
Chŏnju	5.30 am/11 pm	5-15 min	7100	2¾ hrs
Haenam	7.55 am/5.55 pm	6 daily	12,000	5½ hrs
Ich'ŏn	6.30 am/9.20 pm	20-30 min	2300	1 hr
Iksan	5.30 am/10.30 pm	30 min	7000	3 hrs
Kangnŭng	6 am/11.30 pm	15 min	7400	4½ hrs
Kimje	6.40 am/7.50 pm	1 hr	7400	3¼ hrs
Koch'ang	9.50 am/5.40 pm	30-60 min	8700	4 hrs
Kunsan	6 am/10.50 pm	20-30 min	7600	3¼ hrs
Kwangju	5.30 am/midnight	5-10 min	9600	4 hrs
Mokp'o	5.30 am/10.40 pm	30 min	11,300	5½ hrs
Namwon	6 am/10.20 pm	40 min	8800	4¼ hrs
Nonsan	7 am/7.50 pm	1¼ hrs	6400	2¾ hrs
Puan	6.50 am/7.30 pm	30-50 min	8300	3½ hrs
Sokch'o	6.30 am/11.30 pm	30-60 min	9400	5¼ hrs
Sunch'ŏn	6 am/10.50 pm	20-30 min	11,900	5¼ hrs
Tonghae	6.30 am/11.30 pm	30-60 min	8600	4¾ hrs
Wando	7.45 am/5.30 pm	4 daily	13,100	6 hrs
Wonju	6 am/9 pm	15 min	3800	1¾ hrs
Yong-in	7.30 am/9.30 pm	15-30 min	1300	40 min
Yŏju	6.30 am/9.20 pm	30-40 min	2700	1¾ hrs
Yŏngam	8.40 am/4.40 pm	4 daily	10,900	4¾ hrs
Yŏsu	6.10 am/10.40 pm	30-40 min	12,800	5½ hrs

Add about 50% to the fares for 1st class express buses.

Tong-Seoul & Sangbong Bus Schedules

Destination	First/Last Bus	Frequency	Fare (W)	Travel Time
Ch'ŏngju	6 am/9 pm	30 min	4300	1¾ hrs
Ch'ungju	6 am/8.40 pm	20 min	4480	3¾ hrs
Chŏnju	6 am/8.20 pm	40 min	7500	3¼ hrs
Chŏng-ŭp	6.30 am/6.40 pm	6 daily	8400	3¼ hrs
Ich'ŏn	6.30 am/9.30 pm	1 hr	2200	1 hr
Kangnŭng	6 am/7.40 pm	45 min	7400	3½ hrs
Kuinsa	7.05 am/4.20 pm	7 daily	8200	4 hrs
Kwangju	6 am/7.30 pm	30 min	9800	4 hrs
Pusan	6 am/6.40 pm	30 min	12,900	5¼ hrs
Sokch'o	7 am/6.30 pm	4 daily	9400	5 hrs
Songnisan	7.30 am/6.20 pm	10 daily	7700	2¾ hrs
Taegu	6 am/8 pm	30 min	9300	3¾ hrs
Taejŏn	6 am/8 pm	30 min	5200	1¾ hrs
Tanyang	6.40 am/6.15 pm	6 daily	7200	3 hrs
Tonghae	7 am/6.40 pm	2 daily	8600	4¼ hrs
Wonju	7 am/8 pm	1 hr	3800	1¾ hrs
Yŏju	6.30 am/8.30 pm	40 min	2700	1¼ hrs
Yŏngju	9 am/4.30 pm	4 daily	11,000	3¼ hrs
Yŏngwol	7 am/7 pm	4 daily	6400	3 hrs

Sangbong terminal

Destination	First/Last Bus	Frequency	Fare (W)	Travel Time
Ch'iaksan	6.30 am/2.05 pm	4 daily	5900	2¼ hrs
Ch'unch'ŏn	5.15 am/9.30 pm	15 min	3900	1½ hrs
Inje	5.50 am/6.30 pm	30 min	7600	3½ hrs
Kangnŭng	6 am/6.30 pm	8 daily	10,100	4 hrs
Kwangju	6 am/7.40 pm	1 hr	9800	4 hrs
Pusan	6 am/9 pm	8 daily	12,800	5¼ hrs
Sokch'o	6 am/6 pm	26 daily	10,500	4½ hrs
Taegu	6 am/9 pm	8 daily	9200	3¾ hrs
Taejŏn	6 am/9 pm	1 hr	5100	1¾ hrs
Wonju	6 am/6.50 pm	1 hr	5500	2¾ hrs

Add about 50% to the fares for 1st class express buses.

no night buses between midnight and 5.30 am, but that could change. All night buses are from the Seoul express bus terminal.

Tong-Seoul Express Bus Terminal

The Tong-Seoul (East Seoul) express bus terminal (Map 2, ☎ 458 4851) is also very

useful, especially for getting to places on the east coast or the central part of the country.

You can reach Tong-Seoul bus terminal by taking subway line 2 to Kangbyŏn station.

Sangbong Bus Terminal

Sangbong bus terminal (Map 10, ☎ 435

2122), in the eastern suburbs, is most useful to people heading east. The terminal is connected by bus with Ch'ŏngryangni train station (next to Ch'ŏngryangni subway station on subway line 1). From Ch'ŏngryangni it takes 15 minutes to reach Sangbong on bus Nos 38-2, 165, 165-2, 166 and 522-1; or 50 minutes by bus from Chongno 1-ga on bus Nos 131 and 131-1.

From Sangbong terminal there are buses to dozens of obscure little towns – the Tong-Seoul & Sangbong Bus Schedules table lists the major destinations only.

Other Terminals

Other bus terminals, in descending order of usefulness, include these:

Shinch'on bus terminal
  (Map 9, ☎ 324 0611) Offers nonstop bus services to Kanghwado every 10 minutes from 5.40 am to 9.30 pm.
Nambu (south) bus terminal
  (Map 2) Operates buses to destinations in Kyŏnggi-do, such as Kanghwado, Yong-in Everland and Ansung.
Sŏbu (west) bus terminal
  (Map 2, ☎ 355 5103) Easily accessible from subway line 3, and runs buses bound for the north-western part of Kyŏnggi-do, including Freedom Bridge, Imjingak, Kwangt'an, Pogwangsa, Munsan, Munbong, Pobwonni, Choksong, Pyokche, Songch'u and Ŭijŏngbu.

TRAIN

There are no international trains, but South Korea has an extensive domestic rail network operated by Korea National Railroad (KNR). There are four classes of train in Korea: super express (saema'ul-ho), express (mugunghwa-ho), ordinary (t'ongil-ho) and local (pidulgi-ho). The local trains stop at every station. Most trains depart from Seoul station (Map 3) – Korea's busiest. Seoul's second major station is Ch'ŏngryangni station, which serves trains heading eastward towards Ch'unch'ŏn.

There's a monthly timetable (shigakp'yo) available from bookshops – this contains schedules for all forms of transport throughout the country, but only the rail portion is in English.

BULLET TAXI

Long-distance share taxis are affectionately known as 'bullet taxis' (ch'ong'al t'aekshi) because their drivers tend to drive like maniacs. These taxis are found at two places – at some major tourist sites and at bus or train stations. For example, bullet taxis often meet incoming ferries departing from Inch'ŏn. But you are most likely to find them around the Seoul express bus terminal at night when the regular buses stop running.

Along with the bullet taxis are bullet minibuses, which are just a larger version of the same thing. The minibuses usually cost less per person, but of course you have to cram more passengers inside the vehicle to make it worthwhile. Meters are not used, so you must negotiate the fare in advance.

HITCHING

Hitchhiking on Seoul's gridlocked streets is a pretty loony idea and it probably won't even occur to you to try it. However, out in the suburbs it's almost feasible, and it becomes distinctly possible in the rural backwaters of Korea.

Although no part of Korea is a particularly high-crime area, hitchhiking is never entirely safe in any country and we don't recommend it. Travellers who do choose to hitch should understand that they are taking a small but potentially serious risk. People who do choose to hitch will be safer if they travel in pairs and let someone know where they are planning to go.

BOAT

Ship departure tax costs W2000. Children under age two are exempt from paying.

China

International ferries connect the South Korean port of Inch'ŏn with six cities in China: Shanghai, Tianjin, Qingdao, Weihai, Dalian and Dandong. Weihai and Qingdao are in China's Shandong Province (the closest province to South Korea), and boats are operated by the Weidong Ferry Company. Tianjin is near Beijing, and boats are run by the Jinchuan (also spelled Jinchon) Ferry

Company. The Dandong Ferry Company operates the boats to Dandong and Dalian. Shanghai is furthest of all from Korea.

The phone numbers for the Weidong Ferry Company are: Seoul (☎ 02-711 9111), Inch'ŏn (☎ 032-886 6171), Weihai (☎ 0696-226 173) and Qingdao (☎ 0532-221 152). Phone numbers for the Jinchuan Ferry Company are: Seoul (☎ 02-517 8671), Inch'ŏn (☎ 032-887 3963) and Tianjin (☎ 022-2311 2843). Dandong Ferry Company can be contacted in Seoul (☎ 02-713 5522), Inch'ŏn (☎ 032-881 2255) and Dandong (☎ 0415-315 2666). For the Shanghai-Inch'ŏn Ferry Company, the numbers are: Shanghai (☎ 021-6596 6009), Inch'ŏn (☎ 032-886 9090) and Seoul (☎ 02-777 8080).

In Seoul, tickets for any boats to China can be bought from International Union Travel Service (☎ 02-777 6722, fax 777 4971), room 707, 7th floor, Daehan building, 340 Taepyungro 2-ga, Chung-gu, just across the street (south) of Tŏksugung (Tŏksu Palace).

In China, tickets can be bought at the pier, or from China International Travel Service (CITS), which has branches in Tianjin (☎ 022-2835 0092) and Beijing (☎ 010-6512 0508).

To reach the international ferry terminal, take the Seoul-Inch'ŏn commuter train (subway line 1 from central Seoul) and get off at Tonginch'ŏn station. The train ride takes 50 minutes. From Tonginch'ŏn train station it's either a 45 minute walk or five minute taxi ride to the ferry terminal.

You must arrive at the terminal at least one hour before departure (two hours is preferable) or you won't be allowed to board the ship.

Inch'ŏn-Shanghai The ferry runs weekly in each direction and the journey takes about 40 hours. Departures from Inch'ŏn are on Friday at 6.30 pm, while departures from Shanghai are on Tuesday at 11 am. The one-way fares are: 2B class US$70, 2A class US$75, 1B class US$85, 1A class US$115, special B class US$145, special A class US$180.

Inch'ŏn-Weihai The trip takes approximately 14 hours. Departures from Inch'ŏn are on Tuesday, Thursday and Saturday at 6 pm. Departures from Weihai are Wednesday, Friday and Sunday at 5 pm. The fares are: 2nd class US$110; 1st class US$130; special class US$180; royal class US$220; and royal suite class US$300. There is a 5% discount on a return ticket.

Weihai is no place to hang around, so if you arrive there it's best to hop on the first bus to Qingdao. If that's not available, take a bus to Yantai and then to Qingdao.

Inch'ŏn-Qingdao This trip takes about 20 hours. Departures from Qingdao are on Monday and Thursday at 5 pm. Departures from Inch'ŏn are on Wednesday and Saturday at 2 pm. Fares are exactly the same as for the Inch'ŏn-Weihai route.

Inch'ŏn-Tianjin The schedule for this ferry is a little irregular. The boat departs once every four or five days, usually on Monday, Wednesday or Friday. The trip takes a minimum of 28 hours. Departures from Tianjin are at 11 am, while the boat departs from Inch'ŏn at 1 pm. The fares are: 3B class US$120, 3A class US$130, 2B class US$150, 2A class US$160, 1st class US$180 and VIP class US$230.

The boat doesn't dock at Tianjin proper, but rather at the nearby port of Tanggu. Unfortunately, accommodation in Tianjin is outrageously expensive, but Tanggu has at least one economical place to stay, the *Seamen's Hotel*. Tanggu also has trains and minibuses directly to Beijing.

Third class on the boat is a huge vault with around 80 beds, and horrid toilets.

Inch'ŏn-Dalian This journey takes 18 to 21 hours depending on which direction the boat is heading (go figure).

The boat departs Inch'ŏn on Wednesday and Saturday at 6.30 pm. It departs Dalian at noon on Tuesday and Friday. Fares are: 2B class US$120, 2A class US$125, 1st class US$150, special class US$180 and royal suite US$230.

Inch'ŏn-Dandong Departures from Dandong are on Sunday and Thursday at 3 pm, arriving in Inch'ŏn the next morning at 8 am. Departures from Inch'ŏn are on Monday and Friday at 5 pm, arriving the next morning at 9 am. Expect this schedule to get cut back somewhat during the frigid winter season. Fares are: economy US$120, deluxe C US$130, deluxe B US$150, deluxe A US$160, deluxe special US$190, suite US$210 and royal suite US$230.

Japan

There are several ferries linking Japan with South Korea. Purchasing a return ticket gains you a 10% discount on the return half, but fares from Japan are higher and there is a 600 *yen* departure tax in Japan. Korea-Japan-Korea tickets work out to be the same or less than a straight one way Japan-Korea ticket. So for the numerous travellers who work in Japan and need to make visa runs, consider taking a one-way ticket to Korea the first time if you intend to cross the waters more than once a year.

Pusan-Shimonoseki This is the most popular boat, and is serviced by the Pukwan Ferry Company. The one way journey takes 14½ hours. Daily departures from Pusan (South Korea) or Shimonoseki (Japan) are both at 6 pm and arrival is at 8.30 am. Fares on tickets bought in Korea for 1st class are US$80 to $90; 2nd class costs US$55 to $65. Students can receive a 20% discount, and bicycles are carried free. Tickets are available in Shimonoseki (☎ 0832-243 000), Pusan (☎ 051-463 3165) or Seoul (☎ 02-738 0055).

The same company also runs hydrofoils daily between Pusan and Shimonoseki. The journey takes 3½ hours and costs US$62 to $88 (Korean prices). These depart from Shimonoseki at 9.30 am, while departures from Pusan are at 1.40 pm.

Pusan-Fukuoka/Hakata Fast hydrofoils connect Pusan with this city, (usually called Hakata on ferry schedules, but also known in air travel as Fukuoka). The trip takes only three hours and costs US$50. Departure from Hakata is at 8.45 am and 3.45 pm on Tuesday and Thursday; at 10 am on Monday, Saturday and Sunday; and at 12.15 pm on Wednesday and Friday. Departures from Pusan are at 8.45 am and 3.45 pm on Wednesday and Friday; 12.15 pm on Tuesday and Thursday; and at 2 pm on Monday, Saturday and Sunday. These hydrofoils (called 'Beetle') are operated by Korea Marine Express (Pusan ☎ 051-465 6111, Seoul ☎ 02-730 8666 or Hakata ☎ 092-281 2315).

Camellia Line operates ferries thrice weekly between Pusan and Hakata. Because of their slow speed, these are no longer popular and it's possible this service will soon end. The journey takes 16 hours and costs US$44. Departure from Hakata is at 5 pm on Monday and Wednesday, and at 7 pm on Friday. Departures from Pusan are at 5.40 pm on Tuesday, Thursday and Sunday. Call Camellia Line for bookings (Pusan ☎ 051-466 7799, Seoul ☎ 02-775 2323 or Hakata ☎ 092-262 2324).

Note that in Hakata, the name of the wharf for Pusan (and for boats to Okinawa) is Chuo Futoh and it is across the bay, a long walk from Hakata Futoh (bayside place), which has other domestic boats.

Seoul-Osaka There is a wonderful combination ferry-train ticket: super-express train to Pusan, hydrofoil to Fukuoka/Hakata, plus a rail ticket to Osaka (or someplace else in Japan). Seoul-Osaka costs US$178, and Pusan-Osaka costs US$160. Tickets are sold at Aju Tours in Korea and Nippon Travel in Japan. Tickets can be obtained as late as two days in advance. Aju Tours has an office in Seoul (☎ 02-753 5051, 754 2221) and Pusan (☎ 051-462 6661). Nippon Travel has its office in Osaka (☎ 06-312 0451).

TRAVEL AGENTS

You can get pretty good deals on air tickets purchased in Seoul. Just be sure that you buy from a discount travel agent, because tickets purchased directly from the airlines cost nearly double! There are hundreds of travel agencies in Seoul, but English is not widely spoken and they are unlikely to be accustomed to westerners' preoccupation with getting the cheapest price.

Joy Travel Service (Map 4, ☎ 02-776 9871, fax 756 5342), on the 10th floor at 24-2 Mukyo-dong, Chung-gu (directly behind City Hall), offers good deals and has some English-speaking staff.

The large YMCA building (Map 4) on Chongno 2-ga (next to Chonggak station) houses two discount travel agencies. On the 5th floor (and also in the basement) is Top Travel (☎ 02-739 4630), said to have the cheapest fares in Seoul, but zero English-speaking ability. Also on the 5th floor (room 505) is another discount outfit, the Korean International Student Exchange Society, or KISES (☎ 02-733 9494, fax 732 9568).

Numerous other travel agencies advertise in the English-language newspapers. Advertised prices routinely look good, though often there are inconvenient restrictions (prices may be for group travel only, or the date of departure may be permanently fixed, and so on).

ORGANISED TOURS

Booking organised tours outside of Korea is possible, but you'll get a much better deal if you book after you've arrived in Seoul. See the Organised Tours section in the Getting Around chapter for a list of tour agencies in Seoul.

> **Warning**
>
> The information in this chapter is particularly vulnerable to change: prices for international travel are volatile, routes are introduced and cancelled, schedules change, special deals come and go, and rules and visa requirements are amended. Airlines and governments seem to take a perverse pleasure in making price structures and regulations as complicated as possible. You should check directly with the airline or a travel agent to make sure you understand how a fare (and ticket you may buy) works. In addition, the travel industry is highly competitive and there are many lurks and perks.
>
> The upshot of this is that you should get opinions, quotes and advice from as many airlines and travel agents as possible before you part with your hard-earned cash. The details given in this chapter should be regarded as pointers and are not a substitute for your own careful, up-to-date research.

Getting Around

THE AIRPORT

Kimp'o airport (Kimp'o Konghang) is 18km west of the city centre, and handles both domestic and international flights. However, this is due to change with the opening of Inch'ŏn international airport in the year 2002 (just in time for World Cup 2002). When the new airport is up and running, Kimp'o will continue to function as a domestic airport only.

The airport has a number of convenient money-changing facilities, and there is a Korean National Tourism Organisation (KNTO) information desk dishing out maps and hotel reservations. Smoking is permitted inside the airport in certain designated areas. There are a few snack bars, but don't come here looking for great cuisine. Shops in the airport sell the usual very overpriced souvenirs, as well as duty-free booze, cigarettes and chocolate-coated macadamia nuts.

One of the confusing things about Kimp'o airport is that there are three terminals – two for international and one for domestic flights. The terminals are too far apart to walk from one to the other, but a free shuttle bus zips around the airport every few minutes. Note that buses heading to the airport first stop at international terminal No 2, then the domestic terminal and finally international terminal No 1 – tell the bus driver which one you need. Thanks to the Asian economic crisis, a number of airlines which previously flew to Korea have suspended service but will re-enter the market when conditions improve. Therefore, the following information will no doubt change, but at the time of writing the airlines were distributed as follows:

International terminal No 1 Aeroflot, Air Canada, Air India, All Nippon Airways, Ansett Australia, British Airways, Cathay Pacific Airways, Delta Air Lines, Grand Air, Japan Air Systems, Japan Airlines, KLM Royal Dutch Airlines, Northwest Airlines, Philippine Airlines, Singapore Airlines, Thai Airways International, United Airlines, Uzbekistan Airways, VASP Brazilian

International terminal No 2 Air China, Air France, Air New Zealand, Asiana Airlines, China Eastern, China Northern, Garuda Indonesia, Korean Air, Lufthansa Airlines, Malaysia Airlines, Qantas Airways, Swissair, Vietnam Airlines

It's also worthwhile knowing that Korean Air does check-in for the following airlines: Alitalia, Air China, China Northern, Vietnam Airlines and Vladivostok Air. Asiana Airlines handles check-in for China Eastern and Uzbekistan Airways.

TO/FROM THE AIRPORT

You can avoid Seoul's maddening traffic by taking subway line 5, which connects the airport to the city subway grid. From the centre, the subway ride costs W550 rather than the usual W450.

There are five kinds of bus providing transport to the airport, all charging different prices. Some buses are express, but it makes little difference – traffic jams are the key factor in determining how long the journey takes. Ironically, the fancy buses are less frequent, which means you might have to wait longer if you want to travel in style. On the other hand, the fancier buses do offer fancier facilities and extra room to store luggage.

At the bottom of the barrel are the local buses which cost W500. The No 63 bus stops next to Tŏksugung (Tŏksu Palace, Map 5) and just north of the Koreana Hotel (Map 4) at the Donghwa Duty-Free Shop. The No 68 bus also stops close to City Hall (Map 4) and Metro Midopa department store (Map 5). The disadvantage of both these buses is that they will allow standing passengers and there is very little room to stow baggage.

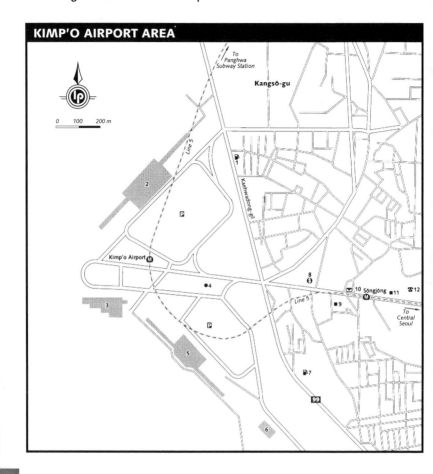

KIMP'O AIRPORT AREA

More popular is bus No 600 or 601, both of which cost W1000 and guarantee a seat for all passengers. The No 601 bus goes into central Seoul (Map 3), stopping at Shinch'on station (Map 9), Seoul station, City Hall, Koreana Hotel, Chongno 1-ga, Chongno 3-ga, Chongno 6-ga and the Eastern Hotel. The No 600 bus goes from Kimp'o airport into the areas south of the Han River (Maps 2 & 7), stopping at the National Cemetery, Palace Hotel, Seoul express bus terminal, Yŏngdong market,

Novotel Ambassador Hotel, New World Hotel, KOEX and KWTC, the Seoul Sports Complex and Chamshil station (Lotte World). There is also a bus No 600-2, which follows the same route as No 600 but terminates at the Seoul express bus terminal (Map 7). These buses leave every 10 minutes from 6 am to 10.30 pm.

Another option is bus No 1002, which costs W1000. It follows much the same route as the No 63, stopping at the Garden Hotel, Kwanghwamun and City Hall. Departures

KIMP'O AIRPORT AREA 김포공항

PLACES TO STAY
9   Kimp'o-jang Hotel
    김포장호텔
11 Airport Hotel
    에어포트호텔

OTHER
1   Petrol Station
    주유소
2   International
    Terminal 2
    국제선신청사(2청사)
3   Domestic Air Terminal
    국내선청사
4   Fountain
    분수대
5   International
    Terminal 1
    국제선신청사(1청사)
6   Cargo Terminal
    화물청사
7   Petrol Station
    주유소
8   Chohŭng Bank
    조흥은행
10 Post Office
    공항동우체국
12 Telephone Office
    공항전화국

are every 10 minutes and operating hours are from 6 am to 10.30 pm.

Airport limousine buses travel between Kimp'o airport and the Korea City Air Terminal (KCAT) in the Korea World Trade Centre (Map 7) in the Kangnam area, south of the Han River. These buses cost a steep W4500. Buses run every 10 minutes and operate from 7 am to 10.15 pm starting from the airport, or 5.55 am to 8.50 pm starting from KCAT.

There are also KAL limousine buses which offer cushy seats, air-conditioning, videos, cellular phones and cellular fax machines. All that's missing is the sauna and massage service. The price tag for this luxury is W4500. These buses run from 7 am

to 10 pm, every 15 to 20 minutes. There are five routes covering 19 luxury hotels, as follows:

Line No 1 (City Hall) Kimp'o airport, Koreana Hotel, Plaza Hotel, Hotel Lotte, Westin-Chosun Hotel, KAL building
Line No 2 (Namsan) Kimp'o airport, Seoul Station, Hilton Hotel, Grand Hyatt Hotel, Shilla Hotel, Sofitel Ambassador Hotel, Tower Hotel
Line No 3 (South Seoul) Kimp'o airport, Seoul Palace Hotel, Seoul Express Bus Terminal, Ritz-Carlton Hotel, Novotel Ambassador Hotel, Seoul Renaissance Hotel
Line No 4 (East Seoul) Kimp'o airport, Lotte World Hotel, Tong Seoul bus terminal, Sheraton Walker Hill Hotel
Line No 5 (Korea World Trade Center) Kimp'o airport, Seoul Express Bus Terminal, Amiga Hotel, New World Hotel, Inter-Continental Hotel, Riviera Hotel

Taxis are convenient if you don't mind paying for one. There are often traffic police handing out official complaint forms at the taxi ramp outside the airport to discourage naughty behaviour from the drivers, and most now seem resigned to using their meters. In a medium sized taxi, the trip to the city centre should cost about W10,000, while you should expect to pay approximately W15,000 to the Kangnam district. In a deluxe taxi, a trip from the airport to central Seoul or Kangnam should be about W25,000 or W35,000, respectively.

BUS

City buses run from about 5.30 am until midnight. The ordinary *(ilban)* buses are colour-coded: either purple-and-white or blue-and-white. They cost W500 (exact change please). You get a discount by using a token (the same word in Korean) or a bus card which can be bought from one of the booths found at most major bus stops. Magnetic bus cards *(bŏsŭ k'adŭ)* cost W10,000 – don't throw it out when it's used up because you can trade it in for W1500 when you buy a new one (the cards can be recharged). The green and white *chwasŏk* buses (the ones with seats) cost W1000 or W1100, and no tokens are available.

Seoul has an extensive bus network, with around 350 routes. The problem is trying to figure out just where these 350 routes will lead you. The token booths sell a *Bus Route Guide (Bŏsŭ Nosŏn Onnae)*, but it's written entirely in Korean even though some editions have an English title on the cover. Unfortunately, there are no bus route maps. Some bus stops have a list of destinations in both Korean and English with red buttons next to them. Press a button and a bus number will light up.

SUBWAY

The expansive Seoul subway now has eight lines, though line 6 was not quite up and running at the time of writing. The subway system extends a fair way out of the city proper – see Map 1 for routes and stations.

Like most urban mass transit systems, the Seoul subway loses money (millions of *won* a day). This is not for lack of passengers – the cars are so crowded that if you drop dead during rush hour, you'll never hit the ground.

The lines are colour coded, and free subway maps of the entire network are available at KNTO offices. The basic charge is W450, which covers most of the city. There are additional charges for connections with Korean National Railroad (KNR) lines running out to destinations such as Suwon or Inch'ŏn, with the most expensive ticket costing W850. At major stations you can buy these long-distance tickets from machines.

On lines 1 to 4, you press the button first on the ticket machine, then put in the money. On lines 5 to 8, you put in the money first, then press the button to select your ticket. If you run into problems, you can also purchase tickets from a real human at the ticket windows.

If you do much commuting, it's worth purchasing a multiple-use subway ticket which gains you a 10% bonanza. A W11,000 ticket actually costs W10,000, and a W22,000 ticket can be purchased for W20,000. Be sure to ask for a 'case' *(kaesu)* to protect the ticket from damage.

There is a subway information office in Kwanghwamun station on line 5, and the staff speak English. Free subway maps are also available here.

Smoking is prohibited on the trains and in the stations. Littering or spitting carries a fine of W70,000. Eating is legal, though it violates a Korean social norm that condemns eating in public places. Sneaking on the train without purchasing a ticket can land you a penalty equal to 30 times the ticket price.

CAR & MOTORCYCLE

Driving in Seoul is a near-death experience and renting a car is not particularly recommended. Finding parking places is also a problem and you'll have to contend with slow-moving (or nonmoving) traffic. During rush hours traffic can become gridlocked. Driving is on the right side of the road (usually). You can turn right on a red traffic light (after stopping first), but if there is a crosswalk and the light is green for the pedestrians, you must stop and wait for them before proceeding.

To rent a car in South Korea, you must have at least one year's driving experience, a valid international driving licence and passport, and you must be 21 years of age. Usually, rental prices include insurance, but it is a good idea to confirm this. Only Korean cars are available for hire. Prices start at W29,000 for a 10 hour period, or W42,000 for 24 hours. There are discounts for longer-term rentals. In general, there is no limit to how far you can drive the car during the rental period.

It is also possible to hire chauffeur-driven vehicles by contacting the Korea Car Rental Union (☎ 533 2503) or Young Nam Rent-A-Car (☎ 7913 7427). The cost for the driver is W70,000 for a full day (this does not include the cost of the vehicle).

Some of the main rental agencies include: 88 (P'alp'al, ☎ 665 8881), Daehan (☎ 585 0801), Hanyang (☎ 376 3491), Korea Express (☎ 719 7295), Kŭmho (☎ 798 1515), Seoul (☎ 474 0011) and Young Nam.

Motorcycles are far less numerous than cars in Seoul because motorcycle drivers often get creamed. Another factor that dampens enthusiasm for two-wheeled transport is the cold winter weather. Nevertheless, motorcycles have found a niche as delivery vehicles, especially for transporting bottled natural gas and kerosene. The delivery men are highly skilled riders, weaving their overloaded vehicles and deadly flammable cargo through the dense traffic and up onto the pedestrian footpaths. Scarier still seeing drivers performing these acrobatics while smoking a cigarette. The law requires that motorcyclists wear a safety helmet.

For vehicles 50cc and under, no driving licence is required. For 51cc to 125cc, any international driving licence can be used (even if the licence is not marked valid for motorcycles). Anything over 125cc will require that you obtain a Korean driving licence specifically validated for operating two-wheeled vehicles (see the Driving Licence entry under Documents in the Facts for the Visitor chapter for more information).

TAXI

Until very recently, Seoul had a severe shortage of taxis. Locals solved this problem by creating unofficial 'share taxis'. Although now supposedly illegal, the practice is still common (though less so as time goes by), so it's worth knowing how the system works. Once the driver has a passenger and is following a major boulevard, he will continue to slow down to listen out for the calls of other hopefuls – as long as there is spare seating in the taxi. If he does pick up another passenger, this won't make your fare any cheaper, although it does make sorting out the exact fares a bit more complicated. If there are passengers in the taxi when you get in, the meter will already be running. Make a mental note of (or better yet, write down) what the meter says when you get in and subtract it from the meter fare when you disembark. If two or more of you get in the taxi at the same time for the same destination you should pay a single fare, not the same fare multiplied two or more times.

Single women travelling late at night should be especially wary about getting into a taxi with other passengers – rapes have occurred when the driver and other 'passengers' turn on the unsuspecting victim.

The two official types of taxis are 'medium sized' and 'deluxe' ('small' disappeared some time ago). Flagfall for medium sized taxis is W1300, which takes you 2km, and W100 for every further 210m. At speeds less than 15km/h, W100 for every 51 seconds is added to the basic fare. Fares are raised 20% between midnight and 4 am.

A deluxe taxi *(mobŏm t'aekshi)* is black with a yellow sign on the roof and the words 'deluxe taxi' written in English on the sides. These special taxis were originally created for foreigners, though there is nothing to prevent locals from using them. The designation 'deluxe taxi' not only means that the vehicle is very comfortable inside, but also that the driver wears a crisp uniform, speaks some English and is polite to a fault.

Flagfall is accordingly higher at W3000, which takes you 3km, and W200 for each additional 250m (or 60 seconds when the speed drops below 15km/h). On the other hand, there is *no* late-night surcharge for the deluxe taxis. When you pay, the driver will issue you a receipt.

Taxis can be hailed on the street or ordered by telephone (☎ 414 0150, 666 9595). Although there is no extra charge for this service (other than an expected tip), call taxis are almost always deluxe taxis.

Complaint forms are available from the Ministry of Transport, and the public has been encouraged to record details of taxi drivers who drive dangerously or attempt to charge more than the amount on the meter. However, the authorities won't entertain any complaint about taxis not stopping for you.

In the countryside, many taxis are not metered, so you'll have to negotiate the fare before you set off.

If you take a metered taxi to a place where the driver won't necessarily get a return fare (eg to a temple outside a town), he will usually demand you pay 1½ times what the meter indicates at the end of the journey. This can work in your favour if you don't arrive by taxi but want to take one for the return journey.

BOAT

Old timers may remember the Han River as an open-air sewer, but it has been cleaned up considerably since the mid-1980s, and parklands have been established along the banks. Pleasure cruises on the river are now on offer, and although these theoretically run year-round, they're really only popular during the warmer months.

There are several routes, the longest being 15km (Yŏŭido-Chamshil). This can be done as a straight 30 minute one-way jaunt, or as an evening dining cruise (called the Green Cruise). Nature lovers will probably most enjoy the cruises that take in Pamsŏm Islet, a nesting area for migratory birds.

The cruises are operated by Semo Corporation (☎ 785 4411), which you can contact for reservations and information. In the peak season (summer), boats run from 10 am to 9.20 pm. The routes are as follows (see Maps 2, 7 & 9 for locations):

Green Cruise (dining cruise); Chamshil Ferry Pier, Yŏŭido, return to Chamshil Ferry Pier; from 7.30 to 9.20 pm; costs W49,500 to W60,500

Yanghwa Bridge, Chŏldusan Martyr's Shrine, Pamsŏm Islet, Tongjak Bridge, return to Yanghwa Bridge; duration one hour; W6800

Yŏŭido, Yanghwa Bridge, Chŏldusan Martyr's Shrine, Pamsŏm Islet (bird nesting area), Tongjak Bridge, return to Yŏŭido; one hour; W6800

Yŏŭido, Ttuksŏm Riverside Park, Chamshil Ferry Pier; 30 minutes; W7000

Chamshil Ferry Pier, Ttuksŏm Riverside Park, Yŏŭido; 30 minutes; W7000

Yŏŭido, Ttuksŏm Riverside Park; 25 minutes; W6000

Ttuksŏm Riverside Park, Yŏŭido; 25 minutes; W6000

Ttuksŏm Riverside Park, Panp'o Bridge, return to Ttuksŏm Riverside Park; one hour; W6000

Chamshil Ferry Pier, Panp'o Bridge, return to Chamshil Ferry Pier; one hour; W6000

BICYCLE

There are bicycles for hire in Yŏŭido Park (Map 9), but these are just for riding in endless circles around the plaza area itself. As for serious riding in traffic, it's feasible but dangerous. This is not to say that you should refrain from cycling in Seoul, but merely to suggest that it would be a damn good idea not to.

WALKING

Unlike many other Asian cities, where the footpaths are clogged with motorcycles, bicycles and food stalls, Seoul is an excellent city to explore on foot. Footpaths are broad and well kept, and there are underpasses for crossing busy roads. Some of the underpasses are a little confusing at first – you won't always resurface where you had intended – but this is a small gripe when you consider the risks of trying to cross the road at traffic level.

The central city area is particularly good for walking. Almost all the major sights can be reached on foot, and there is plenty to see along the way. The areas south of the Han River are less suitable for walking, mainly because the distances are greater, but also because there's very little of interest in these areas. Fortunately, the south is well served by the subway lines.

ORGANISED TOURS

There are a wide variety of tours available in Seoul and they can be booked at the KNTO office (see Tourist Offices in the Facts for the Visitor chapter for KNTO contact details) or at any of the major hotels.

Examples include morning tours taking in Kyŏngbokkung (Kyŏngbok Palace), the Korean Folk Museum and Chogyesa temple for W22,000; afternoon tours to Namdaemun Market, Insa-dong and Ch'angdŏkkung (including Piwon) for W27,000; and full-day tours taking in all of the preceding plus a big luncheon for W65,000.

There are also tours to specific sights such as Korea House (W82,000), Lotte World (W38,000), the Korean Folk Village (W38,000), Everland (W42,000) and Ich'ŏn Ceramic Village (W42,000). Most tour operators offer a Sheraton Night Tour that takes in the casino along with a dinner show for W95,000. Full-day tours always include an elaborate lunch.

The Royal Asiatic Society (Map 3, ☎ 763 9483, fax 766 3796) operates tours every weekend. The day tours are reasonably priced, but overnight trips are somewhat expensive because you stay in good hotels rather than at cheap *yŏgwan* (small, family-run hotels). The RAS is in room 611 of the Korean Christian building (also called the CBS building) off Taehangno. Office hours are from 10 am to 5 pm, Monday to Friday. Take subway line 1 to Chongno 5-ga station.

The USO (Map 2, ☎ 795 3028, 795 3063) runs tours at bargain prices, and you don't have to be a member of the US military to join a tour.

There are, of course, plenty of commercial travel agents which can arrange tours to almost anywhere for a fee. While some of these tours are not horribly expensive, few could be regarded as cheap. Large groups can bargain for a reduced price. Travel agencies catering to foreigners include Global Tour (☎ 335 0011), Grace Seoul Travel (☎ 332 8946), A-One Travel (☎ 701 0947), Star Travel (☎ 564 1232), Hanwha Travel (☎ 757 1232) and the Korea Travel Bureau (☎ 585 1191).

Things to See & Do

HIGHLIGHTS

Undoubtedly the city's major drawcard are the Chosŏn (or Yi) Dynasty **palaces**. Many of the royal residences were destroyed during the 1592 Japanese invasion of the Korean peninsula by Hideyoshi Toyotomi, and were subsequently rebuilt. Still more were destroyed during the Japanese occupation of the country from 1910 to 1945. Add to this the Korean War, when the city changed hands four times and was virtually levelled, and it is a wonder that there is anything of historical interest to look at in Seoul. But remarkably there is.

The palaces may have been greatly reduced in number by Seoul's turbulent history, but there is still enough remaining to keep even the most energetic visitor busy for a few days. See the 'Royal Palaces of Seoul' special section in this chapter for details.

Effectively marking the eastern and southern extents of the central city area are the old city gates of **Tongdaemun** and **Namdaemun**. In both these areas there are large, bustling **markets** and a browse through at least one of them should be on anyone's agenda.

Hidden in the heart of the modern city is **Insa-dong**, where the full-on push of surrounding boulevards gives way to the laid-back lure of traditional shops and studios. West of Insa-dong is **Chogyesa**, Seoul's main Buddhist temple.

To the north is the **old residential area** of Seoul's *yangban* (nobility), where the walls of tile-roofed courtyard houses line a maze of alleyways. Guarded by auspicious peaks to the north, including **Puk'ansan** and **Suraksan** (see the Excursions chapter for both), this 'royal' area is also the site of **Kyŏngbokkung** (Kyŏngbok Palace), the former centre of power in Korea.

To the south is **Namsan** (Mt Nam). At 265m it is not exactly the Matterhorn, but the Seoul Tower at the summit offers excellent views (smog permitting).

Namdaemun (Map 5)

Namdaemun (South Great Gate), also known as Sungnyemun, was once Seoul's chief city gate, in keeping with the geomantic principles that determined the layout of the Yi palaces. It is still an impressive sight, surrounded by tall office buildings and knots of jostling traffic. It was originally built in the late 14th century. The latest reconstruction work was completed in the 1960s for damage sustained during the Korean War.

Tongdaemun (Map 3)

Seoul's other main gate is Tongdaemun (East Great Gate), which is also known as Hŭng-injimun. Tongdaemun dates from 1869, though it had to be renovated after it was damaged during the Korean War.

Insa-dong (Map 4)

Insadong-gil is a fascinating street of antiques, art galleries, teahouses and exotic restaurants. In the post-Korean War era, expats nicknamed the street 'Mary's Alley', and the Korean tourist literature endlessly reminds you of this fact (even though there's scarcely anyone left alive who still calls it that).

Insadong-gil is closed to traffic every Sunday from 10 am to 10 pm, and vendors set up tables in the street to display their wares. This makes for very pleasant strolling if the weather is cooperative. During summer, various **Sunday festivals** are organised (traditional dance, food festivals etc) – check with the Korean National Tourist Organisation (KNTO) for a schedule of events.

The Blue House (Map 2)

One could say that Kyŏngbokkung is actually still the seat of power in South Korea. Just beyond Shinmumun (the north gate of Kyŏngbokkung) is the Blue House (Ch'ŏngwadae), South Korea's answer to America's White House. The Blue House is where South Korea's president lives.

On 21 January 1968, a squad of 31 North Korean commandos was caught just 500m from Ch'ŏngwadae – their mission was to assassinate South Korean President Park Chung-hee. Obviously, security remains tight and the Blue House is not open to the general public. However, the tree-lined street in front of the Blue House has been open to the public ever since former president Kim Young-sam was inaugurated in 1993. As you approach Ch'ŏngwadae on foot, you will encounter plenty of conspicuous plain-clothes police who may question you about where you are going.

PAVILIONS & STATUES

The following sights are all in the north-central area of the city (Map 4).

Close to the YMCA on Chongno is **Poshingak Pavilion**. Chongno, which means 'Bell Street', derives its name from the city bell which hangs in the pavilion. The old city bell, forged in 1468, was struck daily at dawn and dusk to signal the opening and closing of the city gates. That bell has now been retired and is housed in the National Museum. The new city bell was dedicated in 1985, and is only sounded to usher in the new year, and to mark Independence Movement Day and National Liberation Day. The pavilion area is fenced off and there's not a lot to see, but the place is packed on New Year's Eve despite the frigid temperatures.

At the Kwanghwamun intersection is the tiny **Pigak Pavilion**, built in 1903 to commemorate the enthronement of King Kojong. Just north of the intersection is a bronze statue of **Admiral Yi Sun-shin** (1545-98). Admiral Yi was a masterful military strategist and invented the so-called 'turtle ship'. By cladding wooden ships in sheets of armour, Admiral Yi was able to achieve stunning victories over the much larger Japanese navy.

MUSEUMS
National Museum

While arguably the best museum in Korea, the main problem with the National Museum is figuring out where it is. Until 1995, it was

For Whom the Bell Tolls

In ancient royal Seoul, the great bell of Chongno was rung 33 times at dawn and 28 times at dusk. The tolling of the bell in the evenings not only effectively shut the city off from the outside world, but also announced a male-only curfew. In a curious apartheid of the sexes, men caught on the streets after the bell had rung could be subject to arrest as thieves. This provided an opportunity for women, limited to their homes during the day, to throng the streets. At midnight the bell would toll just once to announce a full curfew until dawn.

housed in the former Capitol building on the grounds of Kyŏngbokkung. The Capitol building was a beautiful piece of architecture, constructed in the Renaissance style that was so popular in the first half of the 20th century. However, as part of the reconstruction of Kyŏngbokkung, this building has been demolished and will not be rebuilt.

There is a story behind this. The ruling Japanese built their Capitol building in 1926 on the grounds of Kyŏngbokkung deliberately to symbolically intersect the axis of geomantic power that flowed from the throne hall through Kwanghwamun (Gate of Radiant Transformation), and the building was constructed in the shape of the Japanese character for Japan – all to enforce the notion that Korea was now part of Japan.

Needless to say, Koreans were less than overjoyed at this and have long vowed to get rid of this remaining symbol of Japanese imperialism. Demolition of the National Museum finally began in 1995 and the collection has been temporarily moved to adjacent annexe buildings in Kyŏngbokkung (Maps 3 & 4). Those buildings are also undergoing renovation, so exactly where the collection will be housed at the time of your visit is not easy to say. The National Museum will eventually be moved to Yongsan Family Park (Map 2) near It'aewon. At the time of writing, work on the new museum had not yet started.

Interestingly, there are many other major buildings around central Seoul which were built by the Japanese, including City Hall and Seoul Train Station. However, not much has been said about demolishing these.

National Folk Museum (Map 3)

Like the former National Museum, this place is on the grounds of Kyŏngbokkung. Unlike the National Museum it will not be demolished, but it may be undergoing renovation at the time of your visit. You'll have to check with KNTO to find out its current status.

The collection comprises items from the daily lives of Koreans throughout history, including everything from kitchen utensils to items associated with shamanistic rituals. Altogether there are about 10,000 items housed in nine display rooms.

Admission costs W700, and the museum is closed on Tuesday.

War Memorial (Map 2)

Despite the name, this is a full-fledged museum and certainly one of the best in Seoul. The War Memorial (☎ 709 3114) traces the history of battles in Korea. Many travellers are surprised by the exhibit on the Vietnam War – it's often forgotten that the South Koreans participated in this war at the urging of the USA.

Opening hours are from 9.30 am to 6 pm (to 5 pm from November to February) and the museum is closed on Monday. Admission costs W2000. There is a military parade every Friday at 11 am (but check – the time could change).

The War Memorial is in the Yongsan area, very close to Samgakchi station on subway line 4.

Sejong University Museum (Map 2)

This is a folk museum which has some 3000 exhibits, with an emphasis on traditional dress and furniture. The university (sometimes called King Sejong University) and museum are close to Children's Grand Park, and can be reached by a 10 minute walk from Konkuk University station on subway line 2.

Kimch'i Museum (Map 7)

Unless you're travelling on business, the only thing worth doing in the enormous Korea World Trade Centre is to pop into the Kimch'i Museum in the basement. The museum even has a kitchen for attempting your own *kimch'i* experiments. The museum is open from 9 am to 6 pm from April to October and until 5 pm from November to March; closed on Sunday and public holidays. Entry is free. Take subway line 2 to Samsŏng station.

Postal Museum (Map 5)

Strictly for the keen philatelist, the Postal Museum is on the 4th floor of the central post office (CPO). It has a reasonably extensive collection of 19th century stamps and other items related to the postal industry. The museum is closed on Sunday and public holidays.

Agricultural Museum (Map 3)

Korea's mostly defunct agrarian society is well portrayed at the Agricultural Museum (☎ 397 5676). The museum is open from 10 am to 5 pm, and closed on Sunday. Entry is W300. Take subway line 5 to Sŏdaemun station.

Amsa-dong Prehistoric Settlement Site (Map 2)

More like an open-air museum, this remote place is notable for prehistoric dwellings dating back to 3000 BC. The site has, of course, been restored.

Getting to Amsa-dong (☎ 471 3867) is a bit of a expedition. The site is 1km north of the Han River (Han-gang) yachting area. Take subway line 2 to Sŏngnae station, then bus No 569. There are a couple of *yŏgwan* (family-run hotels) nearby.

CHURCHES & MOSQUES
Myŏng-dong Cathedral (Map 5)

On the outskirts of the fashionable Myŏng-dong shopping district is Myŏng-dong Cathedral. Occupying some of Seoul's priciest real estate, this is the focus of Catholicism in South Korea. More controversially, it is also the focus of much political activity. When the students get restless, sit-ins, spirited speeches and demonstrations are often held near the cathedral. The cathedral itself dates from 1898, and was designed by a French priest.

Anglican Cathedral (Map 4)

This Romanesque building (Asia's largest) is on the north side of Tŏksugung, close to the British embassy. It is beautiful and is an officially designated Seoul Historical Site.

Korean Islam Mosque (Map 8)

Not far from It'aewon's notorious nightclub area is the Korean Islam Mosque. There are good views of Seoul from here, but this just about exhausts the sightseeing possibilities of It'aewon.

From central Seoul the most convenient buses to It'aewon are Nos 23 and 401. These run along Chongno, stop outside the YMCA, then travel up to Kwanghwamun gate and double back on Sejongno to the Sejong Cultural Centre and City Hall.

TEMPLES
Chogyesa (Map 4)

Buried in the alleys south-east of Kyŏngbokkung is Chogyesa. It is the only major Buddhist temple in Seoul, and is named after the Chogye school (the largest Buddhist school in Korea) to which it belongs.

In the vicinity of Chogyesa, out on the main road, are a number of **Buddhist supply shops** selling everything from alms bowls to tapes of Buddhist meditation chants.

The most interesting time of the year to visit Chogyesa and its surrounding streets is Buddha's Birthday. At that time there is the **Lotus Lantern Mass**. On the Sunday prior to Buddha's birthday, there is an evening **lantern parade** from Yŏuido Park (Map 9) to Chogyesa starting around 6.30 pm.

Buddha's Birthday (Puch'ŏnim Oshinal) falls on a lunar date – see the Lunar Holidays entry in the Facts for the Visitor chapter for upcoming dates.

The closest subway station is Chonggak on line 1.

Pongwonsa (Map 2)

Situated north-east of Yonsei University (Map 9), Pongwonsa dates back to the late 9th century. However, the temple was destroyed during the Korean War and has been rebuilt. This magnificent temple is noted for its fine paintings.

Pongwonsa is now the headquarters of the T'aego school of Buddhism, the second largest Buddhist school in Korea. This is an interesting school, in so far as it allows its monks to marry. The Japanese installed this system of married monks during their occupation of Korea, and it remains a controversial issue among Korean Buddhists.

Behind the temple is Ansan (Mt An). At 296m, it's a worthy climb that will reward you with a great view of Seoul.

Pongwonsa can be reached by bus No 135 from the Kyobo building (Map 4) on Chongno. The nearest subway station is Shinch'on on line 2.

Pomunsa (Map 2)

Pomunsa is north of Tongdaemun gate. There's not a lot to see, but the temple is distinguished by being the largest nunnery in Korea. The nearest subway station is Sŏngshin Women's University on line 4.

Pongŭnsa (Map 7)

Located slightly north of the Korea World Trade Centre (KWTC) in the Kangnam area, Pongŭnsa has been relocated to this sterile southern part of Seoul (no doubt kicking and screaming all the way). Next to the main temple is **Kyongp'anjon** (Building of Scriptures), which houses 3479 plates of important wood-block scriptures. The original temple dates from the 8th century and was an important Zen centre in its time.

In the 17th century, King Injo escaped to Namhansansong fortress during an invasion by the Qing dynasty Chinese. Panicked Korean civilians fleeing the Chinese invaders tried to board the king's boat, but were pushed back into the river by soldiers and subsequently drowned. To soothe the angry souls of those who drowned, a ceremony called Suryukche is held at the temple every leap year.

The nearest subway station is Samsŏng on line 2.

MODERN SEOUL

The southern side of the Han River has been criticised for being 'Korea's answer to Los Angeles', but it is worth visiting if you've exhausted everything that central Seoul has to offer.

Yŏŭido (Map 9)

Touted as Seoul's answer to Manhattan, the small island of Yŏŭido is an administrative and business centre. There are a few sights here, but nothing to hold your interest for long. During office hours the streets are eerily deserted, but that changes dramatically on Sunday (weather permitting) when the Yŏŭido and Riverside parks fill up with Seoulites on an afternoon outing.

The only way to see Yŏŭido is on foot. The natural starting point is the massive **Yŏŭido Park**. The park started its life as a landing strip, and was later turned into a treeless venue for cyclists. The plaza was long criticised for being a monotonous asphalt desert among the skyscrapers, but it was about the only place in Seoul where one could safely ride a bicycle. In 1998, the asphalt was finally ripped up and the plaza was transformed into an 'ecologically planned' scenic park.

At the far north-western end of the island is the **National Assembly** building. It is an ugly structure, and as it is a longish trudge from the park, with nothing else of note in its vicinity, it is not really worth the effort.

The massive **Full Gospel Church** is not an architectural triumph, but its Sunday services are a huge multimedia event. The church claims to have the largest congregation in the world, and with some 50,000 faithful they are probably not wrong.

You may want to take a peek at the **LG Twin Towers** building, a post-modern structure composed of gleaming glass and angles. Inside are some boutiques, restaurants and the small **LG Science Hall**, which offers free tours every 10 minutes from 10 am to 3.30 pm.

A couple of blocks to the south is the **Korea Stock Exchange**. There's a free observation room on the 4th floor, with English explanations of the stock exchange activities provided by phones. It is a rather sleepy place. Opposite the stock exchange is the bustling headquarters of the **Munhwa Broadcasting Corporation** (MBC).

From the MBC it is a 10 to 15 minute walk eastwards to the **DLI 63 building** (usually just called 'Yuksam' in Korean), which is open to the public from 10.30 am to 7 pm. Despite the name, the building is only 60 storeys tall (three levels in the basement are included to make it seem higher). Nevertheless, it's Korea's tallest office tower. The top floor has an **observation deck** which costs W5500, but the views here aren't as good as from Seoul Tower. The building also contains the **63 Sea World Aquarium** (admission W8000), which offers about 20 performances daily of dolphins and other marine creatures. Most important is the **Imax theatre** (admission W6000), with a viewing screen 10 times larger than the average cinema. Imax is open from 10.10 am to 7.40 pm and has shows starting 10 minutes before each hour. The ground level of the DLI 63 sports a wide selection of places to eat, plus a few pricier restaurants on the two highest floors.

Close to the DLI 63 building is **Riverside Park**. The park is a vast expanse of lawn (pity the poor soul who has to cut it) and has a large outdoor swimming pool, plus other sporting facilities. If you wander down into the park, you'll find a pier for **Han River ferry tours**. See Organised Tours in the Getting Around chapter for details of riverboat cruises.

Along the south-west side of the island is **Cherry Blossom Park**, which follows the channel that separates Yŏŭido from the mainland. The cherry blossoms are a seasonal event, occurring sometime in mid-April. The rest of the year, don't expect to see anything but some trees.

The easiest way to get to Yŏŭido is to take subway line 5 to Yŏŭido or Yŏŭinaru station.

Olympic Stadium (Map 7)

The 1988 Olympics held in Seoul was an event of great consequence for South Korean national pride, and the slogan 'Keep the Olympic torch burning' crops up frequently in tourist literature. Despite all the hype, it is doubtful whether it is worth heading down to the Olympic Stadium for a look. When all is said and done, the Olympic Stadium is just that: a stadium. Granted, with seating for 100,000, it's big. Entrance to the Olympic Stadium is through Gate 1-14, and there is a charge of W100. Don't confuse the Olympic Stadium with the adjacent Chamshil Baseball Stadium. The Olympic Stadium is at the Seoul Sports Complex – the best way to get there is from the Sports Complex station on subway line 2.

Apartment Blocks

Korea's bloated *chaebŏl* (business conglomerates) dominate the housing construction industry, and it's not hard to get the impression that each building is stamped out on one of their assembly lines. Indeed, the matchbox apartment towers carry the logos of Hyundai, Samsung etc, just like all the other widgets these companies make.

On the upwardly mobile south side of the Han, it's not unusual to find endless rows of residential buildings marching into the distance, each one identical right down to the colour scheme. The **Chamshil Apartments**, near Olympic Park (Map 2), will give you a good look at modernistic hell. Take subway line 2 to Sŏngnae station and walk east.

Lotte World (Map 2)

If you are a fan of mall culture, you'll love Lotte World. Like the Japanese models it's drawn from, Lotte World is a city within a building, and includes an ice skating rink, the Lotte World Hotel, Lotte department store, Lotte Super Store, Lotte World Shopping Mall, Lotte World Sports, Lotte World Swimming and Lotte World Plaza. If this is not enough, there's a Disneyland lookalike next door in Lotte World Adventure, which includes Magic Island and the Lotte World Folk Museum. All that's missing is the southern California weather.

It would easy to spend an entire rainy day exploring the place, and it's be ideal for children. You could leave them there for good, and they might never miss you.

The basic entry fee to Lotte World Adventure is W14,000 for adults, W12,000 for students and W9000 for children, but this doesn't include the rides or the Folk Museum, which all carry surcharges. You can, however, buy all-inclusive tickets for W22,000/W18,000/W13,000. After 5 pm there is a night discount. Also look for discount coupons at KNTO.

Getting to Lotte World is no problem. Chamshil station on subway line 2 has clearly marked signs leading the way – you don't even need to poke your head above ground. Lotte World is open daily from 9.30 am to 11 pm.

Seoul Dream Land (Map 2)

The largest amusement park within the city limits is Seoul Dream Land (☎ 982 6800). Popular facilities here include the dragon coaster, cycle monorail, skyrider, mini train,

(continued on page 84)

ROYAL PALACES OF SEOUL

Though their splendour has been greatly reduced by wars, conflagrations, and Japanese colonial policy, the royal palace compounds of Seoul are still among the best places to gain an appreciation for the aesthetic of old Korea, especially its architecture, landscaping, and use of geomantic *feng shui* principles, so popular in the west these days. All of the palaces but one date from the Chosŏn (Yi) Dynasty (1392-1910). Containing hundreds of structures of various types, grids of lanes and alleyways, and even small parks with formal gardens, they used to function as little cities-within-the-city.

Unfortunately, most of the buildings were razed or dismantled and moved during the Japanese occupation (which formally began in 1910 and lasted until the end of WWII), and their contents – including the finest examples of Korean ceramics, paintings, calligraphy and furniture – were carted off to Japan, where they remain to this day mostly hidden away in private collections.

Still, there is a great deal to see in the palaces. Take special note of the bracketwork in the eaves of the buildings with its psychedelic decoration. The stonework, all original, is especially interesting. Be sure to keep your eyes open for the humorous stone creatures you'll find staring at you here and there, some guarding stairways or railings, some overlooking ponds and miniature waterfalls.

Besides their historical and aesthetic significance, the palaces are also a great place to get away from the noise, crowds, and pollution of the metropolitan concrete jungle.

Tŏksugung (Map 5)

Tŏksugung (Tŏksu Palace) was originally built in the mid-15th century as the private manor of King Sŏngjong's elder brother Wolsan. It was first used as a royal residence from 1593 because all the palaces of Seoul had been destroyed in the Hideyoshi invasion of the previous year. Even after the king moved back to Ch'angdŏk Palace in 1618, Tŏksu Palace continued to be used for a while as a residence for a widowed royal consort and later as a royal villa. King Kojong, who ruled during the tumultuous period when the Japanese and Russians were vying for hegemony in Korea at the turn of the 20th century, moved to Tŏksugung after a year of asylum in the Russian legation. After he abdicated in favour of his son in 1907, he remained here until his death in 1919.

Tŏksugung is open from 9 am to 6 pm, Tuesday to Friday, from March to October, and to 5.30 pm from November to February. The grounds stay open to 7 pm on Saturday and Sunday and the palace is closed on Monday. Adult admission is W700. The nearest subway stop is City Hall on lines 1 and 2.

TŎKSUGUNG PALACE

1 P'odŭkmun Gate
2 Sŏkchojŏn (Exhibits of Chosŏn Dynasty Relics)
3 Sŏkchojŏn West
4 Fountain
5 Wŏlgokmun Gate
6 Kwangmyŏngmun Gate ; Hungch'ŏn Temple Bell
7 Chunghwamun Gate
8 Chunghwajŏn (Royal Audience Hall)
9 Chunmyŏngdang
10 Chŭkchodang
11 Sŏgŏdang
12 Statue of King Sejong the Great
13 Tŏkhongjŏn
14 Chŏnggwahŏn
15 Hamnyŏngjŏn
16 Kŭmch'ŏn Bridge
17 Lotus Pond
18 Tehanmun Gate (Main Entrance)

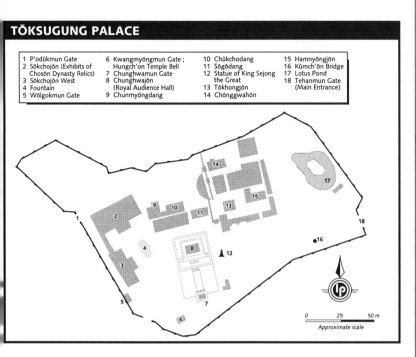

0   25   50 m
Approximate scale

Changing of the Royal Guard If you visit Tŏksugung on a Saturday or Sunday afternoon, you can also take in the spectacle of the changing of the royal guard, a re-enactment held at **Taehanmun**, the main gate of the palace (the one facing City Hall Plaza) beginning at 2 pm. Even if you're not at the palace, you might catch a glimpse of a troop of guards parading down the main street from Kwanghwamun intersection on their way to the ceremony.

It's an arresting departure from the usual parade of cars, buses and business suits – the ceremony is accompanied by a Chosŏn Dynasty military band dressed in brilliant yellow and white, playing various traditional wind and percussion instruments.

Kyŏnghŭigung (Map 3)

Of Seoul's five major palaces, Kyŏnghŭi Palace has suffered the most at the hands of history. Until early in the Japanese colonial period, this was a very large compound surrounded by a wall with four gates. It contained dozens of structures, but only a few of the original elements of the palace remain today, including stone stairways, the carvings of dragons' heads that guard the spring hidden behind the public rest room, and the main gate.

Sungjŏngjŏn, the royal audience hall in the centre of the compound, is a replica built during a recent restoration. The original, built in 1616, was moved to the campus of Dongguk University in 1926 when most of the palace was razed. Renamed Chŏnggagwŏn, it still stands there today.

The **main gate**, also built in 1616, has literally toured Seoul. It served as the gate of a Japanese shrine and then as the gate to the grounds of the Shilla Hotel before being returned to its original home in 1988.

Kyŏnghŭigung is about 500m west of the Sejong Cultural Center. There is no admission charge and the grounds are open at all times. However, visitors to the site are still few. The nearest subway stop is Sŏdaemun on line 5.

Kyŏngbokkung (Maps 3 & 4)

The construction of Kyŏngbokkung (Kyŏngbok Palace) was begun by Yi Sŭng-gye, the founder of the Chosŏn Dynasty, in 1395. The palace served as both a residence for the royal family and as the seat of the government until 1592, when it was destroyed in a great fire during the Hideyoshi invasions. Kyŏngbokkung lay in ruins for 273 years until restoration work was begun in 1865 by King Kojong's father and regent, the Hŭngsŏng Taewongun. The 17-year-old Kojong moved here from Ch'angdŏk Palace in 1868.

Under the Japanese colonial government the geomantic qualities of the palace were purposely spoiled and more than 200 of the compound's buildings were razed, leaving only 10. The Japanese then constructed the office building of the governor-general – the largest ferroconcrete structure in Asia at the time – in the south courtyard.

In 1995, 50 years after liberation at the end of WWII, that building was razed and a program of restoration which will return the palace to

Left: In many ways as important to the long history of dynastic Korea as its wonderful temples pagodas come in all shapes and sizes on the peninsula, from carefully arranged yet simple stacks of rough stones to intricately carved, refined works of art. This elaborate 10 storey pagoda graces the grounds of Kyŏngbokkung.

Korean kings received guests at Kyŏngbokkung's throne hall, Kunjongjon.

Kyŏngbokkung's regal halls are eerily deserted.

Ŏksugung was originally a manor in the 1400s.

Hwangwonjon pavilion floats at Kyŏngbokkung.

ROBERT STOREY

SIMON ROWE

SIMON ROWE

Latticed wooden doors are emblematic of Korean simplicity and elegance (top right). Tonhwamun is an open invitation to Ch'angdŏkkung (top left). Tŏksugung (Palace of Virtuous Longevity) got its current name in 1907, and King Kojong lived here until his death in 1919 (bottom).

some of its former glory was begun. The royal residential quarters have been completed. This project, which will involve even moving the palace walls and the main gate back to their original locations, is scheduled for completion in 2020.

If you visit the temporary **National Museum** currently in the south-west corner of the grounds (see the National Museum entry in this chapter), you can gaze down from the lobby at two big models of what the palace looked like before and after the Japanese, to get some idea of how drastic the changes were.

Kyŏngbokkung is at the north end of Sejongno, the broad boulevard in central Seoul. If you take the subway, get off at Kyŏngbokkung station on line 3. The station itself is worth a visit: it's designed as a vast underground art gallery.

The palace is open daily except Tuesday. From May to October it is open from 9 am to 6 pm and from September to April it's open to 5 pm. Adult admission is W700.

Ch'angdŏkkung (Map 3)

SIMON ROWE

Located to the east of Kyŏngbokkung and adjacent to Ch'anggyŏnggung, is Ch'angdŏk Palace. Because members of Korea's last remaining royal family continued to live here until quite recently, Ch'angdŏkkung is the best preserved of Seoul's main palace compounds.

Visitors are normally not allowed into the grounds except on regularly scheduled 1½-hour guided tours. There are tours in English three times a day, but thanks to plentiful historical markers with explanations in English, you should have no trouble trailing along on a Korean or Japanese-language tour.

The **Piwon** (Secret Garden) in the back part of the palace grounds is the highlight of the tour. Its 32-hectare grounds contain ponds and pavilions, ancient gnarled trees and interesting gates such as **Pullomun** – passing under this gate is said to guarantee everlasting youth.

Tours take around 1½ hours, and although English tours are only available at 11.30 am, 1.30 and 3.30 pm, there are Korean-language tours on the hour from 9 am to 5 pm (until 4 pm from November through February). The tours cost W2200 for adults and W1100 for children.

The nearest subway station is Anguk on line 3.

Ch'anggyŏnggung (Map 3)

Ch'anggyŏng Palace is the oldest of Seoul's royal residences, having originally been built in 1104 as a villa for the kings of the Koryŏ Dynasty (918-1392), who would come here for the summer from Kaesŏng, the Koryŏ kingdom's capital. Later, Yi Sŭng-gye lived here temporarily while Kyŏngbokkung was being built. During its colonial occupation (1910-45) the Japanese administration turned the palace into a public park with a zoo and amusement rides, but now the palace has been restored.

Ch'anggyŏnggung is open from 9 am to 6 pm, March to October, and to 5 pm from November to February. Adult admission is W700. The palace is closed on Tuesday.

Chongmyo (Map 3)

The Chongmyo royal shrine has been designated a World Cultural Heritage site by UNESCO. Chongmyo's two great halls, **Chŏngjŏn** and **Yŏngnyŏngjŏn**, were built to enshrine the ancestral tablets of deceased Chosŏn Dynasty kings.

The halls are fronted by broad, stone courtyards to accommodate the orchestras, officiants, and attendants at the royal ancestral rites. These days, the rites are held only once a year, on the first Sunday in May. They are open to the public.

A footbridge connects Chongmyo with Ch'anggyŏnggung, so you can cross over and see both for the price of one admission ticket. If you want to take advantage of this, don't go too late in the afternoon: the footbridge is closed to traffic 1½ hours before Chongmyo closes its gates.

Chongmyo is open from 9 am to 5 pm, March to October, and to 4 pm from November to February. Admission is W700 for adults.

The nearest subway stop is Chongno 3-ga on lines 1, 3 and 5.

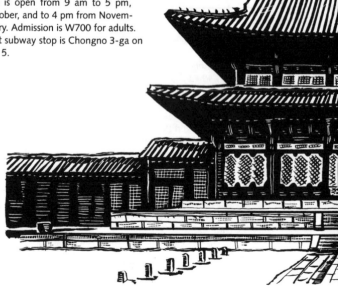

Full Page: Originally built in 1405 as an annexe to Kyŏng-bokkung, Ch'angdŏk-kung managed to escape Kyŏngbokkung's indignity at the hands of imperial Japan. Thus, the plan is to restore the latter palace to its ideal, 'pre-Japanese' appearance. However, modernising Korean touches at Ch'angdŏkkung, such as the royal garages which housed the country's first car (a Cadillac brought over in 1903 by King Sunjong) will remain.

Unhyŏn-gung (Map 3)

Besides the five major palace compounds and the royal shrine described above, Chosŏn Dynasty Seoul also had several minor palaces. Thanks to the fact that until recent years it was still lived in by descendants of the royal family, Unhyŏn-gung is the best-preserved of these.

This manor was originally the home of the Hŭngsŏng Taewongun, the father of King Kojong, second-to-last monarch of Chosŏn. Kojong ascended the throne in 1863 at the age of 12 – too young to rule – so his father was designated to act as his *taewongun*, or regent.

While in the major palaces you are limited to exterior views except for the royal audience halls, here the buildings in the southern half of the compound have their doors thrown wide open so the visitor can see the interior of the rooms, which are fully furnished in the style of the *yangban* (nobility) of old Korea.

The northern half of the compound contains a small **institute** that offers classes in court etiquette, a **research studio** where Chosŏn Dynasty court costume is studied and made, and a **teahouse** where you can experience a tea ceremony, Korean style. There is also a tiny **museum** with displays of personal effects and other items related to the taewongun.

Unhyŏn-gung is open every day from 9 am to 7 pm, March to October, and to 5 pm from November to February. Adult admission is W700. The palace is just a short walk south of Anguk subway station on line 3.

Gary Rector

(continued from page 77)

haunted house, swimming pool and miniature golf course. Seoul Dream Land is open from 10 am to 7 pm, Monday to Friday, and from 9 am to 8 pm on weekends and holidays. General entry for adults is W1100, but the rides cost extra (the astrojet is the most expensive at W2000).

The park is in Tobong-gu in northern Seoul. Take subway line 4 to Miasamgŏri – from there it's 2km by bus or taxi.

Yongma Land (Map 10)

A new tourist attraction, Yongma Land (☎ 208 2222) was once a quarry but has been converted into a small amusement park. Entry to the park is free, though there are charges for the various facilities. Take subway line 7 to Myŏnmok station. Yongma Land is open from 9.30 am to 9 pm.

PARKS

Unlike many other Asian cities, Seoul is well endowed with parks. Even in the central city area you are never far from some greenery, most of it in the palace areas. New parks have also been established on the Han River's south side.

Namsan Park (Maps 3 & 5)

Namsan once marked the southern extent of royal Seoul, and remains of the old city walls can be seen in the park's wooded grounds. The peak was also once crowned with defensive fortifications, but these have vanished.

In the western section, not far from Namdaemun Market, is **Namsan Botanical Gardens**, a library and a number of statues.

At the top of Namsan is **Seoul Tower** (☎ 775 6222). With the help of Namsan, the tower reaches 483m, though minus the mountain it's a mere 240m.

The goal for most visitors is the tower's observation deck. Other attractions in the tower include the Game Room, World Musical & Animal Land, Fairyland and the Global Village Folk Museum. If you enjoy this kind of tourist-oriented action, a comprehensive ticket includes all the attractions for W7000. For those content with just the view from the observation deck, a W2000 ticket will suffice.

You can reach the tower by walking from the botanical garden area (about a 15 to 20 minute exhilarating climb), taking a taxi or by taking the cable car. The cable car runs at 30-minute intervals from 9 am to 10 pm, March to October, and from 9 am to 8 pm, November to February. The cost is W1400 one way or W2100 for a round trip.

Namsankol Traditional Korean Village is at the northern end of the park, a short walk from Ch'ungmuro subway station on lines 3 and 4. The courtyard houses here are genuine, though they have been moved from other parts of the city and restored to their original grandeur. It's really worth a look around and English-speaking guides are available. There is also a small handicrafts shop and an interesting display of traditional Korean furniture.

T'apkol Park (Map 4)

On the corner of Insadong-gil and Chongno is T'apkol Park (formerly called Pagoda Park). There are always crowds of friendly pensioners sitting around, and it's very easy to strike up a conversation with someone. A prominent feature of the park is the statue of **Son Pyong-hui** (1861-1922), reader of the Korean Declaration of Independence. In the vicinity of the park are roadside vendors selling maps of Korea and copies of the Declaration of Independence. In the evenings fortune tellers set up shop in small candlelit tents in the same area.

Hongnŭng Arboretum (Map 10)

Hongnŭng Arboretum is administered by the Forestry Research Institute (☎ 961 2651). Both the institute and the arboretum got their start when the Japanese colonial authorities set up the Forestry Experimental Centre in 1922. The Korean War turned the whole site into smouldering ashes, but it has been restored, although it's shrunk dramatically from its pre-war size. At present, the arboretum covers 10 hectares, plus an experimental forest of 28 hectares. There

Son of Independence

T'apkol (Pagoda) Park is named after the 10 tier marble Wŏngaksa Pagoda inside, but it is remembered first for its role in Korean resistance to Japanese rule.

During the Koryŏ Dynasty (918-1392) this was the site of Hungboksa, the temple later burned to the ground during the Chosŏn Dynasty to make way for Wŏngaksa. Wŏngaksa in turn was demolished in 1515, though Wŏngaksa Pagoda was spared and remains to this day.

The temple site remained in ruins for the next 382 years. It was an Englishman working for the Korean customs service, Sir John MacLeavy Brown (1842-1926), who designed T'apkol Park. The park was dedicated in 1897, making it the first public park in Korea.

During the Japanese era (1910-45), an attempt was made to dismantle Wŏngaksa Pagoda. The three top levels of the structure were removed but fortunately the marble pieces were not destroyed. The US Army Corps of Engineers reassembled the pagoda in 1946.

Mounted on a pedestal in the park is a statue of Son Pyong-hui (1861-1922), leader of the independence movement. The pedestal on which Son now stands was until 1961 occupied by a statue of Syngman Rhee, the incompetent first president of South Korea.

On 1 March 1919, Son Pyong-hui and other Korean dissidents drew up a Declaration of Independence. The declaration was read aloud in the park two days later. It unleashed a torrent of anti-Japanese feeling and the *sam-il*, or 'March 1st movement' was born. The entire contents of the Declaration of Independence are reproduced on a brass plaque alongside Son Pyong-hui's statue. Look also for the murals along the wall of the park which depict the activities of the independence movement.

are more than 2000 species of plants and 65 species of wildlife (mostly birds).

Smoking, barbecuing and carrying food and drink are all prohibited here. These strict prohibitions may be in part to drum up business for the arboretum's restaurant, but also to protect the delicate environment. Growing all these rare plants and raising birds is, after all, a tricky business in a big city like Seoul.

At present, the arboretum is only open to the public on Sunday from 7 am to 7 pm, though in the future this may be extended to include Saturday. Admission is free.

To reach the arboretum, take subway line 1 to Ch'ŏngryangni station. From there it's a 15 minute walk north.

Along the way you'll pass a compound housing **Hongnŭng Tomb** (Map 2, ☎ 962 0556), which is worth a visit. Within the compound you'll also find **King Sejong Memorial Hall**. Admission to the Hongnŭng Tomb site costs W340.

Sajik Park (Map 3)

Sajik Park is not far to the west of Kyŏngbokkung. It was originally the site of two ceremonial altars established by the first Yi king, T'aejo. Agricultural rites and sacrifices were held here twice yearly until 1897. The remains of the altars are still here, though today they are two visually unimpressive mounds. The park is a pleasant retreat, and worth a stroll from Kyŏngbokkung.

Tongnim Park (Map 2)

Patriotic resistance against the Japanese is a theme Koreans never seem to tire of, and one place to pursue the matter further is Tongnim (Independence) Park. The park was built on the site of a former prison where patriotic Koreans were martyred during the Japanese occupation. The city government has left several Japanese-era buildings standing, including the execution chamber.

Adjacent to the park is **Tongnimmun** gate, which was built in 1898. Curiously, it's claimed that Tongnimmun was modelled after the famed Arch of Triumph in Paris, though in fact it looks nothing like the French original.

Nonetheless, the dearly departed North Korean dictator Kim Il-sung was inspired by Tongnimmun to build his own version in P'yŏngyang, which indeed looks like an exact copy of the original Arch of Triumph. However, in a classic case of 'mine is bigger', the North Korean version is a full 3m taller than its Parisian counterpart.

Tongnim Park can be reached by taking subway line 3 to Tongnimmun station.

Yongsan Family Park (Map 2)

The government has big plans for this park, so far mostly unrealised. The former golf course for the US military base in Yongsan, this will eventually be the site of the National Museum. At the moment it's chiefly a place for picnics and barbecues.

The nearest subway station is Ich'ŏn on line 4.

Children's Grand Park (Map 2)

Out near the Sheraton Walker Hill Hotel in eastern Seoul, Children's Grand Park has plenty to keep the kids amused. There are rides, play areas, fountains and ponds, and even a small zoo.

The park is open daily from 9 am to 7 pm, and entry costs W1000 for adults, W500 for teenagers aged 12 and up, and free for children under 12. Take subway line 5 to Ach'asan station, or line 7 to the Children's Grand Park station.

Samnŭng Park (Map 7)

Samnŭng (Three Tombs) Park is close to Sŏllŭng station on subway line 2. The three tombs in the park belong to two Chosŏn Dynasty kings (the 9th and 11th) and, as they were father and son, their wife and mother respectively.

The tombs themselves just look like grass-clad mounds, but some of the surrounding stone statuary is fascinating. Surfacing from Sŏllŭng station, you wouldn't expect a site like this to be so close by, and

consequently it is one of the least visited historical sites in Seoul – by foreigners anyway.

Samnŭng park is open daily from 6 am to 6 pm (to 5 pm from November to February) and is closed on Monday. Entry for adults costs W400.

Olympic Park (Map 2)

Not far from the Olympic Stadium, Olympic Park is a more interesting outing than the former. Its grounds contain numerous sporting facilities from the 1988 Olympics, as well as outdoor art exhibits and remains of the Paekche Dynasty **Mongch'on Fortress**, which dates from the 4th century. There is also a small **museum** housing Paekche artefacts. The park is a short walk from Songnae or Chamshil station on subway line 2.

Military Academy Museum (Map 10)

This musuem is one of the less visited sights in Seoul, but it is interesting. The Military Academy Museum (☎ 970 2471, 976 6454), 77-1 Kongnung-dong, Nowon-gu, is housed within a three storey building (don't forget to check the basement) inside the Korean Military Academy complex.

Some of the items on display from Korea's long experience with war include various ancient and recent armaments such as swords, bows, arrows, pistols, rifles and cannons. You can also inspect old uniforms, horse-drawn equipment, classic texts on military strategy and paintings of various military campaigns. Lastly, there's a cadet's parade every Saturday.

The museum is open from 10 am to 4 pm and is closed Monday. Admission is free, but you need some identification (passport, resident card etc) to obtain a visitor's pass.

The museum is a five minute walk from Seoul Women's University bus stop. The nearest subway station is Mŏkkol on line 7.

ACTIVITIES

If you are interested in sport, fitness and games, Seoul has a good range of venues. For information on spectator sports, see the Entertainment chapter.

Archery

Both traditional Korean-style archery *(kungdo)* and the western form are practised in South Korea. Archery ranges are usually out of town. More information can be obtained by contacting the Korea Amateur Sport Association (☎ 420 3333), 888 Oryun-dong, Songp'a-gu, Seoul.

Billiards

Koreans are keen on billiards *(tanggu)*, and billiard halls are to be found everywhere around town – an unmistakable sign identifies these places.

Operating hours are from approximately 10 am to midnight.

Bowling

There are 23 public bowling *(polling)* alleys in Seoul (not counting the ones in five-star hotels):

ABC
  (☎ 546 7524) 114 Nonhyŏn-dong,
  Kangnam-gu
AMF
  (☎ 231 7782) 117-6 Shinsŏl-dong,
  Tongdaemun-gu
Ch'ŏnggu
  (☎ 545 5927) Ch'ŏngdam-dong, Kangnam-gu
Ch'ŏngryangni
  (☎ 966 5067) Ch'ŏngryangni-dong,
  Tongdaemun-gu
Chamshil
  (☎ 423 9787) 7 Shinch'ŏn-dong,
  Kangdong-gu
Crystal I
  (☎ 324 9977) 57-1 Nogosan-dong, Map'o-gu
Crystal II
  (☎ 784 6633) 43-3 Yŏŭido-dong,
  Yŏngdŭngp'o-gu
Diamond
  (☎ 567 1571) 151-7 Samsŏng-dong,
  Kangnam-gu
DLI 63 building
  (☎ 789 5921) 5th & 6th floors,
  60 Yŏŭido-dong, Yŏngdŭngp'o-gu
Giant
  (☎ 546 0141) 278-4 Nonhyŏn-dong,
  Kangnam-gu
Han-gang
  (☎ 794 7041) 543-1 Hannam-dong, Yongsan-gu
Hannam Cheil
  (☎ 792 5724) 110-1 Hannam-dong, Yongsan-gu

Hansŏng
  (☎ 324 6913) 49-55 Nogosan-dong,
  Map'o-gu
Hanyang
  (☎ 295 8866) 319-39 Haengdang-dong,
  Sŏngdong-gu
Hyundai (☎ 567 4295) 1004-1 Taech'i-dong,
  Kangnam-gu
Kumkang
  (☎ 918 1252) 3-1237 Chong-am-dong,
  Sŏngbuk-gu
Kyŏngnam
  (☎ 246 5197) 366-7 Chang-an-dong,
  Tongdaemun-gu
Life
  (☎ 265 2215) 289-3 Chongno 6-ga, Chongno-gu
Nagwon
  (☎ 743 7191) 284-6 Nagwon-dong, Chongno-gu
Osong
  (☎ 267 7171) 12-1 Ch'ungmuro 4-ga, Chung-gu
Piccadilly
  (☎ 745 1005) 139 Tonŭi-dong, Chongno-gu
Royal
  (☎ 496 0070) Chunghwa-dong, Chungnang-gu
Sŏngdong
  (☎ 444 9115) Chayang-dong, Sŏngdong-gu

Canoeing & Rafting

Canoeing *(k'anu)* and rafting *(kŭmnyut'agi)* are catching on, but Korea only has three rivers which attract whitewater enthusiasts. Naerinchŏn River (Naerinchŏn-gang) near Inje in Kangwon-do is considered the best. In the southern part of Kangwon-do near Yŏngwol is the Tong River (Tong-gang). About 50km north of Seoul is Han-t'angang Resort, which also offers some rafting activities.

For further information, contact the Pine River Canoe School (☎ 3473 1659) in Seoul, or ring its office in Inje (☎ 0365-461 4586).

Computer Clubs

The Seoul Computer Club is an English-speaking organisation founded by US military personnel at the base in Yongsan. However, the club is open to all – you do not need to be a member of the military. Monthly meetings are held at the Seoul USO (Map 2), and no military ID or base pass is required. Check out the club's Web site (www.seoulcc.org).

THINGS TO SEE & DO

Diving & Snorkelling

You won't find tropical coral reefs, but Korea does have a small group of enthusiastic divers. For more information call the Korea Underwater Association (☎ 420 4293).

Golf

For club-swinging Japanese, South Korea is golfing (*golpŭ* in Korean) mecca, as prices are so much cheaper than at home. But for many western visitors, prices won't seem quite so ridiculously cheap. You can expect to pay from W50,000 to W75,000 for a game, and club rental is in the vicinity of W25,000. Golf clubs should be declared at customs when you enter the country.

Miniature golf is much more accessible to those on a budget. However, about the only venue for this at present is in Seoul Dream Land (Map 10).

There are two 18-hole golf courses within Seoul: Namsungdae (☎ 403 0071), 419 Changji-dong, Songp'a-gu; and Taenung, also called Yuksa, (☎ 972 2111), 230-30 Kongnung-dong, Nowon-gu.

There are 48 golf courses in the province of Kyŏnggi-do. There's no need to list all of them here, but the following is a list of all the 36-hole golf courses:

Asiana
(☎ 0335-348 800) 281-1 Taetae-ri, Yangjimyŏn, Yong-in
Gold
(☎ 0331-283 8111) 18 Komae-ri, Kihŭng-ŭp, Yong-in
Hanil
(☎ 0337-847 000) 69 Yanggwi-ri, Kanammyŏn, Yŏju-gun
Hanyang
(☎ 0344-969 0811) 38-23 Wondong-dong, Tŏkyang-gu
Kihung
(☎ 0339-376 4011) 46-1 Shin-ri, Tongt'anmyŏn, Hwasŏng-gun
Lakeside
(☎ 0335-342 111) 5-12 Nŭngwan-ri, Mohyŏnmyŏn, Yong-in
New Seoul
(☎ 0347-625 672) 1-3-ri Kwangju-ŭp, Kwangju-gun

Pal Pal ('88')
(☎ 0331-282 0881) 80-2 Ch'ŏngdŏk-ri, Kusŏng-myŏn, Yong-in
Plaza
(☎ 0335-326 761) 257-1 Pongmu-ri, Namsamyŏn, Yong-in
Suwon
(☎ 0331-281 6613) 313 Kugal-ri, Naehŭng-ŭp, Yong-in
Taegwang
(☎ 0331-281 7111) 66 Shingal-ri, Kihŭng-ŭp, Yong-in

There are also five driving/putting ranges within the city limits, as follows:

Eagle Golf Club
(☎ 501 2929) 1006-2 Li Taech'i-dong, Kangnam-gu. Inside a five storey building. Take subway line 2 to Samsŏng station and walk about seven minutes towards Taech'i-dong. The driving range is 136.5m, with 64 tees. It can accommodate 100 people, and is open daily from 5 am to midnight. There is a putting room, computerised practice room, locker rooms, showers and a pro shop. Rates are W15,000 per hour or W230,000 per month for 80 minutes of use per day. Inquire about memberships and golf lessons.
Gold Sports Indoor Golf
(☎ 454 3691) Kwangjang-dong, Kwangjin-gu. In eastern Seoul, a five minute walk from Kangnaru subway station on line 5. This very large golf range can accommodate 700, and is open from 6 am to 10 pm, closed Tuesday. Fees are very reasonable at W80,000 per month. There are discounts for teenagers.
Kangnam Driving Range
(☎ 544 5282) 633-2 Shinsa-dong, Kangnam-gu (in front of Samwon Garden Restaurant). It's a 10 minute walk from Apkujŏng subway station on line 3. The driving range is 118m, with 35 tees. It can accommodate 50, and the facilities are open from 9.30 am to 5.30 pm, closed Sunday and holidays. Hourly fees are W15,400.
Nonhyŏn Composite Driving Range
(☎ 545 6636) 40 Nonhyŏn-dong, Kangnam-gu. Take subway line 3 to Shinsa station. The driving range is 136.5m, with 72 tees. It can accommodate 110, and is open Monday to Friday from 5.30 am to 9 pm and weekends and holidays from 6 am to 8.30 pm. Rates are W15,000 per hour, or W230,000 per month for 80 minutes of use per day.
Tongnim Golf Plaza
(☎ 545 4246) 105-4 Nonhyŏn-dong, Kangnam-gu. Take subway line 3 to Shinsa station, then bus No 576 and get off at Cine House

Cinema (Map 7). The driving range is 210m, with 36 tees. It can accommodate 50, and is open from 5 am to 9 pm daily, except for major public holidays. Rates are W15,400 per hour or 100 minutes for W20,400.

Hang Gliding & Paragliding

The art of gliding has taken off in Korea. Within Seoul itself, enthusiasts launch their gliders along the shores of the Han-gang at the various riverside parks (ie Yŏuido, Ttuksŏm, Chamshil and Kwangnaru). Even better is to get into the mountainous rural areas where updraughts are good and the skies are uncrowded.

Gliding looks like a solo activity, but in fact this sport is best pursued with a club. Some clubs are nonprofit, while others are very much cash-raking machines. Some organisations that can help you cultivate the fine art of floating on air are:

Air Dream
(☎ 337 3146) 3rd floor, Sambok Bldg, 182-4 Tonggyo-dong, Map'o-gu
Airman School
(☎ 578 9763) Room 1007, Miliana Officetel Il-ch'a, 99-1 Karakbon-dong, Songp'a-gu
Airmaster
(☎ 294 5397) 132 Hongik-dong, Songdong-gu
Green Leisure
(☎ 231 8900) 4th floor, 361-13 Shindang 2-dong, Chung-gu
Han-uri
(☎ 561 0840) 4th & 5th floors, Posong Bldg, 912-17 Taech'i-dong, Kangnam-gu
Hanbaek Leisure
(☎ 515 6633) Room 403, T'aesung Bldg, 618-4 Shinsa-dong, Kangnam-gu
Hankuk Aviation Association
(☎ 203 0488) Room 301, Shinhwa Bldg, 23-22 Chamwon-dong, Soch'o-gu
Hankuk Gliding Association
(☎ 514 7760) 23-22 Chamwon-dong, Soch'o-gu
Hankuk Leisure Event Association
(☎ 722 8811) 6th floor, Hongik Bldg, 198-1 Kwanhun-dong, Chongno-gu
Korea Chonghap Leports
(☎ 516 2042) 2nd floor, Daewoo Bldg, 2-13 Nonhyŏn-dong, Kangnam-gu
Korea Sky-Flying Association
(☎ 512 9940) Nonhyŏn-dong, Kangnam-gu
Kosan Leisure
(☎ 443 8077) Room 1007, Cheil Officetel, 99-3 Karak-dong, Songp'a-gu

Mirae Events
(☎ 753 5034) 3rd floor, Shina Bldg, 66 Kalwol-dong, Yongsan-gu
Nalgae
(☎ 927 0206) Room 302, Ansong Bldg, 756-3 Yongdu 2-dong, Tongdaemun-gu
Shinsegye
(☎ 597 2121) 6th floor, Sogyong Bldg, 910-13 Pangbae-dong, Soch'o-gu
Tonghwa-enndam
(☎ 722 8811) 6th floor, Hongik Bldg, 198-1 Kwanhun-dong, Chongno-gu

Health & Fitness Clubs

There are many of these around, but the most foreigner-friendly ones are in It'aewon. Two of the most popular are:

Taewon Health Club
(☎ 790 5567) 736-55 Hannam 2-dong, Yong-san-gu; near the It'aewon Hotel (Map 8)
World Health Club
(☎ 790 0010) B1 Sekwang Bldg, 303-17 It'ae-won 2-dong, Yongsan-gu; near the Hyatt Hotel (Map 8)

Ice Skating

Lotte World (Map 2) offers year-round indoor ice skating *(sŭk'eit'ŭ)*, but avoid it on weekends when the ice is hidden under a mass of squirming arms and legs. Lotte World is near Chamshil station on subway line 2.

The other option is the Mok-dong sports complex (☎ 649 8454) near Omokkyo subway station on line 5.

Jogging

Here's an activity you can do all on your own, and as long as you stay off the streets, Seoul isn't a bad place to do it. But if you're an expat who craves social bonding through shin splints and beer, you can always seek out Hash Houses Harriers.

If you're just passing through you might not be enthusiastically welcomed to The Hash, an informal, loosely strung network of hundreds of groups around the world, often fondly (?) described as 'a drinking club with a running problem'.

A typical gathering of The Hash includes a non-competitive run or jog of up to an hour, followed by food, drink and merry socialising in the great outdoors, often continuing elsewhere into the wee hours.

There is no club headquarters, but ask around – Commonwealth embassy staffers often know about meetings and sometimes notices are posted at local expat pubs.

The Seoul Hash also has a Web site (members.aol.com/sngmstr/korea.html).

The Harriers started out as an all-male group, but there are now mixed runs (still no all-female runs in Korea, but it could happen if someone wants to organise it). The all-male group runs on Wednesday evenings from mid-April to mid-October, and on Saturday afternoon in the colder months. Afterwards, members wind down in the Mug Club (Map 8), across from the fire station in It'aewon, and can often be found there on other nights as well. Ask the staff if any Hashers are around.

A mixed Hash runs near the Yongsan Military Base (Map 2) near It'aewon, and also at Osan Air Base south of Seoul. Seoul also has a mixed, monthly 'Full Moon Hash' running one Friday a month.

Mountain Biking

Seoul itself offers few opportunities for this pursuit, but there are good venues in the mountains east of town. Contact the Korea MTB Association (☎ 0346-653 916).

Paduk & Korean Chess

Paduk is virtually identical to the Japanese game of *go*, though it originated in China. Flat black and white stones are positioned on a playing board to 'capture' board space and surround enemy stones. As with western chess, the rules are simple but the techniques can be very complex.

It's easy to find partners who can teach you the art of paduk – try the local pubs. Frequently, a fair bit of alcohol is consumed during these games and wagers often change hands. As with western chess, major championships are followed in the news media.

Changgi is Korean chess. Though not as popular as paduk, this interesting forerunner of western-style chess is still played in the same style it once was in China.

Skiing

The cold winters and mountainous terrain of South Korea make the country an ideal place to practice the art of sliding downhill *(sŭk'i)*. The best slopes are near the east coast, a 2½ to four hour drive from Seoul (and thus a mandatory overnight trip). However, there are some moderately good ski resorts less than an hour's commute from central Seoul. The cost for lift tickets and equipment rentals is somewhat lower than in most western countries, but not by much. Finding ski boots to fit big western feet can be a problem – having your own equipment does have advantages.

Some of the resorts have youth hostels, though you will need an IYH (HI) card to stay in these places. There is usually at least one hotel inside the resort, with some smaller hotels and yŏgwan several kilometres away (if you stay in the latter, you'll probably need your own car). Most of the resorts also have time-share condominiums – these can often be rented for less than a hotel room costs, and may have the added bonus of a kitchen. All of the resorts have skiing classes – figure on about W25,000 for a full day, or W18,000 for a half day of instructions. There are substantial discounts for children on lift tickets, ski rentals and skiing classes.

To check snow conditions and make hotel reservations, call the resorts at their Seoul representative offices (indicated by area code ☎ 02) or call the resorts directly – most of the Seoul offices employ at least one staff person who speaks English. Almost all of the resorts run chartered buses directly from Seoul to the ski slopes – ring up to find out the details, ask KNTO or inquire at any of the larger travel agencies in Seoul.

In most cases, you'd be wise to arrive with a group and thus be eligible for significant group discounts on lift tickets and ski rentals. Some average prices for lift tickets are: full-day W30,000, half-day W17,000, night W12,000, single ride W4000, season W750,000. The typical prices for ski rentals are: full-day W27,000, half-day W21,000, night W19,000.

The following resorts are listed in order of distance from Seoul.

Seoul Ski Resort
(☎ 02-561 1230, 0346-571 1230) Season: 10 December to late February; four slopes ranging in length from 232m to 1002m; three lifts. Accommodation possibilities include one family hotel (66 rooms). The resort is a 40 minute drive east of Seoul at Paekpongsan, Namyangju-gun, Kyŏnggi-do.

Bears Town Ski Resort
(☎ 02-594 7780, 0357-322 534) Season: late November to early March; 12 slopes ranging in length from 500m to 2500m; 11 lifts. Accommodation includes one youth hostel (48 rooms) and condominiums (533 rooms). The condominiums boast a heated indoor swimming pool, sauna, karaoke, bowling alley, game room and tennis courts. The resort is a 40 minute drive north-east of Seoul in P'och'on-gun, Kyŏnggi-do. Public transport from Seoul: bus to Kwangrung or Ildong departing from Sangbong bus terminal.

Yangji Pine Ski Resort
(☎ 02-511 3033, 0335-382 001) Season: 10 December to late February; eight slopes from 500m to 1500m; seven lifts. Accommodation includes one hotel (60 rooms) and one condominium (302 rooms) – the latter has a heated swimming pool and bowling alley. The resort is at the town of Yong-in, not far from the Korean Folk Village – it's a 50 minute drive south-east of Seoul.

Ch'onmasan Ski Resort
(☎ 02-285 6677, 0346-594 2463) Season: 9 December to early March; five slopes ranging in length from 350m to 1300m; seven lifts. Accommodation is limited to one hotel (38 rooms) which boasts a heated swimming pool. The ski resort is a 50 minute drive north-east of Seoul, close to the town of Namyangju. From Seoul, you can catch a train from Ch'ŏngryangni station, get off at Masok station and take a 10 minute taxi ride to the resort.

Jisan Ski Resort
(☎ 02-3406 0122, 0336-638 460) Six slopes and three lifts; the resort is at Ich'ŏn, a 50 minute drive south-east of Seoul.

Taemyong Hongch'ŏn Ski Resort
(☎ 02-222 7000, 0366-434 8311) Season: 9 December to early March; 12 slopes from 287m to 1644m; 10 lifts. The site has one youth hostel (188 beds) and one condominium (1090 rooms). The resort is a two hour drive east of Seoul in Hongch'ŏn-gun, Kangwon-do.

Sajo Maeul, also known as Suanbo Sajo Village Ski Resort
(☎ 02-363 2040, 0441-846 0750) The resort has seven slopes and 13 lifts. Accommodation is primarily a youth hostel with 68 beds, though

there are some nearby yŏgwan. The resort is near Suanbo Hot Springs, Ch'ungch'ŏngbuk-do, a 2½ hour drive south-east of Seoul.

Phoenix Park Ski World
(☎ 02-508 3400, 0374-336 000) There are 12 slopes and nine lifts. Accommodation can be found at one hotel (141 rooms) and one condominium (756 rooms). The resort is a 2½ hour drive east of Seoul at P'yongch'ang-gun, Kangwon-do. The nearest major town is Changp'yong, which can be reached by express bus from Tong Seoul bus terminal From Changp'yong, there is a free shuttle to the resort between about 9.30 am and 6 pm.

Hyundai Song-u Ski Resort
(☎ 02-523 7111, 0372-403 000) Season: 30 November to March; 21 slopes and eight lifts. It's the newest ski resort in Korea and boasts modern facilities. The site has one hotel (86 rooms) and a condominium (767 rooms). The resort is a 2½ hour drive east of Seoul, close to Wonju, Kangwon-do.

Korea Condo Ski Resort
(☎ 02-783 8000, 0374-368 800) There are three slopes and two lifts. As the name implies, accommodation consists of a condominium (198 rooms). The resort is to the south of Odaesan National Park, a 3½ hour drive east of Seoul.

Yongp'yŏng (Dragon Valley) Ski Resort
(☎ 02-561 6271, 0374-355 757) Season: late November to early April; 18 slopes ranging in length from 410m to 1750m; 16 lifts. There is one hotel (191 rooms), one youth hostel (54 beds) and one condominium (825 rooms). The resort is at P'yongch'ang-gun, Kangwon-do. It's a 3½ hour drive from Seoul. A free shuttle bus runs from Kangnŭng airport to Yongp'yŏng. The bus runs six times a day (8.20 and 8.50 am and 12.20, 3.20, 7.20 and 8 pm). Non-stop buses also run from Kangnŭng to Hoenggye (40 minutes), then take a free shuttle bus from Hoenggye to Yongp'yŏng (every 10 minutes throughout the day).

Muju Ski Resort
(☎ 02-3849 5000, 0657-322 9000) There are 30 slopes from 90m to 3220m; 13 lifts. Accommodation consists of one resort hotel (118 rooms), one family hotel (418 rooms) and one condominium (950 rooms). It's Korea's southernmost ski resort (and thus occasionally problematic for snow), but official season is from late November to early March. It's at Tŏgyusan National Park, Muju-gun, Chŏllabuk-do, a four hour drive south of Seoul.

Alps Ski Resort
(☎ 02-756 5481, 0392-681 5030) Season: from late November to late March; eight slopes ranging in length from 550m to 2220m; five lifts. There is an on-site youth hostel (38 beds)

and condominiums (604 rooms). The resort is at Sŏraksan National Park, Kosong-gun, Kangwon-do, a five hour drive north-east of Seoul.

Skydiving & Ballooning

If you have a generous budget and a good life insurance policy, this could be just the sport for you. Two organisations that can help you take the big leap are the Korea Skydiving Association (☎ 318 7943) and the Korea Skydiving School (☎ 3443 0797).

Ballooning also requires a fair bit of capital. If you've got the urge and the financial resources, you can try calling the Korea Balloon Association (☎ 338 0950).

Squash & Racquetball

Neither of these two sports has caught on in Seoul, but there are a couple of venues at which to play. KBS 88 Gymnasium (☎ 600 8807), 1093 Hwagok 6-dong, Kangsŏ-gu, has squash facilities open from 8 am to 4 pm, and charges W8000 per hour. Racquetball can be played from 1 to 5 pm at the Sŏch'o Sports Centre (☎ 591 6060), 114-3 Panp'o-dong, Sŏch'o-gu.

Swimming Pools – Outdoor

Seoul's short summer season and the fact that school children have summer holidays means that the few outdoor public pools tend to be horribly crowded. Using the facilities early in the morning should help you beat the worst of the crowds.

Ich'ŏn
(☎ 798 9632) Open July and August only. This large public swimming pool has a capacity for more than 2000 persons. Admission costs W1100 for adults. The pool is in Ich'ŏn Riverside Park just next to the Han River and the Tongjak Bridge. There are adjacent facilities for playing soccer, basketball, baseball and volleyball. Take subway line 4 to Ich'ŏn station, then walk 15 minutes, or alternatively bus No 15, 38, 57, 61, 76 or 211.

Chamshil
(☎ 421 2574) Han-gang Kosubuji (Riverside Terrace), Chamshil 2-dong, Songp'a-gu. Take subway line 2 to Sŏngnae station. Large outdoor pool with a capacity for 3000 persons. It's open July and August. Admission costs W1100. Nearby facilities on the river for jet skiing, water skiing, motor boating. Other facilities for soccer, baseball, volleyball, basketball plus an ice skating rink.

Yŏŭido
(Map 9, ☎ 783 1539) Riverside Park, Yŏŭido-dong, Yŏngdŭngp'o-gu. The pool is on Yŏŭido, along the Han-gang shore. Take subway line 5 to Yŏŭinaru station. The pool is open in July and August. Other facilities include soccer fields, volleyball courts, basketball courts, boat marina, play grounds, tennis courts, ice skating rink and a 4.5km-long fishing dock. Admission is W1100.

Seoul Dream Land
(Map 10, ☎ 982 6800) 28-6 Pon-dong, Tobong-gu. The swimming pool is in the Seoul Dream Land complex. Take subway line 4 to Suyu station, or line 1 to Sŏkkye station and then catch a shuttle bus. Alternatively, take line 4 to Miasamgŏri station and walk 20 minutes. The pool is open from mid-June to early September from 9 am to 6 pm. Admission costs W5000. The amusement park has many other facilities.

Swimming Pools – Indoor

Heated indoor public pools are the answer if you want to enjoy year-round swimming. Many private health clubs have indoor pools and the added benefit of exercise rooms and sometimes a sauna. If you want to beat (or at least minimise) the crowds, try to use the facilities during business hours when most Seoulites are at work.

AMF Swimming Pool
(☎ 231 7781) 117-6 Shinsŏl-dong, Tongdaemun-gu. Take subway line 1 to Shinsŏl-dong station. It's open year-round from 6 am to 8.30 pm. Additional facilities include an exercise room and a bowling alley. Admission is W4000 each time, or W80,000 per month.

Kop'yong Medith Club
(☎ 519 0700) 203 Nonhyon-dong, Kangnam-gu. Take subway line 2 to Kangnam station and walk 15 minutes. The club is in Kop'yong Group building B, opposite the Ritz Carlton Hotel (Map 7). Admission for single use costs W9900 and a one year membership costs W600,000. The pool is open from 6 am to 9 pm, closed Sunday. Other facilities include exercise machines, racquetball court and a sauna.

Lotte World Swimming Pool
(☎ 411 4502/6) 40-1 Chamshil-dong Songp'a-gu. Take subway line 2 to Chamshil station. This large facility has separate pools for children, adults and diving. It's open from 6 am to

1 pm for groups and swimming classes, and from 1 to 9 pm for individual nonmembers. It is closed during major holidays, and the second Monday and fourth Tuesday of the month.

Olympic Memorial Citizen's Hall
(☎ 745 6701) 1-21 Hyehwa-dong, Chongno-gu. Take subway line 4 to Hyehwa station. The citizen's hall is 200m towards Songbuk-dong from the Hyehwa-dong Rotary Club. The pool is open from 6 am to 8 pm, closed every second and fourth Sunday of the month. In addition to the swimming pool, facilities include exercise rooms, a gymnasium for learning martial arts, fencing, badminton, ping-pong etc. The cost for the swimming pool only is W2500, but inquire about full memberships.

Spa Swimming Pool
(☎ 922 9229) 76-34 Shinsol-dong, Tongdaemun-gu. Take subway line 1 to Shinsŏl-dong station. The pool is open year round from 6 am to 9 pm, and the cost for adults is W3650.

Sports Complex
(Map 7, ☎ 417 8807) 1-10 Chamshil 1-dong Songp'a-gu. Take subway line 2 to the Sports Complex station. The pool is in the Olympic Stadium. This is Seoul's largest indoor swimming pool and can get very crowded. It's open in summer from 9 am to 6 pm, and in winter from 9 am to 5 pm. Admission for adults costs W200.

Uju 'Universe'
(☎ 557 0111) New World Hotel (Map 7), 112-5 Samsong-dong, Kangnam-gu (a 10 minute walk from Sŏllŏng station on subway line 2). The pool is open daily from 6 am to 10 pm. Additional facilities include a snack bar and tanning beds. Admission costs W9900.

Wujung Sports Centre
(☎ 332 0222) Yonhui-dong, Sodaemun-gu. Take subway line 2 to Shinch'on station and walk north-west for about five minutes. There is a swimming pool and sauna at the sports centre, and this is perhaps the best such facility in the trendy Shinch'on area.

YMCA
(Map 4, ☎ 732 8291) 9 Chongno 2-ga Chongno-gu. Take subway line 1 to Chonggak station. This pool is for YMCA members only. It's open daily from 6 am to 9 pm, but it's closed on holidays. The YMCA has a branch swimming pool in Tongdaemun-gu which is less crowded – make inquiries at the main YMCA building.

Tennis

Public tennis (*t'enisŭ*) courts exist in city parks, but (surprise) these tend to be very crowded. There are also private facilities. Obviously, it's easiest to get on a court, public or private, if you try to play during regular working hours. Forget about it on weekends and holidays.

A few major tennis facilities include:

Ch'onghak
(☎ 542 9481) 632 Shinsa-dong, Kangnam-gu; 11 courts
Changch'ung
(☎ 279 7721) 14-68 Changch'ung-dong 2-ga, Chung-gu (in Changch'ung Park); nine courts
Cheil
(☎ 782 0486) 28-2 Yŏŭido-dong, Yŏngdŭngp'o-gu; 16 courts, night lighting
Elgreen
(☎ 423 5334) 7-18 Shinch'on-dong, Kangdong-gu; 23 courts, night lighting
Garden Park
(☎ 556 5964) 1009 Taech'i-dong, Kangnam-gu; 19 courts
Giant
(☎ 794 7801) 302-6 Tongbu-ich'on-dong, Yongsan-gu; 46 courts
Hosu
(☎ 414 7597) 35 Songp'a-dong, Songp'a-gu; 12 courts, night lighting
Hyoch'ang
(☎ 714 4479) 7 Hyoch'ang-dong, Yongsan-gu; 16 courts
Ich'on
(☎ 798 0444) 302-87 Tongbu-ich'on-dong, Yongsan-gu; nine courts
Kkottongnae
(☎ 599 8600) 185-12 Soch'o-dong, Soch'o-gu; 30 courts, night lighting
Kwangjang
(☎ 445 5659) 453-2 Kwangjang-dong, Songdong-gu; 14 courts, night lighting
Le Caf
(☎ 562 6970) 972-2 Taech'i-dong, Kangnam-gu; 32 courts
New Town
(☎ 532 9765) 59-16 Chamwon-dong, Soch'o-gu; 21 courts
Seoul
(☎ 993 2560) 419 Ssangmun-dong, Tobong-gu; 31 courts
Seoul Tennis Park
(☎ 602 5914) 25-1 Shinwol-dong, Yangch'on-gu; 30 courts
Shinil
(☎ 980 4170) 190-1 Mia-dong, Tobong-gu; 37 courts
Tongshin
(☎ 832 5453) 425-1 Shingil-dong, Yŏngdŭngp'o-gu; 15 courts

Yongdong A
(☎ 567 0466) 663-4 Yoksam-dong, Kangnam-gu; 16 courts, night lighting
Yongdong B
(☎ 566 4445) 680 Yoksam-dong, Kangnam-gu; nine courts, night lighting
Yongma
(☎ 433 1189) 69-1 Myonmok-dong, Chung-nang-gu; 18 courts

Windsurfing & Water Skiing

Although Seoul lacks a sizeable lake, water sports are possible on the Han River. Of course, the season is short, unless you want to water ski behind an icebreaker.

For the 1988 Olympics, a regatta course for rowing and canoeing competitions was established in Misa-dong, Hanam City, the first suburb south-east of Seoul. The site is now a recreation area, though getting there on public transport may be difficult. It's near the Olympic Expressway, Chungbu Highway and P'altang Bridge. You can ring (☎ 0347-791 3147) for information on up-coming competitions.

COURSES
Language

First, note that it is very important to obtain a student visa *before* enrolling in any kind of course in Seoul – the schools will not tell you this!

This mean that even if you already have a work visa, you cannot legally enrol in a school without first getting permission stamped into your residence permit by immigration. The fine for breaking this rule is at least W100,000.

There are several large government-run language schools in Seoul, including:

Ewha Women's University
(Map 9), 11-1 Institute of Language Research & Education (☎ 312-0067), Pughyŏn-dong, Sŏdaemun-gu
Hankuk University of Foreign Studies
(Map 10), Intensive Korean Language Program (☎ 961 4174), 270 Imun-dong, Tongdae-mun-gu
Konkuk University Language School,
Institute of Language Research & Education (☎ 450 3075), Konkuk University (Map 2), 93-1 Kwangjin-gu

Sŏgang University Korean Language Education & Research Institute
(☎ 705 8081) Sŏgang University (Map 9), No-gosan-dong, Map'o-gu
Sookmyung Women's University
SMU International Centre for Language Education (☎ 710 9165), 53-12 Chungpa-dong 2-ga, Yongsan-gu; Sookmyung Women's University station is on subway line 4, one stop south of Seoul Station.
Yonsei University
(Map 9), Korean Language Institute, Institute of Language Research & Education (☎ 392 6405), Yonsei University, 134 Shinch'on, Sŏdaemun-gu

Private language institutes are the most flexible and may be better located depending on where you live in Seoul. However, if possible talk to some (satisfied?) foreign students first before handing over a wad of cash. Also, be certain that the school can legally sponsor you for a student visa. Some private schools include:

ANC Language Institute
(☎ 508 0081) 2nd floor, Taeyoung Bldg, Taechi-dong, Kangnam-gu
ARC Korean Language Education
(☎ 511 9311) 636-1 Shinsa-dong, Kangnam-gu
Berlitz Language Centre
(☎ 3481 5324) 2nd floor, Sungwoo Academy Bldg, 1316-17 Sŏcho-dong, Sŏcho-gu
Central Language Institute
(☎ 556 9944) 131-1 Sŏch'o-dong, Sŏch'o-gu
Hanyang International Language Institute
(☎ 290 1663) 17 Haengdang-dong, Sŏngdong-gu
Jungjin Language Institute
(☎ 753 5243) 130-1 Hyehyun 1-ga, Chung-gu
The Korea Herald Language Institute
(☎ 727-0271) 9th floor, Korea Herald Bldg, 1-12 Hyehyun 3-ga, Chung-gu
YBM Sisa Yong O Sa
(☎ 278 0509) 55-1 Chongno 2-ga, Chongno-gu, opposite T'apkol Park

T'aekwondo

T'aekwondo is a traditional Korean form of self-defence which has evolved from an earlier form called *t'aekkyŏn*.

Despite its strong emphasis on harmonious physical and spiritual discipline, as actually practiced t'aekwondo occasionally licences a macho streak, especially in overseas schools. It's also the case that these days, almost all Korean males are inducted into the army and are taught t'aekwondo as part of their training – as a result, bar-room brawls in Korea can be pretty nasty.

T'aekwondo also has a following in the west and the more serious students often make the long journey to South Korea to study it at the source. The headquarters of the World T'aekwondo Federation (Map 7, ☎ 566 2505) is south of the Han River in Kangnam-gu. Another local organisation that promotes the sport is the Korean T'aekwondo Association(☎ 420 4271).

Culture

Courses in traditional culture, customs and manners are taught at Yejiwon (☎ 253 2211).

The topics covered depend on student demand but can include traditional Korean dance, cooking (including the all-important art of kimch'i making), *tado* (tea ceremony) etiquette, *hanbok* (traditional clothing) design and so on. Classes are often geared towards locals, but an English-speaking instructor can be arranged for foreign students.

Yejiwon is opposite the National Theatre (Map 3) on the north-east edge of Namsan Park. The nearest subway station is Dongguk University on line 3.

Places to Stay

A major factor in deciding where you want to base yourself in Seoul is what you are going to be doing there. It may be that visitors on business trips will prefer to be based in the booming Kangnam and Songp'a districts on the south side of the Han-gang (Han River). Another option for business travellers is sterile-looking Yŏŭido in the middle of the Han-gang. For those who want to see the sights and get a taste of what's left of the more traditional Seoul, the heart of central Seoul is the best choice. But some people will like the upmarket hotels on the scenic slopes of the Puk'ansan area to the north.

Prices in hotels are usually (but not always) calculated per room rather than per head, so many travellers save money by sharing. Note that mid-range and top-end prices quoted here will be 20% higher in reality because of the VAT and services tax.

The Korean national Tourism Organisation (KNTO) has an official rating system for hotels, though this does not include the budget end *(minbak, yŏinsuk, yŏgwan* and motels*)*. In descending order, hotels are rated super-deluxe, deluxe, 1st, 2nd and 3rd class.

Minbak

Paying a fee to stay in people's homes is known as minbak. In many rural parts of Korean, elderly women congregate at bus stations and solicit tourists to stay in their homes. The idea of seeking out minbak is that it's either cheaper than a hotel, or else (at least in resort areas) it's the only thing available during peak holiday times when hotels are full.

This is not the case in Seoul. A home stay in Seoul is not necessarily cheap (minimum W35,000 a night), nor will you find elderly women standing in bus terminals drumming up business for their minbak. Furthermore, Seoul does not suffer from a shortage of hotel space, especially during holidays because everybody leaves town.

In Seoul, home stays are organised by the Ministry of Culture & Tourism as a sort of cultural exchange program. You get to experience life in a Korean home, the Koreans get a little foreign language practice and perhaps earn some money, and hopefully the arrangement makes everybody happy.

If you would like to stay in the home of a Korean family in Seoul, you can check out a Web site (homestay.andyou.com). Otherwise, contact one of the following organisations in Seoul:

Labo International Exchange Centre
  (☎ 817 4625, fax 813 7047, email klabo@chollian.co.kr)
  Room 403, Sejong Bldg, 343-7 Sindaebang-dong, Tongjak-gu; Web site:www.labostay.or.kr
Korea Youth Exchange Promotion Association
  (☎ 817 6325, fax 817 6326, email kyepa2@kyepa.or.kr)
  Room 303, Sejong Bldg, 343-7 Sindaebang-dong, Tongjak-gu; Web site: www.kyepa.or.kr
WAWO
  (☎ 254 2916, fax 261 3166)
  Room 208, Seo-am Bldg, 114-22 Sinsul-dong, Tongdaemun-gu; Web site: www.wawo.co.kr

Guesthouses

Budget travellers usually head straight for the traditional Korean inns known as yŏinsuk or yŏgwan. Unlike western-style hotels, yŏinsuk and yŏgwan sometimes have beds but usually do not – you sleep on the floor, which is padded with a Korean-style futon. Warmth in the winter months is provided by an underfloor heating system called *ondol*, which makes the floor particularly comfortable.

The name of the guesthouse gives a clue to what facilities you can expect and the price you'll pay. Yŏgwan usually have at least some rooms with private bath, while yŏinsuk never do. The more classy yŏgwan are called *jang yŏgwan (*often just abbreviated to *jang)*. Rooms in jang yŏgwan all have private baths, and some of these places

The pagoda-topped National Folk Museum at Kyŏngbokkung is well worth a visit.

Tonhwamun, the oldest remaining gate at Ch'angdŏkkung, is also the palace's main entrance.

Above the din (but sometimes below the smog) is a view of central Seoul from Namsan.

Hidden by clouds of urban 'development' are many neighbourhoods of courtyard houses.

even have beds, which means that they are actually small family-run hotels.

Yŏinsuk are disappearing – the few remaining in Seoul attempt to disguise their low standards by calling themselves yŏgwan. Yŏgwan are more numerous, but jang yŏgwan are gradually taking over. In other words, Seoul is moving upmarket, which definitely puts a squeeze on budget travellers. If you can find one, a basic yŏinsuk room generally costs no more than W8000 a night. Yŏgwan prices start around W15,000, but W20,000 is almost standard for jang yŏgwan.

There are yŏgwan scattered throughout Seoul, and once you learn to recognise the *han'gŭl* for the word yŏgwan (see the Language chapter) you'll be seeing them all over the place. If you can't read han'gŭl, the next best thing to look out for is the public bathhouse symbol, which is found on all jang yŏgwan (but also on bathhouses). If you show up with your bags, staff will either show you a room or give you a good scrubbing down. The symbol is as follows:

Since yŏinsuk have such primitive bathing facilities, you might indeed want to visit a bathhouse *(mogyokt'ang)*. This can be a very pleasant experience – it's a great way to get the winter chill out of your bones. Men and women have separate facilities, and you can rent towels and soap, and bathe for as long as you like for around W3000 to W4000. Many bathhouses employ staff to give massages (legitimate massage, not prostitution), but inquire about the price first. In large cities, bathhouses are typically open from about 5 am to 9 pm. Most bathhouses shut down for a 10 day break in early August.

Many of the old bathhouses have recently been converted into saunas *(tchimjilbang)*. However, the vast majority of these places (so far) are for women only. At W6000, they cost more than bathhouses, but the saunas give you more. For one thing, they are usually open all night, which means you can sleep in a lounge chair wearing a bathrobe (supplied by the sauna) and thus save a night's hotel bill.

Many yŏgwan are transformed into short-time love hotels on weekends. As a result, they typically raise the price another W5000 on Saturday night. However, some yŏgwan will give you a discount if you rent a room by the week or month, in which case you shouldn't be charged extra on weekends.

One other thing worth bearing in mind is that most yŏgwan lock their doors at midnight. If you arrive at your yŏgwan after midnight, you'll probably have to knock on the door and get the owners out of bed. They will usually overlook this on the odd occasion, but if it occurs regularly, you can be sure it won't make you too popular.

PLACES TO STAY – CENTRAL

The central area of Seoul consists mainly of two large districts, Chung-gu and Chongno-gu, both to the north of Namsan.

Budget

Kwanghwamun (Map 4) The venerable *Inn Daewon (Map 4, ☎ 738 4308, 26 Tangju-dong, Chongno-gu)* is basically a yŏinsuk, although its Korean name is *Daewon Yŏgwan*. A bed in a shared room costs W7000 and a private room is W11,000. All 20 rooms share one grotty washroom with barely functional plumbing. Check the place out carefully before you pay – it looks like it's been through the Korean War.

The same family that operates Inn Daewon also runs *Inn Sung Do (Map 4, ☎ 737 1056, 120 Naesu-dong, Chongno-gu)*. This place is in considerably better condition than its cousin and is only slightly more expensive. Dorm beds are W8000. Doubles with shared bath cost W11,000 and a private bath raises the tab to W16,000.

The Nest (Map 3, ☎ 725 4418) is a lovely little hostel just east of the National Folk Museum. This very clean and charming hostel is owned and operated by the Net House Cyber Cafe (Map 4), and you might want to stop in there first to see if rooms are available. Dorm beds cost W8000, with breakfast thrown in free. The hostel boasts a washing machine and kitchen.

T'apkol Park Area (Map 4) An excellent guesthouse that packs in the backpackers is *Munhwa Yŏgwan (☎ 765 4659, 69 Unnidong, Chongno-gu)*. Pleasant single rooms with shared bath cost W10,000 to W11,000, and a few doubles have private bath for W16,000.

Just a few doors south of the Munhwa is the *Motel Jongrowon (☎ 745 6876)*. Beautiful rooms with private bath go for W20,000.

A little north of Chongno 3-ga station, and just west of Chongmyo (Royal Shrine), is an alley where you'll find *Sun Ch'ang Yŏgwan (☎ 765 0701)*. At W12,000 it's cheap, though the rooms are small. There is a small courtyard and the *ajimma* (the woman who runs the place) is very nice.

As you face the YMCA, on the right side of the building, you'll find an alley. If you head up this alley, you'll find a sign indicating the route to the *Taewon Yŏgwan (☎ 730 6244)*. Doubles with shared bath at this popular place cost W12,000.

Other alleys behind the YMCA contain a thick concentration of yŏgwan which all charge W18,000 to W25,000 for a double with private bath. Those charging W18,000 include *Wongap Yŏgwan (☎ 734 1232)* and *Insŏng Yŏgwan*. In the same neighbourhood is *Chongno Yŏgwan*, which costs W20,000 on weekdays and W25,000 on Saturday night.

The *Yong Jin Hotel (☎ 765 4481, 76 Nagwon-dong, Chungno-gu)* is on an alley on the east side of the Nagwon arcade. Pleasant rooms with private bath cost W16,000. Directly opposite the Yong Jin is the *Hwasŏng-jang Yŏgwan (☎ 765 3834)*, which costs W20,000 (W25,000 on Saturday night).

On the same alley is the *Emerald Hotel (☎ 743 2001, 75 Nagwon-dong, Chongno-gu)*. A comfortable double with private bath goes for W28,000, but can be reduced to W25,000 if you stay three or more days. Be sure not to confuse this place with the super-expensive Emerald Hotel in the Kangnam district.

To the west of Tonhwamunno, the *Seahwa-jang Hotel (☎ 765 2881)* houses numerous foreigners working in Seoul. Rooms with attached bath cost W20,000 per night, but it's W400,000 per month, which works out to a very reasonable W13,300 a day. It's a good place for long-termers.

There are several yŏgwan hidden in the alleys running off Insadong-gil, but beware of overcharging, which is common in this neighbourhood. The yŏgwan owners here seem to want you to check out by 8 or 9 am, and may even penalise you if you stay until noon (which is not a common practice in Korea). The favourite place with foreigners is currently the *Hanhŭng-jang Yŏgwan (☎ 734 4265, 99 Kwanhun-dong)*, where a double room with an attached bathroom costs W20,000. The nearby *Kwanhun-jang Yŏgwan* costs W20,000 if you check out by 8 am, but W25,000 if you leave at noon. The *Shingung-jang Yŏgwan (☎ 733 1355)* costs W25,000, but the owner will give a 'discount' if you check out by 9 am.

Taehangno (Map 6) A very clean and pleasant place to stay in this area is *Trek Korea (☎ 743 7631, fax 743 7632, email trekorea@chollian.dacom.co.kr, 78-3 Hyehwa-dong, Chongno-gu)*. As the name implies, trekking tours of Korea's mountains can be arranged here. Dorm beds cost W10,000 and any of the three private rooms are W20,000. Take subway line 4 to Hyehwa station.

Tongdaemun (Map 3) More like a hostel than a motel, *Traveller's A Motel (☎ 285 5511, 274 2162, email pricky@hitel.net, 106-2 Chugyo-dong, Chung-gu)* is a fine place to stay for budget travellers. It's in a four storey building near Ŭlchiro 4-ga subway station on line 5 (exit 1), hidden in an alley just off a major street lined with shops (currently) peddling sewing machines. Beds cost W12,000 per person, and there are seven rooms – which range from twins to a six bed dormitory. The place is kept very clean, and there is a computer on the premises which guests can use to check email. Other features include a small kitchen (with microwave oven), cable TV, free coffee and tea, plus a laundry service for long-term guests. For a detailed map, check out the hostel's Web site (bbs.para.co.kr/~pricky).

Mid-Range

The low end of mid-range has to be the *YMCA (Map 4, ☎ 734 6884, 9 Chongno 2-ga, Chongno-gu)*, on the north side of Chonggak station on subway line 1. The imposing building is eight storeys tall, and down in the basement you'll find a coffee shop, beauty salon, discount travel agency and even the Boy Scout Shop. Rooms at the 'Y' are no better than at the nearby yŏgwan, but some of the staff do speak English and are very accustomed to dealing with westerners. Singles are W31,404, doubles W37,190, twins W42,975 and triples W52,893. The check-in desk is on the 6th floor. The tiny outdoor car park can only accommodate a few cars, so try to arrive by public transport.

Astoria Hotel (Map 5, ☎ 268 7111, fax 274 3187, 13-2 Namhak-dong, Chung-gu) is a five minute walk from Ch'ungmuro station on subway line 3 or 4. Doubles cost W55,000 to W65,000, twins W66,000 to W77,000 and suites are W85,000 to W100,000. Facilities include a western restaurant, coffee shop, game room and an outdoor car park. KNTO rates it 3rd class.

Central Hotel (Map 4, ☎ 265 4121, 227-1 Changsa-dong, Chongno-gu), one block south of Chongno 3-ga station on subway line 1, is nine storeys tall plus a basement. Singles cost W38,500, doubles (western and Korean-style) are W44,000, twins (western-style) are W49,500 and suites are W80,000. Facilities include a coffee shop, western buffet restaurant, banquet hall, nightclub, sauna and an indoor car park. It's also rated 3rd class.

The 3rd class *Eastern Hotel (Map 3, ☎ 741 7811, fax 744 1274, 444-14 Ch'angshin-dong, Chongno-gu)* is a three minute walk from Tongdaemun station on subway

line 1 or 4. Doubles cost W40,000, twins W45,000, suites W50,000 and Korean-style rooms W45,000. Facilities include a coffee shop, Korean restaurant, nightclub, sauna, game room and two minuscule car parks.

Metro Hotel (Map 5, ☎ 752 1112, fax 757 4411, 199-33 Ŭlchiro 2-ga, Chung-gu), a two minute walk from Ŭlchiro-1 station on subway line 2, is eight storeys tall with a basement (there is also a three storey annexe). Singles cost W45,980, doubles W48,400 to W65,340, twins W65,340 to W84,700, suites W133,100 and Korean-style rooms are W53,240. Facilities include a Japanese and a western restaurant, a banquet hall, coffee shop, cocktail lounge and a micro-sized outdoor car park. It's rated 2nd class.

Savoy Hotel (Map 5, ☎ 776 2641, fax 755 7669, 23-1 Ch'ungmuro 1-ga, Chung-gu) is rated 2nd class and is two minutes walk from Myŏng-dong station on subway line 4. Singles cost W54,000, doubles W68,000 to W80,000, twins W74,000 and suites are W112,000. Korean-style rooms cost W80,000. Facilities include a coffee shop, Japanese and western restaurants, a shopping arcade, karaoke, gift shop and a small outdoor car park.

Prince Hotel (Map 5, ☎ 752 7111, fax 752 7119, 1-1 Namsan-dong 2-ga, Chung-gu) is two minutes walk from Myŏng-dong station. Singles cost W30,640, doubles W45,000, twins W45,450 and suites W80,108. The Prince is a 2nd class hotel and facilities include a western restaurant, coffee shop and a small car park.

Seoul Hotel (Map 4, ☎ 735 9001, fax 733 0101, 92 Ch'ongjin-dong, Chongno-gu), three minutes walk from Chonggak station, offers 2nd-class doubles for W65,340 to W67,760, twins for W70,180, suites for W83,490 and Korean-style rooms for W79,860. The Seoul has a western and a Japanese restaurant, coffee shop, banquet hall, bar, sauna, game room, gift shop, barber shop, and a tiny indoor and a slightly larger outdoor car park.

New Oriental Hotel (Map 5, ☎ 753 0701, fax 755 9346, 10 Hoehyon-dong 3-ga, Chung-gu) is a three minute walk from

Myŏng-dong station. Singles cost W48,400, doubles W60,500, twins W72,600 and suites (western and Korean-style) are W96,800. Facilities include a cocktail lounge, coffee shop, banquet hall and a small outdoor car park. It's rated 1st class.

New Kukje Hotel (Map 4, ☎ 732 0161, fax 732 1774, 29-2 T'aep'yongno 1-ga, Chung-gu) is a five minute walk from City Hall station on subway lines 1 and 2. KNTO rates it 1st class and singles in this 16 storey hotel cost W80,000, doubles W103,000, twins W130,000 and suites W180,000 to W230,000. The Korean-style rooms are W110,000. Facilities include a western and a Korean restaurant, coffee shop, business centre, bar, sauna, barber shop, karaoke and a small car park.

New Seoul Hotel (Map 4, ☎ 735 9071, fax 735 6212, 29-1 T'aep'yongno 1-ga, Chung-gu) is just by the New Kukje. Singles in this 17 storey, 1st class place cost W90,000, doubles are W120,000, twins (western and Korean-style) cost W120,000 to W150,000 and suites go for W220,000. Facilities include a cocktail lounge, coffee shop, restaurants (Korean, Japanese and western), karaoke, gift shop, sauna and a moderately sized car park.

Pacific Hotel (Map 5, ☎ 777 7811, fax 755 5582, 31-1 Namsan-dong 2-ga, Chung-gu) is two minutes walk from Myŏng-dong station. Double rooms cost W100,000 to W120,000, twins W120,000 to W130,000 and suites are W180,000 to W210,000. The Korean-style rooms are W230,000. Facilities include restaurants (Korean, Japanese, Chinese and western), a cocktail lounge, bakery, coffee shop, banquet hall, gift shop, barber shop, and large outdoor and moderately sized indoor car parks. KNTO rates it 1st class.

The 1st class *Poongjeon Hotel (Map 3, ☎ 266 2151, fax 274 5732, 73-1 Inhyon-dong 2-ga, Chung-gu)* is a two minute walk from Ŭlchiro 4-ga station on subway line 2. Doubles (western and Korean-style) are W100,000, twins W110,000 and suites W170,000 to W200,000. Facilities include a cocktail lounge, western and Korean

restaurants, a coffee shop, banquet hall, nightclub, shopping arcade, duty-free shop, game room, sauna, health club, indoor golf driving range, indoor swimming pool, and small outdoor and large indoor car parks.

Puk'ansan (Map 10) The *Pugak Park Hotel (☎ 395 7100, fax 391 5559, 113-1 P'yongch'ang-dong, Chongno-gu)* is 10 minutes by bus from Kwanghwamun, on bus No 135 or 135-1, or a short drive north of Kyŏngbokkung station on subway line 3. On the northern fringe of Chongno-gu, the hotel's location on the southern slopes of scenic Puk'ansan National Park is impressive. Twins (both western and Korean-style) cost W88,572 and suites W157,300, but discounts of 25% are available on weekdays. Facilities include a Korean restaurant, coffee shop, bar, banquet hall, nightclub, game room and a moderately large outdoor car park. It's rated 2nd class.

Top End

The KNTO-rated deluxe *King Sejong Hotel (Map 5, ☎ 773 6000, 61-3 Ch'ungmuro 2-ga, Chung-gu)* is opposite the east end of Myŏng-dong station on subway line 4. Singles in this 16 storey hotel are W140,000, doubles are W180,000, twins W170,000 and suites W350,000. Korean-style rooms go for W200,000. Facilities include a cocktail lounge, coffee shop, restaurants (western, Japanese, Korean and Korean buffet), a banquet hall, conference hall with simultaneous interpretation equipment, health club, sauna, game room, shopping arcade, gift shop, karaoke bar, and indoor and outdoor car parks.

Koreana Hotel (Map 4, ☎ 730 9911, fax 734 0665, 61-1 T'aep'yongno 1-ga, Chung-gu) is five minutes walk north of City Hall subway station. The Koreana has 23 storeys above ground and two storeys below. Doubles cost W145,000 to W115,500, twins W115,5000 to W118,000, suites W337,000 and Korean-style rooms are W117,500. Facilities include a cocktail lounge, coffee shop, restaurants (Korean, Japanese, Chinese and western), a banquet hall, game room, barber shop, shopping arcade, gift shop, and indoor and outdoor car parks. The Koreana is rated deluxe.

President Hotel *(Map 5, ☎ 753 3131, fax 752 7417, 188-3 Ŭlchiro 1-ga, Chung-gu)*, five minutes walk from City Hall subway station, has 33 storeys above and three storeys below. Singles cost W95,000, doubles and twins W140,000, suites W200,000 to W250,000 and Korean-style rooms W145,000. It's rated deluxe and facilities include a cocktail lounge, coffee shop, restaurants (western, Korean, Japanese and buffet-style), a banquet hall, conference hall with simultaneous interpretation equipment, game room, shopping arcade, gift shop, barber shop, beauty salon and an indoor car park.

Royal Hotel *(Map 5, ☎ 756 1112, fax 756 1119, 6 Myŏng-dong 1-ga, Chung-gu)* is also rated deluxe and is five minutes walk from Myŏng-dong station. The hotel is 21 storeys tall plus two floors underground. Single rooms cost W127,000, doubles are W145,000, twins go for W173,000, suites are W245,000 to W336,000, and Korean-style rooms cost W145,000 to W336,000. Facilities include a cocktail lounge, coffee shop, restaurants (western, Japanese and buffet-style), a banquet hall, nightclub, sauna, gift shop, barber shop, and small indoor and outdoor car parks.

The deluxe-rated ***Sofitel Ambassador Hotel*** *(Map 3, ☎ 275 1101, fax 272 0773, 186-54 Changch'ung-dong, Chung-gu)* is a three minute walk from Dongguk University station on subway line 3. The Sofitel is 19 storeys tall plus two storeys underground. Singles cost W180,000, doubles and twins W200,000 and suites W400,000 to W900,000. Facilities include a coffee shop, bakery, Korean restaurant, sauna, swimming pool, health club, safe-deposit box, currency exchange and a large outdoor car park.

The ***Tower Hotel*** *(Map 3, ☎ 236 2121, fax 235 0276, 5-5 Changch'ung-dong 2-ga, Chung-gu)* is rated deluxe. The main hotel is 19 storeys tall with two basement levels, and there is a three storey annexe with two basements. Singles cost W121,000, doubles W169,400, twins W181,500 and suites are W242,000 to W884,000. The Korean-style rooms are W181,500. Facilities include a cocktail lounge, coffee shop, restaurants (Korean, Japanese, Chinese and western), a banquet hall, health club, outdoor swimming pool, tennis court, golf driving range, golf shop, sauna, shopping arcade, conference room with simultaneous interpretation equipment, business centre, barber shop and a medium-sized outdoor car park.

Hilton Hotel *(Map 5, ☎ 753 7788, fax 754 2510, 395 Namdaemunno 5-ga, Chung-gu)* is 10 minutes walk from Seoul train station and is rated super-deluxe by KNTO. This large hotel is 23 storeys tall plus two basement levels. Singles at the Hilton cost W240,000, doubles and twins W260,000, suites W440,000 to W390,000 and Korean-style rooms W440,000. Facilities include a lobby lounge, coffee shop, numerous restaurants (Korean, French, Italian, Japanese and Chinese, and western buffet), a banquet hall, health club, indoor swimming pool, sauna, shopping arcade, duty-free shop, business center, conference hall with simultaneous interpretation equipment and a large indoor parking garage.

The super-deluxe ***Lotte Hotel*** *(Map 5, ☎ 771 1000, fax 756 8049, 1 Sogong-dong, Chung-gu)* is a two minute walk from Ŭlchiro 1-ga station on subway line 2. If bigger is better, stay here – it's the largest hotel in Korea. The old building has 38 storeys and three basements, the new wing has 35 storeys and five basements, with a total of 1316 western and two Korean-style rooms – it's so large they ought to sell maps of the place. Doubles cost W230,000 to W260,000, twins W250,000 to W270,000, suites W280,000 to W4,500,000 and Korean-style rooms W300,000. Facilities include a cocktail lounge, coffee shop, many disparate restaurants (Korean, Japanese, Chinese, French, Italian, western buffet and of course a Lotteria fast food joint), a banquet hall, conference hall with simultaneous interpretation equipment, health club, sauna, indoor swimming pool, indoor golf practice range,

PLACES TO STAY

nightclub, shopping arcade, and a large outdoor and even larger indoor car park.

Plaza Hotel *(Map 5, ☎ 771 2200, fax 755 8897, 23 T'aep'yongno 2-ga, Chung-gu)*, two minutes walk from City Hall station, and rated super-deluxe, is 22 storeys tall plus three floors underground. Singles here cost W210,000 to W260,000, doubles are W230,000 to W280,000, twins W250,000 to W300,000 and suites W450,000 to W400,000. The Korean-style rooms go for W250,000 to W450,000. Facilities include cocktail and lobby lounges, a coffee shop, bar, restaurants (Korean, Japanese, Chinese and western), a banquet hall, conference hall with simultaneous interpretation equipment, business centre, voice mail, in-room safe-deposit boxes, shopping arcade, and large indoor and outdoor car parks.

Shilla Hotel *(Map 3, ☎ 233 3131, fax 233 5073, 202 Changch'ung-dong 2-ga, Chung-gu)* is a five minute walk from Dongguk University station on subway line 3. The building has 23 floors above ground plus three levels in the basement. Doubles and twins cost W235,000 to W370,000, western-style suites are W385,000 to W450,000 and Korean-style suites cost W385,000. Facilities here include a lobby lounge, bar, coffee shop, restaurants (Korean, Chinese, Japanese, Italian and French), banquet rooms, disco, conference hall with simultaneous interpretation equipment, business centre, executive floors, health club, indoor and outdoor swimming pools, tennis courts, indoor golf driving range, sauna, weight and exercise room, barber shop, beauty parlour, travel agent desks, car rental desk, shopping arcade, duty-free shop, open-air sculpture park, plus an enormous outdoor car park. The Shilla is rated super-deluxe.

Westin Chosun Hotel *(Map 5, ☎ 771 0500, fax 752 1443, 87 Sogong-dong, Chung-gu)*, two minutes walk from City Hall station, has 18 floors above ground plus one basement level. Twins here cost W223,000 to W230,000 and suites are W438,000 to W1,450,000. Facilities include a cocktail lounge, lobby lounge, bakery, restaurants (Korean, French, Italian,

Japanese and Chinese, and western buffet), Irish Pub and Sports Bar, grand banquet hall equipped with simultaneous interpretation system, health club, sauna, swimming pool, business centre, barber shop, beauty salon, pharmacy and a large car park. It's also rated super-deluxe.

Puk'ansan (Map 10) The ***Olympia Hotel*** *(☎ 287 6000, fax 353 8118, 108-2 P'yong-ch'ang-dong, Chongno-gu)* is in the north of Chongno-gu, near the Pugak Park Hotel (see the previous Mid-Range section). Besides having a spectacular location, the deluxe-rated Olympia is a good choice for people who enjoy outdoor activities. Singles cost W145,000, doubles and twins W169,000, suites W302,500 to W847,000, and Korean-style rooms W194,000 to W303,000. Facilities include a cocktail lounge, sky lounge, coffee shop, bakery, restaurants (Korean, Japanese, western and buffet), a banquet hall, conference room with simultaneous interpretation equipment, health club, indoor and outdoor swimming pools, indoor golf driving range, aerobics room, sauna, game room, nightclub, theatre restaurant, shopping arcade, gift shop, art gallery and an outdoor car park.

PLACES TO STAY – IT'AEWON

Yongsan-gu is the official name for It'aewon and the surrounding area. If you're intrigued by redneck bars and the possibility of getting mugged at night, consider staying in It'aewon.

Budget

The budget places to stay in this section are all on Map 8.

Right at the heart of the action, at the top of that infamous stretch of alley known to locals as 'hooker hill', is the ***Hilltop Motel*** *(☎ 793 4972, 732-20 Hannam 2-dong, Yongsan-gu)*, where there are western-style doubles with attached bathroom, colour TV and air-con costing W23,000. The hotel's sign is in English and some English is spoken by the staff. This place is a favourite with backpackers.

Just down the hill from the Hilltop is an alley where you'll find the *Kwangsŏn-jang Yŏgwan*. Rooms cost W22,000.

Back on the main drag is the *Mido Hotel*, which is in fact a yŏgwan. The closet-like hovels with private bath at this place go for W22,000. Nearby is the similar *Hannam Yŏgwan*, which has an English sign saying 'Motel'.

At the western end of It'aewonno up on a hill is *Ihwa-jang Yŏgwan*, which is also W22,000.

Mid-Range

Kaya Hotel (Map 2, ☎ 798 5101, fax 798 5900, 98-11 Kalwol-dong, Yongsan-gu), a one minute walk from Namyŏng station, is one stop south of Seoul station on subway line 1 and very close to the USO. The Kaya offers easy access to It'aewon without actually being right in it, and the hotel gets very good reviews from travellers. However, if you want to be in the centre of It'aewon's frenetic action, don't stay here. There are 47 western-style and four Korean-style rooms here, all very comfortable. Other features include a sauna, outdoor car park, good restaurant and overall great service. Singles cost W40,000, doubles W43,000, twins W50,000 and Korean-style rooms are W43,000. KNTO rates it 3rd class.

The 1st class *Crown Hotel (Map 8, ☎ 797 4111, fax 796 1010, 34-69 It'aewon-dong, Yongsan-gu)* is south of the It'aewon tourist zone. Doubles and twins (both western and Korean-style) cost W100,000 and suites are W195,000. Facilities include a western restaurant, coffee shop, banquet hall, nightclub, sauna, indoor golf driving range, and an indoor and outdoor car park.

Hamilton Hotel (Map 8, ☎ 794 0171, fax 795 0457, 119-25 It'aewon-dong, Yongsan-gu) is deep in the heart of It'aewon and rated 1st class. The hotel is nine storeys above ground and three storeys underground, and has western-style rooms only. Doubles cost W121,000, twins W145,200 and suites W205,700. Facilities include restaurants (Korean, Indian and western), a banquet hall, outdoor swimming pool, shopping arcade, nightclub, disco, beauty salon, travel agency, and indoor and outdoor car parks.

Top End

It'aewon Hotel (Map 8, ☎ 792 3111, fax 798 8256, 737-32 Hannam-dong, Yongsan-gu) is in the It'aewon tourist zone. The hotel has 11 storeys above and four storeys below ground. Singles cost W52,600, doubles and twins W100,000 and suites W165,000 to W400,000. The Korean-style rooms cost W100,000 to W200,000. Facilities include Japanese and western restaurants, a banquet hall, cocktail lounge, bar, nightclub, shopping arcade and an indoor car park. The hotel is rated 1st class.

The super-deluxe *Grand Hyatt Hotel (Map 8, ☎ 797 1234, fax 798 6953, 747-7 Hannam-dong, Yongsan-gu)* is a short walk north-east of It'aewon. The hotel boasts 20 storeys above ground and two storeys underground, with 605 rooms. Doubles/twins here are W220,000/270,000 and suites are W330,500 to W440,000. Facilities at the Hyatt include some of Seoul's more popular restaurants (The Terrace, Hugo's and JJ Mahoney's), a Chinese and a buffet restaurant, a bar, lobby lounge, banquet hall, health club, aerobics room, squash court, indoor and outdoor swimming pools, tennis courts, nightclub, sauna, shopping arcade, conference hall with simultaneous interpretation equipment, business centre and an outdoor car park.

Capital Hotel (Map 2, ☎ 792 1122, fax 796 0918, 22-76 It'aewon-dong, Yongsan-gu) is south of the It'aewon tourist zone. The hotel has 16 storeys above and six storeys below ground. Doubles and twins cost W163,350, suites are W290,400 to W726,000 and Korean-style suites are W726,000. Facilities include a coffee shop, bakery, bar, Korean-Japanese buffet restaurant, banquet hall, health club, indoor swimming pool, tennis courts, nightclub, shopping arcade, conference room with simultaneous interpretation equipment, indoor golf driving range, sauna, indoor and an outdoor car park. It's rated deluxe.

PLACES TO STAY

PLACES TO STAY – SOUTH SIDE

The glass-and-concrete southern side of the Han River is Seoul's most prestigious and expensive area, the place where almost every Korean dreams of living. Though totally lacking in character, this zone is where many business travellers wish to be based. The two adjacent districts of Kangnam-gu and Songp'a-gu are chock-a-block with luxury hotels.

Budget

The *Olympic Parktel Hostel (Map 2, ☎ 410 2114, fax 410 2100, 88 Pang-i-dong, Songp'a-gu)* in Chamshil is the only genuine youth hostel in Seoul, but it's hardly worth seeking out. While the facilities are comfortable, it's inconveniently located and not worth the price at W13,000 a bed. But if you're determined to try it, take subway line 2 to Sŏngnae station and walk about 500m. There are 1234 beds, and the building is closed from 10 am to 3 pm.

Mid-Range

Kangnam (Map 7) A short walk northeast of Shinsa station on subway line 3, *Youngdong Hotel (☎ 542 0112, 6 Nonhyŏn-dong, Kangnam-gu)* offers doubles/twins for W59,900/69,900. Facilities include three restaurants, banquet hall, nightclub, sauna, game room, outdoor and indoor car parks. It's rated 1st class.

Dynasty Hotel (☎ 540 3041, fax 540 3374, 202-7 Nonhyŏn-dong, Kangnam-gu) is a 15 minute walk from Kangnam station on subway line 2 (airport bus No 600 stops in front of the hotel). The building has six storeys above ground and four storeys underground, with more Korean-style rooms (20) than most hotels. It's rated 2nd class and doubles, twins and Korean-style rooms all cost W80,000; suites are W180,000. Facilities include Japanese and western-style restaurants, a banquet hall, nightclub, karaoke bar, and indoor and outdoor car parks.

Green Grass Hotel (☎ 555 7575, fax 554 0643, 141-10 Samsŏng-dong, Kangnam-gu) is five minutes walk from Sŏllŭng station on subway line 2. The hotel reaches 10 storeys

above ground and has three storeys underground. Doubles (western and Korean-style) cost W108,900, twins W133,100 and suites W169,400 to W242,000. Facilities include a western-style restaurant, cocktail lounge, lobby lounge, coffee shop, banquet hall, sauna and game room, and it's rated 1st class.

The 2nd class-rated *Sunshine Hotel (☎ 541 1818, fax 547 0777, 587-1 Shinsa-dong, Kangnam-gu)*, 10 minutes walk from Apkujŏng station on subway line 3. Singles are W45,000, doubles (western and Korean-style) W63,000, twins W63,000 and suites W121,000. Facilities include a cocktail lounge, banquet hall and sauna.

Samhwa Hotel (☎ 541 1011, 527-3 Shinsa-dong, Kangnam-gu), just north of Shinsa station on subway line 3, distinguishes itself by being more Korean-style than usual, even boasting ondol-style suites. At four storeys tall, it's also stunted by Kangnam standards. Western and Korean-style doubles are W49,000, Korean-style deluxe rooms are W55,000 and suites (both western and Korean-style) are W70,000. Facilities include a Korean/western restaurant and coffee shop. It's rated 3rd class.

Samjung Hotel (☎ 557 1221, fax 556 1126, 604-11 Yŏksam-dong, Kangnam-gu) is about five minutes walk from Yŏksam station on subway line 2 and rated 1st class. The hotel has 11 storeys above ground and two floors below ground. All its singles, doubles and twins (Korean and western-style) cost W120,000; western-style suites are W240,000. Facilities include a Korean-Japanese-Chinese buffet restaurant, cocktail lounge, western-style coffee shop, banquet hall, sauna, nightclub, beauty salon and outdoor car park. It's rated 1st class.

Amiga Hotel (☎ 3440 8000, 248-7 Nonhyŏn-dong, Kangnam-gu), 15 minutes walk from Sŏllŭng station (or catch bus No 235 at Sŏllŭng station), has 11 storeys above ground and four storeys below ground. Doubles and twins are W210,000, western-style suites are W330,000 to W550,000, Korean-style standard rooms are W210,000, Korean-style suites are W330,000. Facilities include a cocktail lounge, coffee shop, Japanese and western-style buffet restaurants, a banquet hall, tennis courts, game room, disco and outdoor car park. The Amiga is rated deluxe.

The 2nd class *New Hilltop Hotel (☎ 540 1121, fax 542 9491, 152 Nonhyon-dong, Kangnam-gu)* is 10 minutes by foot from Yŏksam station or Apkujŏng station. The hotel has 15 storeys above the ground and four storeys underground. Doubles (both western and Korean-style) cost W87,000, western-style twins are W99,000 and suites are W107,000. Facilities include a coffee shop, bar, restaurant, banquet hall, nightclub and a car park.

Yŏuido (Map 9)

The *Manhattan Hotel (☎ 780 8001, fax 784 2332, 13-3 Yŏuido-dong, Yongdŭngp'o-gu)* is on Seoul's soulless Yŏuido. If you're a business traveller or just someone with a passion for skyscrapers, this could be the place for you. The hotel is 15 storeys tall (Lilliputian by Yŏuido's standards), but there are two more levels underground. Doubles, twins and Korean-style rooms cost W110,000 and suites are W210,000. Facilities include a cocktail lounge, lobby lounge, coffee shop, Japanese and western restaurants, banquet hall, health club, nightclub, sauna, game room, gift shop and a large outdoor car park. It's rated 1st class.

Top End

Chamshil (Map 2)

This area east of Kangnam is home to the *Lotte World Hotel (☎ 419 7000, fax 417 3655, 40-1 Chamshil-dong, Songp'a-gu)*, a two minute walk from Chamshil station on subway line 2. The main feature here is the adjacent Lotte World shopping mall-cum-amusement park – a godsend if you have children and need to keep them entertained. The hotel has 33 storeys above ground and four levels underground. Double rooms and twins cost W215,000, and suites are W270,000 to W1,000,000; Korean-style rooms cost W300,000. Facilities include restaurants (Korean, Chinese, Japanese and western buffet), a coffee shop, lounge, bar, banquet

hall, sauna, shopping arcade, conference hall with simultaneous interpretation equipment, duty-free shop, swimming pool, indoor golf course, and a small outdoor but gargantuan indoor car park. KNTO rates the hotel super-deluxe.

Kangnam (Map 7)

The large, new, deluxe-rated *Elle Lui Hotel (☎ 514 3535, 129 Ch'ongdam-dong, Kangnam-gu)* is a five minute drive from Shinsa station on subway line 3. The hotel has 13 storeys above ground and five storeys underground, but just three Korean-style rooms. Doubles (western and Korean-style) cost W135,000, twins W140,000 and suites W350,000. Facilities include a western restaurant, cocktail lounge, banquet hall, health club, shopping arcade, sauna, conference room with simultaneous interpretation equipment, and indoor and outdoor car parks.

Novotel Ambassador Hotel (☎ 567 1101, fax 562 0120, 603 Yŏksam-dong, Kangnam-gu) is deluxe and a short drive from Kangnam station on subway line 2. This is a very large hotel with all the trimmings, boasting 17 storeys above ground and six storeys below ground (with 332 western-style and six Korean-style rooms). Doubles and twins (western and Korean-style) cost W180,000 to W200,000, and suites are W400,000 to W600,000. Facilities include a Korean-Japanese buffet restaurant, banquet room, lobby lounge, cocktail bar, coffee shop, health club, sauna, indoor swimming pool, golf course (with both indoor and outdoor facilities), and indoor and outdoor car parks.

New World Hotel (☎ 557 0111, fax 557 0141, 112-5 Samsŏng-dong, Kangnam-gu) is 10 minutes walk from Sŏllŭng station on subway line 2. The New World has 12 storeys above and five storeys below ground. Doubles and twins (western-style) cost W134,000, and suites are W330,000 to W970,000. Korean-style standard rooms are W130,000, or W300,000 for an ondol suite. Hotel facilities include a coffee shop, Chinese-Japanese restaurant, buffet restaurant, banquet hall, pub, health club, indoor swimming pool, nightclub, sauna, shopping

PLACES TO STAY

arcade, indoor golf driving range, barber shop, beauty salon, and indoor and outdoor car parks. It's rated deluxe.

Seoul Renaissance Hotel (☎ 555 0501, fax 553 8118, 676 Yŏksam-dong, Kangnam-gu) is a five minute walk from Yŏksam station on subway line 2. KNTO rates it super-deluxe. The hotel is enormous, with 24 storeys above ground and two floors in the basement. Doubles and twins (western-style) cost W210,000 to W260,000, Korean-style rooms W210,000 to W490,000, and western-style suites are W420,000 to a whopping W2,500,000. Facilities include a cocktail lounge, coffee shop, buffet restaurants (Korean, Chinese and Italian), a banquet hall, health club, indoor swimming pool, tennis court, nightclub, sauna, shopping arcade, conference hall with simultaneous interpretation equipment, indoor golf driving range, game room, business center, and indoor and outdoor car parks.

Riviera Hotel (☎ 541 3111, fax 541 6111, 53-7 Ch'ongdam-dong, Kangnam-gu) is about a 10 minute drive from Apkujŏng station on subway line 3. This deluxe-rated hotel has 15 storeys above ground and five storeys below. Western and Korean-style doubles cost W135,000, western-style twins are W140,000, and suites are W300,000 to W800,000. Facilities include the 'sky lounge', a lobby lounge, coffee shop, buffet restaurants (Korean, Japanese and Chinese), banquet hall, health club, indoor swimming pool, nightclub, sauna, shopping arcade, conference hall with simultaneous interpretation equipment, indoor golf practice range, and indoor and outdoor car parks.

The super-deluxe *Inter-Continental Hotel (☎ 555 5656, fax 559 7990, 159-8 Samsŏng-dong, Kangnam-gu)* is a three minute walk from Samsŏng station on subway line 2. It's one of Seoul's largest hotels, with 32 storeys above ground and four storeys underground. Deluxe rooms (Korean and western) are W205,000, executive (western-style) rooms are W250,000 and suites are W300,000. Facilities include a lobby lounge, coffee shop, western buffet

restaurants, other restaurants (Korean, Japanese, Chinese, Italian and French), banquet hall, health club, indoor swimming pool, nightclub, sauna, duty-free shop, shopping arcade, conference hall with simultaneous interpretation equipment, business centre, business library, indoor and outdoor car parks, and a late check-out option (4 pm).

Ritz-Carlton Hotel (☎ 3451 8000, 602-4 Yŏksam-dong, Kangnam-gu) is near Yŏksam station on subway line 2. This huge hotel has 18 storeys above ground and six storeys underground. Western-style deluxe rooms cost from W230,000 to W305,000, while suites are W330,000 to W3,000,000. The two Korean-style rooms are W230,000. Facilities include Japanese, Chinese and western restaurants, a steak house, buffet restaurant, banquet hall, coffee shop, nightclub, karaoke, beauty salon, barber shop, shopping arcade, and indoor and outdoor car parks. As befits its name, the Ritz-Carlton is rated super-deluxe.

PLACES TO STAY – SHINCH'ON
Budget

There are a couple of dozen *yŏgwan* and *love motels* in the maze of alleys just to the north-east of the Shinch'on subway station (Map 9) on line 2.

Mid-Range

Mirabeau Hotel (Map 9, ☎ 392 9511, 104-36 Taehyon-dong, Sodaemun-gu) is a three minute walk from Ehwa Women's University subway station on line 2. The 2nd class hotel has twins for W66,000, Korean-style rooms at W81,000 and suites for W114,000. Facilities at the Mirabeau include a coffee shop, western restaurant, bar, karaoke lounge, steam baths, and small indoor and outdoor car parks.

Seokyo Hotel (Map 9, ☎ 333 7771, 354-5 Sogyo-dong, Map'o-gu) is a two minute walk from Hongik University subway station on line 2. Rooms in the 13 storey building cost W110,000/W120,000/W200,000. Facilities include a banquet hall, coffee shop, restaurants (Korean, Japanese, Chinese, western and buffet style), a bar, health club, indoor swimming pool, nightclub, sauna, shopping arcade, gift shop and a large outdoor car park. KNTO rates it 1st class.

Top End

The deluxe *Holiday Inn (Map 9, ☎ 717 9441, fax 715 9441, 169-1 Tohwa-dong, Map'o-gu)* is just south of Shinch'on proper, a 10 minute walk from the Map'o subway station on line 5. Its location just on the north side of the Han-gang is a bit puzzling, though it's only one subway stop away from the concrete jungles of Yŏŭido. The hotel rises 15 storeys above and two storeys below the surrounding area. Singles (western and Korean-style) cost W120,000 to W132,000, twins W140,000 to W160,000 and suites W330,000 to W700,000. Facilities include a cocktail lounge, coffee shop, lobby lounge, restaurants (western, Japanese, Chinese and Korean), a bar, bakery, nightclub, sauna, barber shop, beauty salon, game room, health club, banquet hall, conference hall with simultaneous interpretation equipment, shopping arcade, indoor golf putting green, and large indoor and outdoor car parks.

PLACES TO STAY – KIMP'O AIRPORT

Staying near the airport (see the Kimp'o Airport Area map in the Getting Around chapter) has little to recommend it other than the convenience of being able to make a fast getaway.

Airport Hotel (☎ 662 1113, 11-21 Konghang-dong, Kangsŏ-gu) is not surprisingly the name of the main hotel (2nd class) near the airport. It's one subway stop (towards central Seoul) on line 5 – get off at Songjŏng station. By taxi, it's about a three minute ride. The hotel is a five storey building plus a basement. Doubles cost W58,000 to W64,000, suites are W107,000 to W124,000, and the Korean-style rooms go for W58,000 to W74,000. There are Korean and western restaurants, a coffee shop, banquet hall, karaoke lounge and a small outdoor car park.

Kimp'o-jang Hotel (☎ 663 1311, 42-10 Konghang-dong, Kangsŏ-gu) is a cheaper alternative, and some of the staff speak English. It's on the other side of the road and to the east of the Airport Hotel, and slightly closer to Songjŏng subway station. There are 26 western-style and 14 Korean-style rooms here, costing W28,000 to W30,000.

ELSEWHERE IN SEOUL

There are a few mid-range and top-end hotels which are not in any of the aforementioned districts, but are nevertheless noteworthy because of their special facilities or location.

Sheraton Walker Hill Hotel (Map 2, ☎ 453 0121, fax 452 6867, 21 Kwangjang-dong, Sŏngdong-gu) is super-deluxe and 2km east of Children's Grand Park, about a 10 minute walk north of Kwangnaru subway station on line 5. It distinguishes itself by having Seoul's only casino (see the Entertainment chapter for details).

The Sheraton is 17 storeys tall plus four basement levels. Doubles and twins cost W200,000 and suites cost W430,000 to W2,300,000 (the high end is for the 'Diamond Suite'). Facilities include a cocktail lounge, coffee shop, restaurants (western buffet, Korean, Chinese and Japanese), a banquet hall, health club, indoor and outdoor swimming pools, tennis courts, nightclub, sauna, theatre restaurant, shopping arcade, conference hall with simultaneous interpretation equipment, golf course and a game room. Airport limousine bus service connects the hotel to Kimp'o airport every 15 minutes between 6.05 am and 7.50 pm.

Swiss Grand Hotel (Map 2, ☎ 3216 5656, fax 3216 7799, 201-1 Hong-un-dong, Sodaemun-gu) is in the north-west part of Seoul, a 10 minute walk from Hongje station on subway line 3. It boasts a Swiss-like setting at the base of scenic Paengnyŏnsan (216m), but another feature are the unique 'apartment-style' suites, which include a kitchen. The hotel is 12 storeys above and three storeys below ground, with 397 western-style rooms, three Korean-style rooms and 111 apartments. Singles are W220,000, twins W250,000 and suites W420,000 to W2,500,000. Facilities include a famous Swiss buffet restaurant, 'international' restaurants (Japanese, Chinese and Italian), a cocktail lounge, bar, bakery, banquet hall, health club, indoor swimming pool, nightclub, sauna, shopping arcade, conference room with simultaneous interpretation equipment, barber shop, beauty salon, jogging track, golf driving range, business centre and a disappointingly small car park. KAL Limousine Bus No 5 makes a stop here. The Swiss Grand is rated super-deluxe.

LONG-TERM RENTALS

An increasing number of foreigners are basing themselves in Seoul for long periods. In many cases they come to an agreement with the owners of a yŏgwan for a better monthly deal on a room. However, it's advisable to spend at least one night in the yŏgwan first before handing over a month's rent – you may discover that the place is unsuitable for your needs.

Yŏgwan living has drawbacks, like not being able to cook for yourself and having to be home by midnight when the yŏgwan closes. It's also impractical to have your own telephone installed, though you can bypass the problem with a pager or cellular phone.

Renting houses and apartments in Korea works very differently than in most western countries. The problem is the astronomical deposits required on rented accommodation – it's (another) bad custom borrowed from Japan. The deposits are known as 'key money' *(chonsei)*, and a figure of W30 million is not unusual in the better parts of Seoul. The way it works is that if you pay chonsei, you do not have to pay any monthly rent at all, and when you move out your deposit will be refunded. This sounds like a good deal, but as the locals point out, the tenant takes all the risks. Although the landlord is required to refund the deposit when you leave, in some cases your money will be channelled into dodgy investments

(or outright gambling) and may be lost. Theoretically, you would have an excellent legal case against a landlord who loses your deposit, but in practice you could spend months or years pursuing the matter in a Korean court without good results.

The western system of paying a small deposit and then a monthly fee *(wolsei)* does exist in Seoul, and has become more common in recent years thanks to an oversupply in the housing and business rental market.

Finding an apartment in the city is mainly a matter of deciding on an area that you want to live in and then seeking out real estate agents. It helps considerably to bring a Korean-speaking friend along.

The ideal solution is to find an apartment or rent a room in a boarding house, known locally as *haksuljip*. Boarding houses are probably a better alternative to the expense of renting an apartment, but conditions in these houses are not always ideal. Before committing to anything, check to see whether there are cooking facilities and if a curfew is in effect.

Best of all, if you're working in Seoul, inquire as to whether a provision of accommodation can be built into your employment contract. Many employers provide accommodation for their foreign staff, and there's no particular reason why *your* employer shouldn't make some effort towards helping you get set up in Seoul too.

If you do end up looking to rent, take note that real estate is measured in *p'yŏng* (1 p'yŏng is 3.3 sq metres). A medium-sized flat in Seoul is about 30 p'yŏng, though smaller budget flats of 15 to 20 p'yŏng are common. There are even some super-tiny studios of 7 to 10 p'yŏng, which are only suitable for a single person. At the opposite end of the scale are enormous flats of 50 to 60 p'yŏng.

Places to Eat

FOOD
The four generic cuisines available in Seoul are Korean, Chinese, Japanese and western.

Korean
The one element of Korean cooking which receives the most comments, both positive and negative, is that staple of the Korean diet, *kimch'i*. Kimch'i is basically grated or chopped vegetables mixed with various other ingredients – notably chilli, garlic and ginger – and left to ferment in an earthenware pot. The result is served as a side dish or as the principle component of any Korean meal, even breakfast. It has a raw, tangy taste, and most varieties are very spicy.

While most westerners can't face kimch'i at 7 am, it does make a tasty addition to lunch or dinner. However, some foreigners simply can't get used to kimch'i at all. If you fall into this latter category, you'll have to be more picky about what you eat, though you won't starve – there is always something good to eat on virtually every street corner in Seoul.

An omelette with rice *(omŭ raisŭ)* is a cheap dish which has sustained many a backpacker. Another budget travellers' special is *kimbap*, which is the Korean version of Japanese *maki-zushi*: rice *(bap* in Korean*)* and sliced vegetables wrapped in dried seaweed (actually 'laver' rather than common seaweed). If it's not wrapped in laver (eg it can be wrapped in fried egg), it's called *ch'obap*. Kimbap is always served with some yellow-coloured pickled *daikon* radishes.

Unless you're vegetarian, you should definitely try *pulgogi*, almost certainly the favourite dish of foreign visitors. Pulgogi, which literally means 'fire beef', is often translated as 'Korean barbecue'. Strips of beef marinated in soy sauce, sesame oil, garlic and chilli are grilled on a hot plate right on the dining table. Basically, you do your own table-top cooking. Eating this way is a leisurely social affair, and it makes

Silk worm larvae tastes better than it sounds.

sense to share it with at least one other person rather than do it solo. Prices vary, but should be in the W6000 to W10,000 range.

Similar to pulgogi is *kalbi*, which uses short ribs instead of strips of beef. Most pulgogi restaurants also serve kalbi.

A dish that uses kimch'i as an ingredient is *pibimbap*. Basically it's a bed of rice with kimch'i, vegetables, meat and a dollop of hot chilli on top. There are variations on the theme which exclude meat, a boon to vegetarians. Pibimbap is usually served in a thick, heated iron bowl, so that the dish is still cooking when it is placed in front of you. The whole thing should be stirred up with a spoon before eating.

Shinsŏllo is similar to Japanese *shabu-shabu*. Meat, fish, vegetables and tofu *(tubu* in Korean*)* are simmered together in a broth right at your table. This is another dish that most foreigners enjoy.

A notable Korean speciality is *naeng myŏn*, or cold noodles *(myŏn)*. The noodles are made of buckwheat and are very healthy. *K'ong kuksu* is a noodle dish made in a soy milk broth. More appealing to western tastes is *mak kuksu*, a combination of vegetables and meat slices with noodles in chicken broth.

Korean *haute cuisine* is best represented by *hanjŏngshik*, a banquet meal with a vast array of dishes. At the other end of the scale are cheap but filling dishes like *mandu guk*, a Korean version of Chinese won-ton soup.

Stews Korean stews *(tchigae)* are very tasty. There seems to be an almost endless variety of tchigae, but one of the most delicious is *tubu tchigae*, or tofu stew. Another variation is *toenjang tchigae* (bean paste stew). The broth is made with a bean paste mixture that is very similar to Japanese *miso*.

Another excellent though more expensive stew is *kalbi-tchim*, which uses short ribs as the main ingredient. These dishes come with rice and a serving of kimch'i.

Cow intestine stew generally gets mixed reactions from westerners – definitely an acquired taste. There is also *kimch'i tchigae* for those who can't get enough of the stuff in the side dishes provided.

Soups Probably the most famous Korean soup is *samgye t'ang*, or ginseng chicken soup. A small, whole chicken stuffed with ginseng and glutinous rice is served with soup in a clay pot.

Kalbi t'ang is beef short rib soup served with rice and kimch'i. *Sŏllŏng t'ang* is a hearty beef stock soup mixed with rice. *Kom t'ang* (beef soup) is simple beef with bones cooked in broth. *Kkorikom t'ang* (ox tail soup) is self-explanatory. *Yukkaejang* (spicy beef soup) often contains cows entrails, which doesn't always cheer western diners. *Maeun t'ang* (pepper pot soup) is excellent but *very* spicy.

Street-Stall Food Street stalls are a good option, both for the traveller on a tight budget and for others interested in sampling the full gamut of Korean cuisine. A very palatable example is *t'wigim*, a slightly Koreanised version of Japanese *tempura* – vegetables, seafood and *mandu* (dumplings) deep fried in batter. Also very common are the stalls specialising in Korean pancakes. These come in various forms, the most basic being *p'ajŏn*, or green-onion pancakes. Tasty mung bean pancakes *(pindaettŏk)* contain bean sprouts and pork.

Spicy rice rolls *(ttŏkpokki)* are a popular snack, consisting of pressed-rice dough rolled into the shape of hot dogs and simmered in hot sauce.

Styrofoam Cuisine The 24-hour convenience stores are a possibility for a cheap meal or midnight snack. These places invariably sell instant noodles packaged in a styrofoam bowl. The noodles are 'Koreanised' in the sense that they are typically loaded with enough hot red pepper *(goch'u)* to make your tattoos sit up and take notice. Most of the convenience stores have hot water, disposable chopsticks and a table (though no chairs), so you can consume your instant banquet on the premises. This should cost around W700 from *7-Eleven* or *Family Mart*, but *Bestore* and *Buy The Way* charge double.

A Most Memorable Meal

While walking down a street in Seoul you might catch a whiff of some new and exotic stench. More than likely it will be coming from a local street vendor preparing *ppŏndaegi*, or boiled silk worm larvae. This unforgettable dish, especially popular with Korean kids, is easy to spot – a thick brown broth full of floating insects, bubbling away in big cauldrons by the roadside. The odour alone should deter all but the most intrepid culinary explorers from slurping down a bowl. But if you dare to try it, be assured that it's a meal you won't forget.

Chinese

Seoul's Chinese restaurants cater mostly to the lower and mid-range scale of the dining market, though there are some ritzy places as well. The smaller and dingier the restaurant, the cheaper it is likely to be.

If you don't know what to order, start with *tchajang myŏn*, a northern Chinese speciality consisting of thick noodles in a heavy beef sauce. Most Chinese restaurants also serve fried rice, which is *poggŭmbap* in Korean. Another time-honoured delicacy is *t'angsu yuk*, more familiarly known to westerners as sweet-and-sour pork.

Japanese

Japanese food typically costs twice as much as an equivalent Korean meal, though there is no reason why it should. Despite the price and the fact that most Koreans will claim to hate Japanese food, there seems to be no shortage of clientele in the Japanese restaurants around Seoul.

The Koreans have adopted sushi as their own, but if you order it in a Japanese restaurant you get the privilege of paying double. A variation on the theme is *tubu ch'obap*, which is prepared similarly to kimbap, except tofu and rice mixed with vinegar are wrapped into a roll with egg which has been fried as a very thin omelette.

Another famous Japanese cold dish is *saengsŏn hoe (sashimi* in Japanese*)*, or raw fish. In Japan it gets served with *wasabi* (hot green horseradish), but the Koreans prefer it with either soy or hot chilli sauce and rice.

The cheaper Japanese hot dishes include tempura *(t'wigim)* – battered, deep-fried cuisine. The most common dishes are shrimp tempura with vegetables *(saeu t'wigim)*, fish tempura *(saengsŏn t'wigim)* and vegetable tempura *(yach'ae t'wigim)*.

Western

Fast Food Connoisseurs of frozen and microwaved cuisine will be delighted with Seoul. The city has yielded itself to the razzle dazzle of the fast-food industry with apparent abandon. Aside from the well known western chains (*McDonald's*, *KFC*, *Hardees*, *Burger King* and *Pizza Hut*), the Koreans have produced a few of their own. *Popeye's Chicken* is sprinkled with red hot spice – 'New Orlean's style', so the management claims, but really more like Korean style. *Lotteria* is a poor imitation of western fast-food culture – it's only saving grace is that it's cheap.

Upmarket Cuisine Seoul's outrageous prices for better western cuisine has long been a sore spot, but the good news is that the 'IMF crisis' has brought down costs significantly. American, Italian, French, German and Mexican food can all be had. The Korean version of western cuisine can be a little odd (steak and kimch'i?), but it has gradually improved over the past few years. Another trend of recent times has been a migration of western upmarket chain restaurants to Seoul. Prominent among these are *TGI Friday's* (American-Mexican cuisine), *Bennigan's* (Irish-American food somewhat cheaper than Friday's but just as good), *Tony Roma's* (famous for ribs), *Chili's* (California cuisine), *OK Corral* and *Outback Steak House*.

Self-Catering While most everyday needs can be catered for in the ubiquitous grocery stores and the basement supermarkets in department stores, there are some items (Swiss cheese, frozen turkeys, whole wheat bread etc) that are scarce in Seoul. Fortunately, there are a handful of western supermarkets that can supply these necessities.

If you have access to the US military base in Yongsan (or have friends inside), then your problem is essentially solved. Indeed, most of It'aewon's booming black market in western goods originates from the base.

Failing that, just north-east of It'aewon is *Hannam Supermarket (Map 2, ☎ 702 3313)*, a landmark for desperate westerners in search of salami, cranberry sauce and other treasured commodities.

Down the hill from the Grand Hyatt Hotel is *Jeil Deli* (Map 8), another important landmark for self-caterers. This place

PLACES TO EAT

features fantastic bread, imported jams, cheeses and other rare delights.

The other area in town to look for these precious items is Yonhui-dong, which is near the Seoul Foreign School (Map 2), north of Shinch'on subway station on line 2. Two big stores to check out in this area are *Saroga* and *Lucky*.

More pricey is the *Deli Plaza* (Map 5) in the Plaza Hotel near City Hall. The delicatessen's bakery is excellent.

DRINKS
Nonalcoholic

Korea produces what are arguably the best herbal teas in the world. Ginseng tea is the most famous, but also check out *ssanghwang* tea, made from three different roots and often served with an egg yolk or pine nuts floating in it. Ginger tea *(saengkang ch'a)* is also excellent. Citron tea *(yuja ch'a)* and five flavours tea *(omija ch'a)* are positively yummy.

Tea or coffee rooms *(tabang)* are great social centres. No food is served (by government edict), though they might come up with some rice crackers.

If you're on a tight budget but can't get going in the morning without a coffee, try *7-Eleven* stores or some of its competitors such as *Family Mart* and *Circle K*. They have fresh, percolated coffee for W400, and also sell doughnuts for the same price. Alternatively look out for the coffee-vending machines, which are common throughout Seoul. Prices range from W150 to W300. Of course, making your own coffee is cheapest, if you happen to have a source of boiling water.

Western-style coffee shops *(k'ŏp'i syop)* are numerous in Seoul. These are good places to grab breakfast and they usually serve cakes and sandwiches at reasonable prices. The coffee shop phenomenon has spawned numerous chain stores: *Doutor*, *Paris Baguette*, *Caravan*, *Mr Coffee* and *Jardin* are a few examples.

Alcoholic

Koreans love their liquor and there is no shortage of drinking spots in Seoul. Boozing

Bread & Water

If you're ever invited out for a meal or even just a drinking session with Korean friends, you'll find it difficult to pay for the bill yourself or even to contribute to it. The same applies even if it's you that's doing the inviting. All manner of ruses will be used to beat you to the cashier, even if it means that the person who pays is going to have to live on bread and water for the next week. The bill for a group is always paid by one person and one only. If you want to contribute, then make these arrangements before you go out and square up after you leave. Never attempt to do it in front of the cashier or you will seriously embarrass your host. Indeed, you may embarrass them to such a degree that they'll never be able to return to that particular restaurant or club.

If you're a man taking a woman out for dinner, you pay. Furthermore, a man is expected to escort his date home to make sure she arrives safely, unless she insists otherwise.

eoul's huge boulevards were built for military manoeuvres and now service a chaotic army of ommuters, but market throughways and side streets are where the real action is.

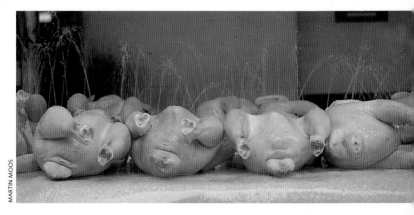

MARTIN MOOS

MARTIN MOOS

MARTIN MOOS

MARTIN MOOS

From fountains built for trussed-up chickens to pork parts on parade, fiery red *goch'u* paste and a monk's vegetarian meal, Seoul food is a sensory trip in itself.

it up is mostly a male group activity in Korea. Visit a typical pub in Seoul and you'll see plenty of Koreans (mostly men) getting drunk, often with a great deal of boisterous toasting and, as time passes, collective singing. Anyone with an aversion to mixing drinks will be made to suffer sorely by these gatherings. Korean drinkers frequently switch from beer to whisky to potato vodka, and from there to anything they can get their hands on short of paint thinner.

A traditional drink is *makkŏlli*, a kind of caustic milky-white rice brew which is cheap but potent enough to embalm a frog. It's sold in raucous beverage halls known as *makkŏlli jip*. *Soju* is the local firewater; a robust drink distilled from rice, yams or tapioca, and potent as toilet bowl cleanser.

Korea's best wine is Kyŏngju Beobjoo. Some drinkers try to mitigate the effects of indulgence by slaking their thirst with *insamju* (ginseng wine). *Maekchu* (beer) comes in several brands; OB, Crown and Red Rock are most popular.

If you drink in a beer hall, the management will expect you to buy some snacks *(anju)* which can include fresh oysters, dried squid, salted peanuts and *kim* (seaweed). All types of Korean booze can be bought in the 24 hour convenience stores at a fraction of the price you'd pay in a club.

PLACES TO EAT –
CENTRAL AREA (MAPS 3, 4 & 5)

We've tried to define restaurants as being budget (fill up for W5000 or less), midrange (W6000 to W15,000) and top end (W16,000 and up), but the definitions are a little stretched since it largely depends on what you order.

Budget

The best place to start is at the beginning – with breakfast. Within the bowels of the Anguk station (Map 4) on subway line 3 is *Paris Croissant*, a fine bakery with coffee, pastries, and a place to sit down and enjoy it all. There is a branch of *Paris Baguette* (Map 4) behind the Sejong Cultural Centre.

Along similar lines is *Doutor Coffee Shop* (Map 4) north-east of T'apkol Park.

Venezia Italian Spaghetti (Map 4), behind Sejong Cultural Centre, is a small place, but the food is scrumptious and amazingly inexpensive.

If you're in the Kwanghwamun area, a place you should definitely visit is the *Koryŏ Supermarket* (Map 4, no English sign). The lunch counters are hidden in the back and to your right – you can eat well for around W2000. The supermarket is one of the best in Seoul and has sustained many a budget traveller.

If you're in the vicinity of a large university (Yonsei, Hongik etc), you can eat well for about W1500 to W2000 at the *student cafeterias*. This doesn't apply at some of the aristocratic schools like Ehwa Women's University, where the food is pricey and portions are stingy. University cafeterias are normally open from about 10 am to 6 pm, but some only serve food from noon to 1 pm and 5 to 6 pm.

When it comes to Korean-style food, check out the basements of large department stores, where you can usually find supermarkets and lunch counters. In the central area of town, *Saerona department store* (Map 5) is a personal favourite, mainly because it's relatively uncrowded. *Shinsegae department store* (Map 5) has some cheap lunch counters in the basement, though selection is limited. *Lotte department store* (Map 5) is the largest, but is very crowded. *Printemps department store* (Map 4) has fine restaurants in the basement and on the 7th floor.

Tongsŏnggak Chinese Restaurant (Map 4) is a fine eatery tucked into an alley just south of the Sejong Cultural Centre. *Tonghwaru Chinese Restaurant* (Map 4) is just west of the Sejong Cultural Centre.

Kabongru Chinese Restaurant (Map 4), near the Sejong Cultural Centre, is one of the more upmarket Chinese restaurants in this neighbourhood, but still very reasonable for what you're getting.

Paejae Chinese Restaurant (☎ 752 7666) and the *Kukil Chinese Restaurant*

(☎ 755 3554) are both in the area (Map 5) just to the south-west of Tŏksugung.

The area around the Chinese embassy in Myŏng-dong is another good place to look for Chinese food. This small collection of restaurants and one or two bookshops is about as close as Seoul gets to a Chinatown. ***Shillawon Chinese Restaurant*** *(Map 5, ☎ 752 2396)* is a favourite with the embassy staff and features (surprise!) an English menu.

Utoo Zone (Map 5) is a department store with a difference – 60 independent vendors in one large building. The 4th floor, called the ***Z-Side***, has a number of small restaurants. Even more important is ***Myŏng-dong Food Alley*** behind Utoo Zone, which has Myŏng-dong's densest collection of restaurants.

Sapporo Restaurant (Map 4) is a small place dishing up inexpensive Japanese food. It's behind the Sejong Cultural Centre.

Restaurants dishing up cheap kimbap are ubiquitous in Seoul, but there are a few that are really outstanding. Near the YMCA are ***Seoul Kimbap*** and two branches of ***Chongno Kimbap*** (both on Map 4). Both have very unusual variations on this quintessential Korean dish (tuna kimbap, cheese kimbap etc).

Shinp'ouri Shikp'um Korean Fastfood (Map 4), just south-west of T'apkol Park, has a difficult name to pronounce, and there is no sign in English. Nevertheless, it's definitely worth seeking out. The food is amazingly good and you can eat your fill for less than W5000. You needn't grapple with the language, as the menu has pictures.

Mid-Range

There is a branch of the popular ***Domino's Pizza*** *(☎ 771 3082, basement 1, Taepyung building, 150 Taepyungro 2-ga, Chung-gu)* that offers home delivery to any place within a 2km radius.

Korea Press Center *(Map 4, ☎ 733 7011)* just north of City Hall is also home to the Foreign Correspondents' Club. The club has a restaurant, and is the spot for local and expat journalists to socialise and interview

each other for tomorrow's news stories (which is why so many newspaper articles quote 'unnamed sources').

Ipanema Brazilian Restaurant *(Map 3, ☎ 779 2756)* is Seoul's first Brazilian restaurant. Brazil is known for tasty barbecued cuisine. You'll find the restaurant off of Tŏksugung-gil, behind Tŏksugung.

Seoul Tower (Map 3) is home to the ***Sky Restaurant***, Korea's only revolving restaurant. Even better, the tower also boasts ***Pulhyanggi***, a superb Korean restaurant where you can eat your fill of scrumptious veggie dishes for around W15,000 to W25,000.

OK Corral *(☎ 771 2771)* does a western buffet, and is also known for steaks and a fine bakery. There is a branch (Map 5) in Myŏng-dong. The closest subway stop is Ŭlchiro 1-ga on line 2 (take exit 5).

TGI Friday's, which does American and Mexican food, has a branch in Myŏng-dong *(Map 5, ☎ 776 0071)*. The Chongno branch *(Map 4, ☎ 738 0321)* is two blocks south of the YMCA.

Tony Roma's *(Map 5, ☎ 771 6164)* is western style and is known for its prime rib dinners. You'll find it in a side street south of Lotte Department Store.

Cafe Little India (Map 4) on Insadong-gil is the only Indian restaurant in this neighbourhood. It's a big hit with expats.

Top End

Westin Chosun Hotel *(Map 5, ☎ 771 0500)* is home to a number of interesting restaurants. The lunch specials can be considered mid-range (around W10,000 to W20,000), but top-notch dinners can be pricey.

Some restaurants to consider at the Westin Chosun include: ***O'Kim's*** (Irish food); ***The Ninth Gate*** (western food), ***Yesterday's*** (Italian food), ***Sushi Cho*** (Japanese food), ***Sheobul*** (Korean food) and ***Hokyungjeon*** (Chinese food).

Shilla Hotel *(Map 3, ☎ 233 3131)* is where you'll find ***La Continentale***, one of the city's finest French restaurants.

Arisoo *(Map 2, ☎ 250 9276)* in the Tower Hotel prepares a posh version of Korean barbecue.

Youngbin Garden (Map 4, ☎ 732 3863) exemplifies an upmarket traditional Korean restaurant. Set in a lovely wooden house in a courtyard off of Insadong-gil, this is one place to get a great kalbi meal and lots of other traditional cuisine.

Koryŏ Ginseng Chicken (Map 5, ☎ 752 9376) specialises in – yes, you guessed it – Korean-style ginseng chicken. The restaurant is near the Korean Air building, southwest of City Hall subway station on line 2.

PLACES TO EAT – IT'AEWON (MAP 8)
Budget
On the western fringe of It'aewan, the *USO (Map 2, ☎ 795 3028, 795 3063)* is operated by the US military, but you don't have to join the army to eat there. The food is American style all the way: fried chicken, hamburgers, French fries and ice cream for dessert. This place only does breakfast and lunch. The USO is within walking distance of Namyŏng station on subway line 1.

Inca Restaurant looks like a corner cafe, but has great breakfasts and some really fine western meals.

On the eastern outskirts of It'aewon is *New York Pizza*. Generous portions make this a good place to fill up.

Manhattan Hof isn't sure if it wants to be Korean or western, but the food is fine nevertheless.

There is a *Domino's Pizza (☎ 792 6660, 683-126 Hannam-dong, Yongsan-gu)* in It'aewon that offers home delivery.

Mid-Range
La Cucina (☎ 794 6005) is It'aewon's premier Italian eatery. Check out the fettuccine and the lasagne.

A few restaurants specialise in food from the Indian subcontinent. The major ones are *Ashoka (☎ 792 0117)* on the 3rd floor of the Hamilton Hotel, *Moghul (☎ 796 5501)* which is behind the Hamilton Hotel shop and *Taj Mahal (☎ 749 0316)* near the mosque. They all have buffet lunches for around W15,000; evening meals are somewhat more expensive.

Up the hill a little, in the direction of the Grand Hyatt, is *Chalet Swiss (☎ 796 6379)*. It's easy to find – the building even looks Swiss. The only thing likely to give you indigestion here is the yodelling session with the Kim Brothers every Thursday to Saturday night. Chalet Swiss is open from noon to 10 pm and reservations (☎ 797 0664) are necessary for dinner.

At the far end of It'aewon is *Deutches Haus* and the food is just as German as the name. It has a pleasant, roomy interior.

One of the few genuinely Korean restaurants in this neighbourhood is *It'aewon Restaurant (☎ 797 1474)*. It has a pleasant atmosphere and is actually not as expensive as it looks.

Le Petite France (☎ 790 3040) is a little pricey, but it easily rates as one of Seoul's best French restaurants.

Churchills Restaurant (☎ 795 7066) is also a serious competitor in western food and the chef was trained in Paris. There are plenty of imported wines, beers and stronger brews. If you have a tobacco addiction, check out the Cuban cigars on sale here.

Thai Orchid Restaurant next to the It'aewon Hotel is one of the finest Thai restaurants in the city.

Top End
The Grand Hyatt Hotel (Map 2) is home to several upmarket restaurants. Chief among them is *Paris Grill (☎ 797 1234)* with 200-plus seats, a fine view of the river and great French food.

PLACES TO EAT – SHINCH'ON (MAP 9)
Budget
Khan Antique Pub, south of Hongik University subway station, specialises in Korean food. This chain store has branches all around Seoul, but the signs are in Korean only.

Jessica's Pizzeria does more than just pizza – check out the exquisite spaghetti and lasagne.

Amato Pizza Buffet (☎ 312 1055) is one of those fantastic all-you-can-eat affairs where budget travellers try to consume enough to last them through the whole week. It's worth coming here just to check out the hi-tech toilets, tourist attractions in themselves.

There is a **Domino's Pizza** (☎ 337 7555) which offers home delivery.

Mid-Range

Ponderosa Steak House (☎ 3141 3473) is a great family restaurant. Aside from steak, the menu also features Mexican food, spaghetti, seafood and chicken. If you want to splurge, check out the buffet meals. Typical costs are W12,000 to W24,000. It's open from 11 am to 11 pm.

La Vecchia Stazione (☎ 363 2160) is an Italian coffee shop with considerable charm. The decor is something like an old train station and classical music is played continuously in the background.

TGI Friday's (☎ 322 6321), a superb American-style restaurant, has a branch near Hongik University station on subway line 2. The hamburgers are outstanding.

Almost in the same league (but not quite) is **Coco's California Restaurant** (☎ 335 1874), which is not to be confused with a similarly named fast-food chain.

Bennigan's New York (☎ 393 6700) is close to Ewha Women's University.

Ch'unch'on Chicken only has chicken dishes on the menu, but everything is delectable. The two bad things about this place are that the seats are uncomfortable (just stools) and it's amazingly crowded (though that attests to just how good the food really is).

Kenny Roger's Roasters Restaurant is a huge place notable for its 'wood fire roasted chicken'. This western chain has been enormously successful with Koreans, in part because of a Koreanised menu (anyone for squid noodles?).

Solomon Chinese Restaurant is definitely one of the classier Chinese restaurants in this part of town.

PLACES TO EAT – TAEHANGNO (MAP 6)
Budget

Coco Fried Rice is a local chain with about 30 branches in Seoul. Its specialities are a sort of Korean-Chinese fast food, which isn't bad at all.

Mozart Coffee Shop is a good place to lounge with tasty pastry and strong coffee.

Pizza Parlour is like a zillion others in Seoul but it's amazingly large, with considerable variations on the menu. This multi-level restaurant is also notable for its good views of Taehangno's main drag.

Mid-Range

Coco's California Restaurant (☎ 742 1031) and **Bennigan's Boston** (☎ 766 9800) are adjacent to each other, and both dish up fine western food.

Golden Gate Chinese Restaurant (☎ 762 0918) at the northern end of Taehangno has excellent food, though we had to compete with a couple of cockroaches for seating.

Hudson Ristorante Italiano is as good as it gets in this neighbourhood for Italian restaurants.

El Paso Mexican Restaurant does tacos, burritos, tostados and enchiladas, along with good tequila sunrises and Corona beer.

Gold Rush Restaurant has a very 'wild west saloon' motif, including epoxy-resin cowboys and horses. Good, hearty western hamburgers and steaks are on the menu.

PLACES TO EAT – KANGNAM AREA (MAP 7)
Budget

Buried deep within the bowels of Kangnam subway station (south side of the river) is **Holly's Coffee**. It resembles the North-American Starbuck's chain, and offers what is reputed to be the best coffee in Seoul.

Domino's Pizza will deliver its product to within a 2km radius. There are branches of this chain outfit at Apkujŏng (☎ 544 1112, 634-6 Shinsa-dong, Kangnam-gu) and Yŏksam (☎ 564 0045, 746-1 Yŏksam-dong, Kangnam-gu) subway stations.

Mid-Range

Uno Chicago Bar & Grill (☎ 547 4111) is a large and very attractive restaurant specialising in Chicago pizza, steak, hamburgers and other western cuisine. The portions are large. It's east of Apkujŏng subway station on line 3.

Ponderosa Steak House (☎ 565 1021) is part of a chain (see the earlier Shinch'on Mid-Range section for details). The restaurant is open from 11 am to 11 pm.

Carne Station has two branches in the south of Seoul. The Kangnam branch (☎ 557 1239) is close to Kangnam subway station on line 2. The Taechi branch (☎ 562 1239) is close to the Inter-Continental Hotel and Samsŏng subway station on line 2. The restaurant dishes up a very tasty Koreanised western buffet complete with salad, beef, seafood and kalbi.

OK Corral (☎ 565 2778) is a western chain. The steaks and buffet meals are superb and the portions are huge. The restaurant is a short walk north of Kangnam subway station.

Chili's Grill & Bar has a branch in Apkujŏng (☎ 3443 7272), near Apkujŏng subway station on line 3; and Chamshil (*Map 2*, ☎ 416 7272), a three minute walk from Chamshil subway station on line 2. The restaurant boasts of its 'American south-west' cuisine, though it's not really that spicy. Some dishes to try include the grilled chicken pasta and the Monterey chicken. Don't forget to try the margaritas. Chili's is open daily from 11 am to 11 pm.

The ***Hyundai department stores*** on the south side of the Han River are known for their cheap Korean-style eateries, but there are upmarket restaurants here too. The Hyundai store next to Apkujŏng station has pricey Japanese, Italian and Chinese restaurants on the top floor. Look out for the ludicrously expensive ***Dragon Palace***, with its braised mushrooms and bean sprouts for W65,000. The Hyundai over by the Korea World Trade Centre (KWTC) has various levels of elegance with prices to match.

Southern Seoul has several branches of ***TGI Fridays***, the American bistro known for fine food and far-out interior decorating (aeroplane parts, baby carriages etc). The Kangnamyŏk branch (☎ 3477 0321) is almost adjacent to the Kangnam subway

station. The Nonhyŏn branch (☎ 512 7211) is close to Shinsa subway station.

Tony Roma's (☎ 3443 3500) is a superb upmarket western restaurant. You'll find it on Tosandaero about halfway between the Apkujŏng and Shinsa subway stations.

Outback Steak House (☎ 3445 4701) pretends to be Australian, though it's really an American chain. It's a short walk south of Shinsa subway station or north of Kangnam subway station.

Coco's California Restaurant has two convenient branches in the area. The Shinsa branch (☎ 548 6904) is in the Apkujŏng area, and the Taechi branch (☎ 561 1112) is close to the Inter-Continental Hotel.

Bennigan's is another popular western chain restaurant with a high profile in Seoul. In the Apkujŏng area is the ***Bennigan's Chicago*** (☎ 517 5007). In the courtyard next to the Inter-Continental Hotel you can find ***Bennigan's Seattle*** (☎ 567 8600).

Chamshil (Map 2) Most of the action in the Chamshil area centres on ***Lotte World***, a mini-city bedecked with small cheap and mid-range restaurants of every variety. Take subway line 2 to Chamshil station.

Top End

Hanmiri Restaurant (☎ 556 4834, *Ildong building, 968-4 Daechi-dong*) in Kangnam is the place to go for elegant Korean food.

The Inter-Continental Hotel is just loaded with opulent restaurants. One good choice is ***Emerald Sea Chinese Restaurant***, which does a mean dim sum buffet.

The Seoul Renaissance Hotel chips in with the upmarket ***Kabin Chinese Restaurant*** and ***Irodori Japanese Restaurant***.

PLACES TO EAT – YŎŬIDO (MAP 9)

On Yŏŭido the logical place to start is the DLI 63 building. The first basement floor has a number of ***Korean restaurants*** dishing up noodles, ginseng chicken soup and dumplings. The same floor has ***Mongnyon Chinese Restaurant***, plus branches of fast-food chains like ***KFC*** and ***Subway***.

Prices on the upper floors are higher – you pay for the view. On the 56th floor is **Wako** (☎ 789 5751), a Japanese restaurant. The 57th floor is home to **Paengnihyang** (☎ 789 5741), one of the city's upscale Chinese restaurants. The 59th floor chips in with the **Steak House** (☎ 789 5904), **Sky Pizza** and **Sky View** (a western restaurant).

Literally top-end is the **63 Roof Garden** (☎ 789 5967), which does Korean and western food, and also has a branch down on the 4th floor.

Entertainment

PUBS

The 'Korean' word for pub is *hof (hop'ŭ)*, a term borrowed from German. Hofs around town wax and wane in popularity with the English-teaching crowd and backpackers passing through. Generally, hofs double as restaurants and it is expected that patrons buy something to eat, even if it is just some nibbles. These small dishes of finger food, or *anju*, are where the hofs make a lot of their money. Just going in for a couple of beers is usually frowned upon. Some hofs do really great roast chicken, and prices are usually quite affordable.

DANCE CLUBS

Dance clubs, which in Korea are still called discos *(tisŭk'o chang)*, have declined somewhat. Apparently, the karaoke business has offered formidable competition.

A pretty steep 'table charge' gets you your first few beers and anju (snacks) at the Korean-style places. This typically costs W10,000 to W15,000, but high-class discos may charge up to W30,000. Some of these places also check ID to make sure that you are young enough (under 30!). The system may differ in places that cater to foreigners, such as in It'aewon.

KARAOKE

Despite the fact that karaoke *(noraebang)* is a Japanese invention, the Koreans have adopted it as their own. For the uninitiated, karaoke (meaning 'empty music' in Japanese) is one big amateur singing contest to the accompaniment of a video tape or laser disk. The idea is to give you the chance to be a star, even if nobody but you gets to hear the performance. The really fancy karaoke lounges have superb audio systems and large-screen videos, but no matter how good the equipment, it's not going to sound any better than the ability of the singer. And with very few exceptions, it usually sounds pretty awful.

Traditional Korean-style drinking establishments are known as *soju bang* (soju parlours). The real budget places are known as *sul jip* and serve *makkoli* and soju rather than beer, and it is expected that you indulge in some *anju* (snacks) as well. Often the snacks will be presented with the drinks. They are not free of charge, but sul jip are usually not expensive places to have a few drinks.

One Korean innovation with a long history is *taep'otjip* (soju tents). These are usually set up in the evening alongside the bank of a river, and feature inexpensive drinks and snacks. The government frowns on these places, believing that they are a relic from the poverty-stricken past which has no place in modern Korea. They are also extremely popular! Soju tents are now banned in Seoul, but as some consolation they can still be found in suburban areas outside of the city.

More upmarket are *kisaeng jip*. A *kisaeng* is the Korean equivalent of the Japanese geisha. Contrary to popular opinion, the kisaeng – like the geisha – was a woman of great conversational and artistic skills employed to amuse male guests, and was generally not involved in transactions for other 'services'. Nowadays kisaeng are selected for their looks and social skills, and work as glorified waitresses, perhaps putting on a song or dance performance at some point in the evening, but mainly catering to the needs of what will almost certainly be an all-male group of diners. An evening out in a kisaeng jip can be shockingly expensive, and most westerners will not get to try one unless they are treated by Koreans, probably in the course of clinching a business deal.

To many westerners, karaoke makes about as much sense as paying to see 90 minutes of test patterns at the local cinema. However, Koreans seem to love it, sometimes dragging their western English teachers along for an evening of sing-along entertainment.

There are two basic variations on the theme. You can sing in front of others at a bar or lounge, where there is usually no cover charge, though you are expected to buy drinks and anju. Or you can sit by yourself (or with a friend) in a little booth and sing along with a video tape or laser disk, record your performance (around W12,000 per hour) and take your recorded tape home to enjoy at your leisure.

The karaoke business is amazingly well organised in Korea. Songs (some in English) are numbered and all the clubs use the same numbering system – if you ask for song No 112, it will be the same at every karaoke venue in the nation.

TEAHOUSES

Teahouses *(tabang)* offer a taste of old-style social life, and they are found anywhere and everywhere. While the drinks may be fairly pricey at around W3000 per cup, you are paying for the space under your bum. One cup of tea or coffee generally entitles you to sit around and chat for as long as you like. Some places may also require you to purchase snacks – don't argue about it, just go with the flow.

An old Seoul landmark in Insa-dong is the *Old Teahouse (Map 4, ☎ 722 5019)*, otherwise known as *Yet Ch'at Chip*. This unique place features live birds that freely flutter around the shop as you drink your tea. You'll find the teashop in an alley off Insadong-gil, upstairs from Arirang Restaurant. It's open from 10 am to 11 pm.

NIGHTLIFE ZONES

Seoul has several major zones especially noted for their bright lights, good food and copious quantities of booze. A list would have to include Shinch'on (including the adjoining Hongik University area), the

Chongno area (near the YMCA), Myŏngdong, It'aewon, Taehangno, Apkujŏng and Kangnam. In terms of relative expense, Apkujŏng, Kangnam and Myŏng-dong are the most expensive places to party.

A word to the wise – for the sake of international relations, try to behave yourself in Korean pubs even if the locals don't. A few thoughtless foreigners have managed to offend the Koreans with their rowdy 'hell-raising behaviour', which has made it tough for those who follow.

Shinch'on (Map 9)

The area behind the Hyundai department store is flooded with coffee shops and nightclubs. Some clubs are multistorey affairs, with each floor geared to a certain clientele. For example, one floor may be reserved for well dressed customers while another floor is kept for those in grubby blue jeans. Furthermore, there are clubs for really young college students, and if you look too old (over age 25) you may not be allowed in.

Woodstock (☎ 334 1310) attracts a foreign clientele with its 60s rock music, though some generation-X foreigners complain that the music is old and always the same.

Voodoo Bar (☎ 336 5021) is a small and cosy place, with barmaids who speak good English. This place is sort of like a smaller version of Woodstock, but with more recent music. Around the corner is *Club Savage (☎ 322 3892)*, a lively place in a basement. Just above it is *The Doors*, named after the infamous 60s band.

Twenty Something has beer at low prices, though the men's urinals are said to be the worst in Seoul. *Bar 33* is another good pub in this vicinity.

Macondo Bar (☎ 332 5752) is very popular with expats, and justifiably so. The pub is known for dark beer (a rare find in Seoul), Latin-style cuisine and salsa music (with dance lessons every evening except Monday at 8 pm). Another plus: films are shown every Saturday at 5 pm and Sunday at 6 pm.

Drug Club is a Seoul institution. This is *the* venue for live music, with up-and-coming bands often making their debut here.

There is a cover charge (the price varies with the band) and no booze is served. Drug Club records live music performances and sells these CDs at the Punk Shop, just above the club.

Movie cafes (see a description of these later in the chapter) abound in this neighbourhood. Some of the notable ones include *Joy of Kino Movie Cafe* and *Black Maria Movie Cafe*.

Freebird Rock & Jazz Bar lives up to its name. Live bands perform here every night.

Bonanza Hole is another live rock music venue. There is no cover charge.

Feedback Live Bar attracts some of Seoul's most popular rock bands.

Be Bop Jazz Club has live bands almost every evening, and for certain on weekends. Being up on the 5th floor also gives it a good view.

Joker Red Disco and *Hodge Podge Disco* are adjacent to each other, and are two of the busiest dance venues near Hongik University. Nearby is *Myŏngwolkwan Disco*. It's tricky to find if you can't read *han'gŭl*, as there's no English sign, but take the stairs to the basement. *Saab Disco* has two branches.

The Rolling Stones Live Bar of course has live music, tending more towards hard rock than mellow sounds. Don't confuse this place with the *Rolling Stone Bar* (above Ch'unch'on Chicken Restaurant), which has good recorded music but no live bands.

Coda Bar is also another live rock music pub, though it's never really busy. Nevertheless, the music's good.

Underground Cafe is managed by a western woman who does a lot of parties and special events. This place is definitely gaining in popularity.

US 66 Bar is very high profile and is usually busy. It features expensive drinks, and lots of women who seem to like expensive drinks.

Apkujŏng (Map 7)
This is the most expensive night-time playground in Seoul, a favourite hang-out for the trendy rich kids (whose activities have only been slightly diminished in this 'IMF era'). The action centres on dozens of so-called 'rock cafes' found just behind the McDonald's opposite Galleria department store. Adjacent to McDonald's is *'Rodeo St'*, known for its pubs and high-fashion boutiques.

The *Hard Rock Cafe* (☎ 547 5671) offers everything from fried chicken with nachos to shrimp cocktails, served in a super-trendy setting with live music. The cafe is open Monday to Friday from 5 pm to 2 am, and from noon to 2 am on weekends. It's in Apkujŏng-dong, a long walk to the southeast of Apkujŏng subway station on line 3.

Kangnam (Map 7)
The area near Kangnam subway station (just behind Tower Records) is illuminated at night by glittering neon – there are heaps of pubs in this area.

On the other side of Kangnam station is an alley where you can find *Woodstock II*, a pub notable for 60s rock music.

Taehangno (Map 6)
Taehangno literally means 'University St', though it's also referred to as the 'Arts & Culture Street'. In fact, the official name is Tongsung-dong. The area is known for its theatres, ultra-trendy cafes and pubs. To get there, take subway line 4 to Hyehwa station.

Street performers set up shop here and live off the donations – look for them in Marronnier Park. The park is also a venue for artists who will be happy to sketch your portrait for a suitable fee.

Up-and-coming bands also get together to give performances. These *jam sessions* are often held in a small, hot, smoky basement, though there may be a steep admission fee. It's impossible for us to tell you where and when these impromptu concerts will be held. If you're interested, ask the local students you see hanging out. There are posters around advertising performances, but these are written entirely in Korean.

Heavy Rock MTV Club has a large-screen video and eardrum-splitting music.

ENTERTAINMENT

Not far away is **Wild Bills**, a busy bar that might as well be a movie set in a Hollywood western.

Boogie Boogie Bar (☎ 744 3626) is instantly recognisable by the 1956 Chevrolet Bel Air on the roof. There's good music, and a menu with lots of Korean and western dishes.

Chicago Jazz Bar (in the basement) provides a good venue for aspiring artists studying at the nearby Seoul Jazz Academy. There is live jazz music Thursday to Sunday evening from 8 to 10 pm.

It'aewon (Map 8)

Most of Seoul's expat bars can be found in It'aewon. Wandering around this foreign ghetto, it's easy to get the feeling that It'aewon has a country-and-western theme – everywhere you look there are bars with names like Cowboy Club, Nashville, Stomper and Grand Ole Opry. Most of the cowboy haunts are hole-in-the-wall hostess bars (more on that in a moment) that can sear quite a hole in your wallet if you're not careful. It's a bit odd that It'aewon doesn't have a much larger number of Japanese and Chinese karaoke joints – a surprisingly large number of Japanese and Chinese tourists come here (literally by the busload).

It'aewon's main strip has a few very crowded clubs that have no cover charge and ask W1500 for a bottle of OB beer. The most popular is **King Club**. It doesn't really get going until around 10 pm, but when it does it can be quite an experience. Off-duty GIs descend on the place in droves and local women turn up in innumerable groups of two and three, many dressed in as little as possible (note that most of the girls *aren't* working).

Hollywood Club (☎ 749 1659) has two dance floors with an excellent sound system (and good DJs). Other entertainment is provided by pool tables, dart games and a plentiful supply of booze. The large collection of Cuban cigars on sale here gives away the fact that this place is run by the same management as nearby Churchills Restaurant.

Next to **Gulliver Disco** are some stairs which ascend a hill. At the top of the steps is **Club Viagra** (another disco) and a steep alley. In local parlance this alley is known as 'hooker hill' and a stroll up here anytime after 8 pm will make it clear why. The alley is lined with bars and out on the alley itself are small knots of freelancers hawking their wares to male passers-by with cries of 'Where you going? You come with me'.

At the top of the alley is **Stomper**, which has no cover charge and inexpensive drinks. Stomper draws in more couples than singles and is a favourite place for a dance.

One other place notable for dancing is **NASA Disco**, which tends to stay open into the wee hours of the morning.

Grand Ole Opry (☎ 795 9155) has country-and-western music on the first floor, but if that doesn't appeal go up to the 2nd floor to find 'old time rock 'n roll'.

All over It'aewon are hostess bars such as **Casablanca**, **Black Jack**, **Ruby's** and **Giorgio's**. Prices for drinks usually start at W3000, which is not that expensive by itself – unfortunately, you will inevitably be hit for a 'lady's drink', which will range between W5000 and W7000 depending on the bar. While it is possible to refuse buying one of the girls a drink, you won't be made very welcome afterwards.

On the main drag is **Nashville**, and it's worth knowing about even though we don't recommend it. On the plus side, it's renowned for its superb hamburgers, reasonable prices, dart games and evening movies shown on a large-size screen. The downside is a prominent sign on the front door saying 'Foreigners Only'. You aren't likely to find any Koreans inside except for the scantily clad female staff.

Woodstock, **Mug Club** and **Prohibition** are known more for good music than for mini-skirted hostesses.

All That Jazz is one of the few places in Seoul where you get an opportunity to catch some live jazz. There are sometimes jam sessions here with local GIs blowing up a storm.

For Members Only

There is an unspoken, usually unofficial, yet palpable apartheid in the It'aewon bar scene. There are numerous clubs that are for locals only, and in some cases foreigners will be turned away. A convenient face-saving excuse is for the management to claim that the club is 'members only', but if the point is pushed this will quickly give way to 'Koreans only'. There are also clubs that turn away Koreans.

Korean feelings about the US military presence in their country are extremely complex, and might charitably described as intense ambivalence. Some Korean men, especially after a few beers, can become quite hostile towards foreigners. Small scuffles can quickly grow into brawls where there are groups of Korean men and military personnel. Consequently, in It'aewon, bouncers are employed to keep foreigners out of the Korean bars and Koreans (the men at least) out of foreigner's bars. This may seem rather grim, but It'aewon is a particularly eccentric neighbourhood. There are plenty of other places where foreigners and Koreans mix without antagonism.

HOTEL BARS

The Seoul hotel scene, mainly centred in the biggies like the Hilton, Westin-Chosun and the Inter-Continental, is worlds away from the lively small bar scene. While the small bars in places like Shinch'on and Tae-hangno cater to a largely student crowd, the big-hotel scene is where you rub elbows with the well heeled business class and ruling elite (which of course doesn't exclude super-rich students). This is not to say that suits or high-heels are mandatory uniforms, but hotel bars lack the casualness of areas like It'aewon and Shinch'on.

A relatively affordable place in this category is Seoul's only Irish bar, **O'Kim's**

(Map 5), in the basement of the Westin-Chosun Hotel. Aside from the booze, there's pricey food available, such as burgers and French fries for W12,000. From Monday to Friday there is usually live Irish folk music. Business hours are from 11.30 am to 2 am.

The Westin-Chosun also hosts **Compass Rose** (☎ 317 0365), which features live music. It's next to the hotel's main lobby.

A trendier location altogether is the flashy **JJ Mahoney's** (☎ 797 1234) in the Grand Hyatt (Map 8). This place is renowned as Seoul's yuppie bar, and has a clientele that is about half expat and half Korean.

Also in the Grand Hyatt (2nd basement) is **Helicon**, which features live music. And the same hotel (1st basement) hosts **The Paris Bar**, which is a piano bar.

Nix and Nox (☎ 3451 8444), south of the river in the Ritz-Carlton Hotel (Map 7), is one of Kangnam's trendiest hotel bars. The Ritz-Carlton is near Yŏksam station on subway line 2.

Also in Kangnam-gu is **Hunter's Tavern** (☎ 559 7619), on the ground floor of the Inter-Continental Hotel (Map 7). The bar features live music, and is open from 7 pm to 2 am.

Yet another Kangnam-gu trend setter is **Maestro** (☎ 3440 8000), a cocktail bar that offers live music. Maestro is in the Amiga Hotel (Map 7).

Pharaoh's *(Map 5, ☎ 317 3244)* is the Hilton Hotel's contribution to Seoul's nightlife scene.

Way out in the far east of Seoul is the Sheraton Walker Hill Hotel (Map 2). Here you can find **Zesty** (☎ 453 0121), a pricey pub not many expats know about. Up on the top floor is **Starlight**, a 'sky lounge' with a great night view.

Firenze *(Map 5, ☎ 773 6000)*, in the King Sejong Hotel, has a quiet atmosphere and looks something like an art gallery. Aside from the drinks, this bar is renowned for its fried beef. Operating hours are from 7 pm to 2 am. The hotel is just in front of Myŏng-dong station on subway line 4.

Bobby London (☎ 771 1000 ext 5291) in the 1st basement of the Lotte Hotel (Map 5)

Seoul Rocks

A couple of years ago when I first came to Korea, the music scene was depressing – nothing but bad dance music, blatantly ripping-off whatever was popular in America. The only interesting band I could find was Pipi Band. They seemed to be doing well, until they spat on a TV camera and gave the finger, and were swiftly banned from all media for a year. They broke up, with Lee Yun-joung going solo and the other two members forming Pipi Longstocking (that band too has broken up, only to reform as Wonderbird).

In the meantime, things started moving. Hwang Shin-hye Band was the next strange group I found. A little too strange to be listenable, but they had some good tunes. They are currently working on a second album, which is supposed to be more electronic than the first.

Drug Club (see its entry in the Nightlife Zones – Shinch'on section of this chapter) opened in 1994, and has taken off. If you think Seoul is musically dead now, imagine how much worse it was then. Drug Club's first band was Drug Band (since disbanded). Crying Nut joined in 1995, followed by Weeper. The club started to make CDs for its own bands, which really helped increase its visibility, including *Our Nation*, featuring Crying Nut and Yellow Kitchen, followed by *Our Nation 2*, and *Here We Stand*. *Our Nation 3* is on the way. The Punk Shop recently opened above Drug Club, providing a place to buy the music, clothes and other accessories required to achieve punkdom.

The first time I went to Drug Club I was expecting a lot of wannabes, too many Nirvana cover tunes (the bane of the Korean music scene), or something equally dull. But as I paid my cover charge, I heard this wonderful sound coming from the club. It was loud and pounding, but it was more than rock music. There were layers of distorted keyboard sounds, an entrancing, powerful pulsing rhythm, and a woman's distorted voice screaming over top of it all. It was the most interesting sound I had heard in ages. The band was Saebomae Pin Ttalgikot (Ttalgikot for short, which means 'strawberry').

Ttalgikot's songs are long (sometimes 15 or 20 minutes) and it's never the same song twice. All of the instruments are subject to improvisations and experimentation. I have seen them play with a zither, oboe and traditional Korean drum. Rumour has it that Ttalgikot will be on Drug Club's latest CD, *Our Nation 3* (teamed with 18-Cruk, a rather strange combination of styles).

A new singing act, Bol Bbal Kan, derives his music from *pong jak*, a style of music you have probably heard, even if you don't recognise the name. It is the music heard in cabaret clubs and karaoke bars, it is that cheesy Casio-organ sound, blasting like a demon from the late 1970s. How one young guy could turn something so pathetically lame into something so good, I have no idea but that is what Bol Bbal Kan does – one dorky-looking guy in a policeman's uniform, standing alone on stage, singing these anachronistic melodies. But somehow it rocks and the crowd of college-aged kids (mostly female) goes nuts.

Actually, it's not just him alone on stage. Usually while he sings, Korean porn videos are screened behind him. Being Korean videos, they are fairly soft and relatively inoffensive by western standards. But there is nudity, and when the risque scenes start, Bol Bbal Kan changes

is more oriented towards Koreans than foreigners, but it has a British pub motif. There are live bands playing nightly from 7 pm to 2 am, and the place sometimes packs

out. Bobby London must be a great success, because it has spawned a clone, **Windsor Bar**, which is also in the 1st basement. In the same hotel but up on the 35th floor is

Seoul Rocks

his singing style to emphasise the action on screen. While the men watch dutifully, it is the women who really seem to enjoy it. And this is a Confucian society?

These days, punk is all the rage. Huckleberry Finn is probably the most rocking band around. Toast is a good, young band, if a little pop-ish. Banana Spoon is regularly on TV and as bubblegum as they might be, they are a significant step forward in Korean pop music. Crying Nut and No Brain are also often on TV.

The meanings of 'punk' and 'techno' and other musical terms are rather loosely applied in Korea. Punk incorporates attitude, fashion, style and an array of different music. Basically, it means loud and anything other than heavy metal. From Clash to Nirvana to Offspring, it's all labelled 'punk'.

Currently, audiences are filled with backpack-wearing kids, mostly around 18 years old. While they sometimes can get quite excited, they still don't know quite how to boogie. In fact, at a couple of concerts, when a friend and I started smashing into each other people thought that we were getting into a fight. An exception is made at Drug Club, where the audiences are often more active.

Audiences are often predominantly female, even at the louder, more cutting-edge places. Often the men are leaning against the wall, looking at the band, but it is the women who bounce around and go crazy. Also, a lot of the better bands have female members.

At a recent concert headlined by Crying Nut, I was really disappointed with the audience. 'Duds', I thought, a typical audience at a Korean show. Then Crying Nut came out, and everyone went totally wild. The audience got up and rushed to the front, packed in together like sardines, practically crushing the band. Sometimes the crowd got so excited that they started grabbing at the instruments and getting in the way of the band. Kids smashed into each other, people flung water and acted completely unreserved and un-Confucian. It was inspiring. Crying Nut's hit song, 'Mal Tal Ri Ja', has made it into the national karaoke scene. Safe to say, this band is catching on.

James Russell

James Russell publishes *Bokonon*, Seoul's underground music-zine

Schoenbrunn Bar (☎ *771 1000 ext 5363*), which has a German motif.

A two minute walk from City Hall station brings you to the Plaza Hotel (Map 5), and in the basement you'll find the ***Plaza Pub*** (☎ *771 2200*). Meals are available from 6 to 9 pm. Live music begins at 6 pm and carries on until 2 am.

CINEMAS

Seoul has no shortage of cinemas (*yŏnghwa gwan* or *kukjang*), some of them luxurious. The only problem is finding out what's on. There is no English publicity for film screenings, though you can find limited information concerning what's on in the Friday editions of the two English-language newspapers. The *Korean Yellow Pages* lists current movie showings on its Web site (www.yellowpages.co.kr) – click on the 'Entertainment' link.

Cinemas usually open their doors around 11 am and show their last two-hour blockbuster from about 9 to 11 pm. Ticket prices average at W8000, but morning matinees are cheaper. A few cinemas won't allow you to eat or drink anything while you watch the film, but most places don't care and sell popcorn, candy and soft drinks.

The current list of places which show foreign films includes:

Broadway
(☎ *511 2301, Nonhyŏn-dong, Kangnam-gu*) Shinsa subway station on line 3

CGV 11
(☎ *3424 1600, 10th floor, Techno Mart, Kuidong, Kwangjin-gu*) Kangbyŏn subway station on line 2

Chung-ang
(*Map 5,* ☎ *776 9024, 48 Cho-dong 1-ga, Chung-gu*) Ŭlchiro 1-ga subway station on line 2

Cine House
(*Map 7,* ☎ *540 4637, 91-6 Nonhyŏn-dong, Kangnam-gu*) Shinsa subway station on line 3

City Cinema
(☎ *540 1637, 816-7 Yŏksam-dong, Kangnam-gu*) exit 7, Kangnam subway station

Core Art Hall
(*Map 4,* ☎ *739 9933, Kwanchul-dong, Chongno-gu*) exit 4, Chonggak subway station on line 1

Daehan
(*Map 3,* ☎ *278 8171, 125 Ch'ungmuro 4-ga, Chung-gu*) Ch'ungmuro subway station on lines 3 and 4

Dong-a
(*Map 7,* ☎ *552 6111, 814-6 Yŏksam-dong, Kangnam-gu*) exit 7, Kangnam subway station on line 2

Dansŏngsa
(*Map 4,* ☎ *764 3745, 56 Myo-dong, Chongno-gu*) Chongno 3-ga subway station on lines 1, 3 and 5

Grandprix
(☎ *518 9091, 501-2 Shinsa-dong, Kangnam-gu*) exit 7, Shinsa subway station

Hoam Art Hall
(*Map 3,* ☎ *751 9614, 7 Sunhwa-dong, Chung-gu*) City Hall subway station on lines 1 and 2

Hollywood
(*Map 4,* ☎ *745 4231, 284-6 Nagwon-dong, Chongno-gu*) Chongno 3-ga subway station on lines 1, 3 and 5

Hwayang
(☎ *362 3149, 126 Migun-dong, Sŏdaemun-gu*) exit 8, Sŏdaemun subway station on line 5

Imax
(*Map 9,* ☎ *789 5555*) DLI 63 Bldg, Yŏŭido

Korea
(*Map 5,* ☎ *778 8361, 50-16 Myŏng-dong 2-ga, Chung-gu*) exit 6, Ŭlchiro 1-ga subway station on line 2

Kukdo
(☎ *266 1444, 310 Ŭlchiro 4-ga, Chung-gu*) Ŭlchiro 4-ga subway station on line 2

Lotte World cinemas 1-4
(*Map 2,* ☎ *417 0213, 40-1 Chamshil-dong, Songp'a-gu*) Chamshil subway station on lines 2 and 8

Lumiere
(☎ *540 5134, 164-7 Nonhyŏn-dong, Kangnam-gu*) exit 7, Kangnam subway station

Myŏng-dong
(*Map 5,* ☎ *752 1444, 83-5 Myŏng-dong 2-ga, Chung-gu*)

Myŏngbo Plaza
(*Map 5,* ☎ *274 2121, 18-5 Ch'o-dong, Chung-gu*) Ŭlchiro 3-ga subway station on lines 2 and 3

Pagoda
(☎ *742 1937, 207 Nagwon-dong, Chongno-gu*) Chongno 3-ga subway station, next to T'apkol Park

Panp'o
(☎ *534 5677), 5th floor, Express Bus Terminal, 19-4 Panp'o-dong, Sŏch'o-gu*) connected to Express Bus Terminal subway station on line 3

Piccadilly
(*Map 4,* ☎ *765 2245, 139 Tonui-dong, Chongno-gu*) Chongno 3-ga subway station

Scala
(*Map 5,* ☎ *266 6303, 41 Ch'o-dong, Chung-gu*) Ŭlchiro 3-ga subway station

Seoul Cinema Town
(*Map 4,* ☎ *277 3011, 59-7 Kwansu-dong, Chongno-gu*) Chongno 3-ga subway station

Shinch'on
(*Map 9, ☎ 336 9431, 5-21 Ch'angch'on-dong, Sodaemun-gu*) Shinch'on subway station on line 2

Shinch'on Art Hall
(*Map 9, ☎ 393 9183, Sodaemun-gu*) Shinch'on subway station

Shinyŏng
(*Map 9, ☎ 392 4450, 20-25 Ch'angch'on-dong, Sodaemun-gu*) Ewha Women's University subway station on line 2

Tongsung
(*☎ 741 3391, 1-5 Tongsung-dong, Chongno-gu*) exit 1, Hyehwa subway station on line 4

MOVIE CAFES

Movie cafes are a variation on the karaoke-inspired theme of 'interactive TV' – essentially, you are buying booze and food while watching films on a big screen video. There are some great classic western films that occasionally appear, but many of the films shown are from Japan (which means Japanese dialogue with Korean subtitles).

There are quite a few of such places in the Shinch'on area (see the earlier Nightlife Zones section). Most movie cafes have a published schedule of films.

THEATRE

Seoul has an amazingly large collection of drama theatres (*sogŭk jang*), especially in the student-oriented Taehangno area.

Unfortunately for non-Korean speakers, the dialogue at these performances is almost entirely in Korean. If you're still keen, KNTO should have a monthly schedule of theatrical events, particularly of those rare performances in English. The local Korean-language newspapers will also have listings of what's on in town. Admission prices are typically around W10,000 to W20,000.

Munye Theatre (Map 6)

The largest of the theatres in the Taehangno area is *Munye Theatre (☎ 760 4800)*. There are many smaller theatres in the vicinity, but it's worth getting an idea of the venue and checking prices first – some places tend to charge steep admission despite sardine-sized facilities.

Hoam Art Hall (Map 3)

This site is a general performing arts centre equipped with up-to-date facilities, with a seating capacity of 1000. Shows on offer include modern and classical dance and music. Films are also shown here. You can ring (*☎ 751 9614*) for information.

Hoam Art Hall occupies the 1st and 2nd floors of the Chung-ang Daily News building at 7 Sunhwa-dong, Chung-gu. Take subway line 2 to City Hall station – the building is on the south-east corner of Sŏso-munno and Ŭijuro.

Post Theatre (Map 9)

This is the largest theatre in the fashionable Shinch'on-Hongik University area. Unfortunately, all the acts are Korean-language only.

TRADITIONAL ARTS

Koreans energetically preserve their traditional culture and are keen to make it accessible to the outside world. Shows on offer may include a drum dance, *salp'uri* (shaman exorcism dance), *t'aep'yong-mu* (court dance), *kanggangsu-wollae* (circle dance), fan dance, mask dance, *shinawi* (an ensemble of eight traditional musical instruments) and other variations on the theme.

To check the times and places of cultural performances, look in the daily English-language newspapers and the tourist literature. KNTO can give you the latest scoop on the more well known venues.

Sejong Cultural Centre (Map 4)

Sejong Cultural Centre (☎ 399 1576) holds performances every Saturday from 3 to 5 pm, often including western-style symphony orchestras. There is seating for 522 persons, and admission costs W3000. The centre is a three minute walk from Kwangh-wamun station on subway line 5.

Seoul Nori Madang (Map 2)

Seoul Nori Madang (☎ 414 1985) lays on the culture with colourful performances typically including folk dancing, drum dancing and occasional martial arts displays. Best of all, admission is free.

ENTERTAINMENT

Performances take place on Saturday, Sunday and holidays from April to October. In April and October show time is from 2 to 6 pm. In May and September it's from 3 to 5 pm. For June, July and August it's from 5 to 7 pm.

Seoul Nori Madang is in Songp'a-gu, a 10 minute walk from Chamshil station on subway line 2.

National Theatre (Map 3)

The *National Theatre* (☎ 274 3507) is at the foot of Namsan in central Seoul. It consists of a grand theatre (1518 seats), a small theatre (454 seats) and an outdoor theatre. Shows are held every Saturday from 6 to 7.30 pm, and admission is free. There is also a ballet on the last Friday of every month at 7.30 pm – the cost is W3000. There are some extra shows in summer – check with KNTO for the latest schedule.

The closest subway station is Dongguk University on line 3 – it's either a 15 minute walk from there or take the shuttle bus that stops in front of the subway station.

Seoul Arts Centre (Map 2)

The *Seoul Arts Centre* (☎ 580 1250) is a massive four storey complex. It is divided into several sections, including the Music Hall (Concert Hall and Recital Hall), Calligraphy Hall, Art Gallery, Arts Library and Opera House.

The *Korean Traditional Performing Arts Centre* (☎ 585 0153) is part of the Seoul Arts Complex, but is in a complex further to the west of the main buildings. There are performances here every Saturday from 5 to 6.20 pm. Admission to the 500 seat theatre costs W5000.

The *National Classical Music Institute* (☎ 585 3131) is also part of the Seoul Arts Centre. The Seoul Arts Centre is a 15 minute walk (or a five minute shuttle bus ride) from Nambu Bus Terminal subway station on line 3.

Chŏngdong Theatre (Map 5)

Chŏngdong Theatre (☎ 773 8960) was opened in 1995. It was meant to be a replica of Wongaksa, which was built in 1908 and regarded as the first modern Korean theatre. Chŏngdong Theatre stages modern and traditional performances.

There are shows every Tuesday and Friday from 7.30 to 9 pm. Chŏngdong Theatre is behind Tŏksugung, a five minute walk from City Hall station on subway line 1 or 2. Tickets cost W15,000 to W25,000.

Munhwa Ilbo Hall (Map 3)

This hall (☎ 3701 5757) shares a building with the *Kyonghyang Daily News* and is just a 15 minute walk from City Hall station. Traditional music and dances are performed here at the beginning of each year as part of a program organised by Munhwa Broadcasting Corporation (MBC). Seating is provided for 1700 persons.

Theatre Restaurants

At Seoul's theatre restaurants you can enjoy power dining while viewing a traditional-style Korean floor show. The most famous restaurant in this class is *Sanch'on (Map 4,* ☎ *735 0312)*. Sanch'on specialises in vegetarian cuisine, which probably has something to do with the fact that the proprietor spent 18 years as a Buddhist monk. The W25,000 special full course allows you to sample 15 courses. There are traditional dance performances every evening from 8 to 9 pm to the haunting twings and twangs of mysterious Korean instruments. Seating is by way of cushions on the floor (which can be tough on the back). Sanch'on is down a small alley off Insadong-gil.

Arirang (Map 4) is adjacent to Sanch'on and offers a similar deal, the main difference being that the meals contain meat.

A more upmarket version of the same thing is *Korea House (Map 3,* ☎ *266 9101)*. It has seating for 170 persons, making it one of Seoul's largest theatre restaurants. Dance performances are held here, and it is possible to make a booking for the performance alone (W21,200). A better deal is the combination show and buffet meal (W27,800). There are also pricier full-course *hanjŏngshik* (Korean banquet) meals costing up to

ROBERT STOREY

ROBERT STOREY

ROBERT STOREY

ROBERT STOREY

Open-air artistic licence is expressed on Taehangno (top left), also known as 'Arts & Culture Street'. Various venues at Seoul Grand Park are also home to modern statuary and sculpture.

T'apkol Park (formerly called Pagoda Park) in central Seoul is a popular spot for the city's seniors to put on a show (top right and bottom). More formal traditional song and dance can be found at the Korean Folk Village near Suwon.

The Kimch'i jars lining courtyards and alleys everywhere in Seoul hold the secrets to Korean cuisine.

T'aewon meets your everyday shopping needs.

Artsy Insa-dong is not immune to kitsch.

Koryŏ Dynasty-style celadon and other ceramics crowd an Insa-dong street.

Standard-issue mega-stores and shopping mall society have made inroads in the city, but the centre of public life remains the vibrant and diverse markets, where everything has a personal touch.

W66,300. From April to November, performances are scheduled twice in the evening from 7 to 8 pm and from 8.40 to 9.40 pm. The rest of the year, performances are once nightly from 8.30 to 9.30 pm. The restaurant is also open for lunch from noon to 2 pm, but there is no performance then. Korea House is at the foot of Namsan in central Seoul, and is open every day. Take subway lines 3 or 4 to Ch'ungmuro station.

Kayagŭm (Map 2, ☎ 453 0121) is in the Sheraton Walker Hill Hotel. The restaurant is named after the *kayagŭm*, a traditional 12-stringed zither, and performances are given twice daily, at 5 and 7.30 pm. Rates for a 'special' dinner are W65,000; regular dinners are W53,000. The champagne show costs W40,000. The Sheraton Walker Hill Hotel is far in the eastern end of Seoul; the nearest subway station is Kwangnaru on line 5.

Kŭmsujang (Map 3, ☎ 273 4445), is in the Sofitel Ambassador Hotel. There are folk dance performances every evening, but they are shown in two parts with an intermission in between. The first part is performed from 6 to 6.50 pm, and the second from 7.40 to 8.30 pm. The hotel-restaurant is a three minute walk from Dongguk University station on subway line 3.

Pan Korea (Map 4, ☎ 267 6105), 101-1 Ŭlchiro 2-ga, Chung-gu, does performances of folk songs, and traditional and modern dance. Shows are more or less continuous from 6 pm until midnight. The nearest subway station is Ŭlchiro 3-ga.

FOREIGN CULTURAL CENTRES

Seoul's various foreign cultural centres often have videos for rent, along with occasional events such as stage dramas, parties and cooking classes. For information, contact the following:

British Cultural Centre
   (Map 4, ☎ 737 7157) 3-7 Chŏng-dong, Chongno-gu; next to Tŏksugung
French Cultural Centre
   (☎ 734 9768) 70 Sagan-dong, Chongno-gu, east side of Kyŏngbokkung

Goethe Institut
   (Map 5, ☎ 754 9831) 339-1 Huam-dong, Yongsan-gu; a short walk south of Namsan public library
Italian Cultural Centre
   (☎ 796 0634) 1-37 Hannam-dong, Yongsan-gu
Japanese Cultural Centre
   (Map 4, ☎ 765 3011) 114-8 Unni-dong, Chongno-gu; near Anguk subway station on line 3

ROCK CONCERTS

Concerts feature both local Korean bands and big-name groups from western countries. The venue most often used is the indoor gymnastic stadium at *Olympic Park* (Map 2). Check the newspapers and KNTO to see what's coming up.

CASINOS

The only forms of legal gambling available to the average Korean is the national lottery (tickets can be bought everywhere) and horse racing (see the Seoul Horse Race Track section in the Excursions chapter).

The situation is different for foreigners, who are invited to part with their cash at *Casino Paradise*, inside the Sheraton Walker Hill Hotel (Map 2) – it's Seoul's only casino. It is open 24 hours a day, seven days a week. As well as all the gambling options you would expect of a casino, Casino Paradise has risque floor shows which are a pale shadow of those in Las Vegas. The floor shows are staged twice every evening at 4.30 and 7.30 pm, and you can ring up *(☎ 450 4554)* for reservations.

VIDEO ARCADES

Video arcades *(orakshil)* are to be found scattered throughout the city. Ask any local teenager where to find one.

SPECTATOR SPORTS
Baseball

Baseball *(yagu)* is big in South Korea and teams are sponsored by the leading *chaebŏl* (business cartels). Seoul's two teams are the OB Bears and the LG Twins. Other notable teams include the Samsung Lions and the Lotte Giants.

Baseball season is roughly from April to October. Games are held in the ***Olympic Stadium*** (Map 7) in the Seoul Sports Complex and at ***Tongdaemun Stadium*** (Map 3). Tickets cost between W2000 and W4000 depending on the seat.

Basketball

Basketball *(nonggu)* also has a devoted following in Korea, and is one of the few spectator sports which can be played in winter. The Korea Basketball League permits each team to have two foreign players, most of whom are Americans. Again, the chaebŏl are big sponsors, with teams like the LG Sakers and SK Knights.

During the season, games are broadcast live on TV. You can go to see the real thing at the ***Olympic Stadium*** (Map 7) in Chamshil and at ***Changch'ung Gymnasium*** (Map 3).

Soccer

Soccer *(ch'uggu)* is big in South Korea; indeed, the country hosts the World Cup in the year 2002, though go part of the competition will also be hosted in Japan. As with baseball, chaebŏl sponsor the major soccer

teams, such as the Hyundai Horang-E, the LG Cheetahs, the Daewoo Royals and the Yukong Elephants.

Soccer season is from April to November. Matches are mostly held at the ***Olympic Stadium*** (Map 7) in Chamshil.

Ssirŭm

To the outsider, *ssirŭm* looks much like the Korean version of Japanese *sumo* wrestling, though it would be best to never let a Korean hear you say this – Korean wrestling most likely derives from its Mongolian cousin to the north-west, not from its eastern islands neighbour.

Unlike sumo, in which the aim is to toss the opponent out of the ring, a win is declared when any part of the opponent's body other than the feet touches the ground. Ssirŭm wrestlers also have more muscle and sinew than sumo wrestlers. The most important matches are held during major national holidays such as Ch'usŏk and the Tano festival. For more information about tournaments, contact the Korea Amateur Sport Association (☎ 420 3333, 888 Oryundong, Songp'a-gu).

Shopping

If you're dreaming of finding such great bargains in Seoul that a shopping expedition will pay for your entire trip, then you are dreaming indeed. The reality is that with the exception of a few locally made products, Korea is generally no cheaper than the west.

This doesn't mean that shopping in Seoul is a waste of time. Aside from the fact that buying things can be fun, the chances are good that you'll wind up with a number of speciality items you could never find at home (wherever that may be).

If it's bargains you're after, Seoul's main strength is in Korean-produced consumer goods such as clothing, shoes and leather goods. Although the Korean design and fashion industry hasn't set the world on fire, the quality of these goods is generally excellent and it's even possible to order something custom-made. However, Seoul really shines in exotic items, such as ginseng, herbal teas, arts and crafts, special interest books, Korean music tapes etc.

When you're shopping for clothes and shoes, the onus is on you to check that the goods are authentic. Brand-name shoes (Reebok, Adidas etc) in particular may be counterfeit. While the counterfeit goods may look just as good as the originals, quality is almost certainly inferior. This may not be a serious problem if you're just buying a T-shirt, but bad quality shoes tend to be uncomfortable and wear out very quickly. Remember that if a price sounds too good to be true, it probably is. Some of the more unscrupulous shops in Namdaemun Market may charge you brand-name prices for fake goods.

Finally, if you wish to return or exchange an item, it's best not to do so in the morning when the shop first opens. Many Korean shop owners believe that the first customer to walk in the shop sets the pace for the entire day – it's bad luck if this customer wants to return something.

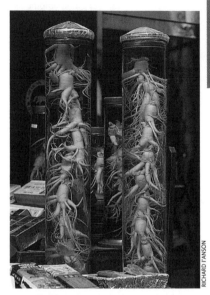

RICHARD I'ANSON

Ginseng is claimed to be the root of all health.

WHAT TO BUY

Seoul's markets are an embarrassment of riches, which makes it hard to understand the government's ceaseless campaigns to get the Koreans to 'reduce consumption'. Perhaps what they really mean is 'reduce consumption of foreign-made products'.

You will find, of course, that there are many foreign-made products around, but the best deals are on Korean-made goods. What follows is just a small sample of the many possibilities available.

Arts, Crafts & Antiques

Insa-dong, Namdaemun, Tongdaemun, Changan-dong and It'aewon all have a wide selection of arts, crafts and antiques ranging from touristy junk to real collector's items. When shopping upmarket for real antiques, bear in mind that the Cultural Properties

Preservation Law forbids the export of 'important cultural properties'. If you suspect that something you've bought or wish to buy falls into this category, it should be assessed by the Art & Antiques Assessment Office (☎ 662 0106). Unless huge amounts of money are changing hands, this is unlikely to be a problem.

Popular antique purchases include ceramics. It is still possible to find examples dating from the Koryŏ Dynasty (918-1392), and chests and furniture from the Chosŏn Dynasty (1392-1910). You can find shops specialising in excellent reproductions of these antiques in the Insa-dong area.

Excellent arts-and-crafts purchases include brassware, lacquerware, silk macrame (*maedŭup*), masks, fans, bamboo-ware and dolls in traditional costume. The best area to purchase these items is Insa-dong, though there are several shops specialising in arts and crafts in It'aewon too. The advantage of shopping in Insa-dong is that there is less pressure to make a purchase, and the sheer number of shops provides more choice.

Namdaemun Market also has a limited selection of crafts and souvenirs. A pricier possibility is one of the big department stores such as Lotte.

Bookshops

Seoul has a number of excellent everything-under-one-roof bookshops. You'll occasionally find some books and magazines in French, German or Japanese, but by far the largest collections of imported publications are in English.

Visiting during the work day is advised – the bookshops can be chock-a-block on weekends and holidays. Although there have not as yet been any big disasters, most of these bookshops look like real fire traps – they're too large, too crowded and have too few exits.

The best places in the city to pick up English-language books are:

Chongno Book Centre (Map 4, ☎ 733 2331)
City Book (Map 7)
Kyobo Book Centre (Map 4, ☎ 397 3500)

Royal Asiatic Society (Map 3, ☎ 763 9483)
Seoul Book Centre (Map 7, ☎ 553 3038)
Ŭlchi Book Centre (Map 5, ☎ 757 8991)
Youngpoong Bookshop (Map 4, ☎ 399 5600)

Determining which one of these is the best depends mostly on what sort of books you're looking for.

Kyobo is the largest, and even boasts an English information desk with staff who really do speak English. Aside from books and magazines, this mammoth store sells CDs, tapes, stationery, clocks, calculators and cutesy items like slogan-bearing coffee mugs and T-shirts. On the downside, prices tend to be higher here than elsewhere, and it's impossible to make a special order. Few people have good things to say about the in-house coffee shop (instant coffee, taste-free donuts) – if you need a break between browsing, go elsewhere. The bookshop (actually an underground arcade) is next to Kwanghwamun subway station on line 5.

Youngpoong has a good collection of paperback novels and English-teaching materials at reduced prices. If you're into fast food, there is a Hardee's hamburger joint inside the bookshop.

Ŭlchi has a good collection of computer books and the friendly manager will do special orders. The bookshop is almost hidden in the bowels of Ŭlchiro 1-ga subway station, just next to Lotte department store.

Many visitors have a love-hate relationship with Chongno Book Centre, which is opposite the YMCA. The store is a multi-level fire trap that is difficult even to walk through – sometimes a few hundred people simultaneously try to cram through the same narrow staircase that serves the whole windowless building. Another complication is that to save space in this very crammed store, many of the bookshelves are mounted on wheels – sliding one of these (very heavy) shelves to the right or left will reveal hundreds of otherwise hidden books! Despite these annoyances, you can find books here that no other store in Korea will stock. The computer book collection is a gold mine – it's probably the best in Asia.

The Seoul Book Centre has little to recommend it other than except that it's the best bookshop on the south side of the Han River. You'll find it in the underground arcade of the Korea World Trade Centre (KWTC). Take subway line 2 to Samsŏng station.

Even worse than the foregoing is City Book, in a basement near Kangnam subway station on line 2. Its only redeeming feature is the magazine collection which – though very complete – is overpriced. In other words, if you want good books, you need to shop in central Seoul, not Kangnam.

The Royal Asiatic Society (RAS) has the widest selection of books on Korea, but nothing on other topics. The staff will happily provide you with a stool to do your browsing in comfort. Members receive a 10% discount. Another drawcard is that the RAS puts out a publications' list providing information on virtually every book relevant to Korea. You'll find the RAS in room 611, Korean Christian building on Tae-hangno. It's open Monday to Friday from 10 am to noon and 2 to 5 pm.

Seoul's major bookshops are open from 10 am to 9 pm on weekdays, or until 8 pm on Sunday and holidays. Kyobo and Ŭlchi bookshops are closed every 2nd and 4th Sunday; Seoul Book Centre is closed on the 2nd Sunday.

Cameras & Film

Seoul is actually a terrible place to buy camera equipment, thanks to a hefty government tax which pushes prices into the stratosphere. The steep taxes may have something to do with the fact that most of the world's cameras are made in Japan, a country not exactly viewed with affection by Koreans. Another reason, no doubt, is to protect Korea's *chaebŏl* (business conglomerates) who also make cameras.

One benefit of the stiff import tax is that it has led to a large and robust market for second-hand cameras and lenses in Seoul. As a result, you do see some ancient leftovers that have disappeared elsewhere. Where else can you easily pick up an old Leica, Hasselbad, Minox or Rollei? However,

Seoul's camera vendors are no fools – they realise that these old cameras are collectors' items and charge accordingly. Still, it's worth checking out if you have a fondness for 1950s technology.

Most of the shops are very small, crowded with equipment and scattered about the city. It'aewon (Map 8) is a good place to shop for cameras, as is the area between T'apkol Park and Chongmyo Plaza on Chongno (Map 4). Also check out the underground arcades around subway stations – the Ŭlchiro Underground Arcade (Map 5) near City Hall and the Hoehyŏn Underground Arcade (Map 5) near the Central Post Office (CPO) have good selections.

Print and slide film are widely available in Seoul. Koreans mostly buy colour print film, which means that slide film and B&W print film can sit on the shelves for eons gathering dust – check the expiration dates before you buy. Same-day and one hour processing for print film is widely available and relatively inexpensive.

Clothes & Shoes

The main centre for clothes and shoes is It'aewon (Map 8). For the sheer convenience of being able to use English on this shopping strip, try things on and check out different shops – it's often worth paying a few dollars more here than you would have done in the markets.

Namdaemun (Map 5) and Tongdaemun (Map 3) markets are also good for clothes, but counterfeit goods abound.

In the clothing department, Seoul offers good deals on everything from three-piece suits to jogging gear. There are numerous tailors specialising in custom suits in the It'aewon area, but these receive mixed reports. The quality is reasonably high, but prices aren't fantastic and you'd best hang around until the final product is completed rather than have it shipped home. There is also the possibility that the final product will require a slight alteration – obviously, this is best accomplished if you are physically present in Seoul.

Hanbok

Until western-style clothing arrived in the 19th century, the brightly coloured *hanbok* was worn by both men and women. Today, only women wear these and only for formal occasions. The hanbok is a very conservative garment – it's floor-length and very baggy, deliberately designed to hide the woman's figure. On seeing a woman dressed in hanbok for the first time, many westerners assume that she is pregnant! Be assured that this is not generally the case, and it would be a major *faux pas* on your part to 'congratulate' her (she might not even be married!). If you have any desire to take home a hanbok as a souvenir, be aware that they are generally custom-made and rather expensive.

Eel-Skin Products

Many shops sell eel-skin wallets, belts, handbags, shoes and boots. Eel-skin enthusiasts claim that the leather is long-lasting and supple.

Electronics

Prices for imported Japanese electronics in Seoul are not competitive with Hong Kong and Singapore, but Korean-made stereos can be very reasonably priced. More importantly, you may find a locally made speciality item that particularly suits your needs. For example, Korean-language software and computer keyboards (which sport *han'gŭl* characters) are certainly useful if you plan to work with this language.

Ginseng

Seoul is the ginseng *(insam)* capital of the world, and for many Asians it is a magical cure-all and aphrodisiac. Japanese and Chinese tourists buy as much of the stuff as they can get their hands on. To protect the tourists from their own raging hormones (and also to protect its lucrative export monopoly)

the ever-paternalistic government has restrictions on how much an individual can take out of the country (3kg in its raw state).

There are two kinds of ginseng: red ginseng, which is sold under a government monopoly with strict quality controls; and white ginseng, which is privately cultivated and treated. Both kinds are fine, but red ginseng has more health claims going for it and is significantly more expensive.

It is possible to buy ginseng in a number of forms – in its raw state in the markets, dried, capsules, tea, powder or as an extract paste. The tea (in foil packets) is generally white ginseng and is easiest to carry while travelling. The extract paste is the best deal for red ginseng – one tiny bottle of the stuff will make dozens of cups of tea.

One of the best areas to look for ginseng is in the shops bordering the northern edge of the massive, covered Tongdaemun Market (Map 3) on Chongno. There are also numerous shops specialising in ginseng on the northern outskirts of the Myŏng-dong shopping area (Map 5).

Herbal Teas

Ginseng is not the only herb the Koreans use, even though it's the most famous. If you like the many delicious kinds of herbal teas served at teahouses, there's no reason why you can't bring some home. This stuff is sold cheaply in foil packets at almost any supermarket in Seoul. Some personal favourites are ginger tea *(saengkang ch'a)* and spicy herbal tea *(ssanghwa ch'a)*.

Jewellery

The stones most used in jewellery in South Korea are amethyst, smoky topaz and jade. All the big department stores carry this stuff, but you can find it cheaper in places like Namdaemun Market (Map 5) and It'aewon (Map 8) – but beware of fakes. Don't expect any enormous bargains on items like gold and diamonds – Korean jewellers know the international price of gold, and Korea does not have a diamond-cutting industry.

If you buy something expensive and authentic, you can request a certificate of authenticity – a refusal to issue one should make you pause.

Bracelets, necklaces and rings are ubiquitously displayed in tourist haunts like It'aewon and the major hotels. Quality varies from excellent to something that could turn your neck, wrist or finger green. Visitors are most enthusiastic about carvings and necklaces made with the local white jade.

Music Tapes & CDs

Musicland (Map 4, ☎ 278 2422, 268 9832), 48-1 Chongno 2-ga, is probably the best source of CDs in Korea. The selection is large, prices are low and all the CDs are well organised for browsing. You'll find Musicland in the basement of the towering ELS building on Chongno 2-ga.

The basement of Metro Midopa department store (Map 5) has one of the best collections for CD buyers, and prices are good. Unfortunately, the CDs are poorly organised and it's difficult to find what you're looking for.

Kyobo Book Centre (Map 4) also has an excellent assortment of music CDs and tapes at good prices. Youngpoong Bookshop (Map 4) also has good prices on CDs but the selection is limited.

Tower Records (☎ 552 0460) has one of the widest selections of CDs in Seoul, but prices are very high. There are two stores: the central branch (Map 4) is near T'apkol Park close to Chongno 2-ga in the centre; the southern branch (Map 7) is near Kangnam station on subway line 2 (almost adjacent to the New York Bakery).

Street vendors plugging music tapes set up shop in various night markets (look for them along Chongno in the YMCA area). It's not hard to find them – indeed, you'd have a difficult time escaping the infernal music that they blast to attract customers. Prices are low and most people claim the tapes are pirated (though the vendors insist this is not so). Legal or not, the music selection is small, but buying here has one advantage – you can *sometimes* listen to the tapes before paying for them.

Name Chops

When Korea adopted the Chinese writing system, it also borrowed the concept of a name chop *(tojang)*, or seal. The traditional name chop has been in use in China for thousands of years.

Until recent times, all official documents in both Korea and China needed to be stamped with a chop to be valid. Today, most Koreans have abandoned the use of Chinese characters, preferring the much simpler han'gŭl system. Furthermore, the use of chops as a valid signature on legal documents is now optional in Korea. Nevertheless, traditions die hard – Korean mail carriers, for example, still ask for your chop when they deliver a registered letter. You will find plenty of shops in Korea which carve name chops using highly decorative Chinese characters, though you can indeed have one carved in han'gŭl. Only red ink is used when stamping your 'signature' with a name chop.

There are many different sizes and styles of chops available with prices to match. Inexpensive small chops can be carved from wood or plastic for about W2000 or so. Chops costing W50,000 and up can be carved from jade, marble or steel. Of course, you will first need to have your name translated into han'gŭl or Chinese characters.

Silk

The place to buy silk and silk brocades is Tongdaemun Market (Map 3) next to Tongdaemun gate. The more inexpensive varieties are likely to be mixed with synthetics.

WHERE TO SHOP
Arcades

Underground Sometimes it seems like half of central Seoul is underground. You'll find when exploring the central city area on foot that you are constantly being forced underground to cross busy intersections. Many of these underpasses connect with the subway system and the underground arcades. Exploring the underground arcades at least offers you refuge from Seoul's maddening traffic, and it is a nice way to do some walking when there is a blizzard or pouring rain.

Mostly, the arcades are warrens of small hole-in-the-wall restaurants, CD outlets, bookshops and clothing shops. Camera supplies and electronic goods are also widely available, and there is even the odd ginseng shop.

The longest arcade (though not necessarily the best) in town is the Úlchiro Underground Arcade (Maps 3 & 5), which runs from City Hall all the way to Tongdaemun Stadium (almost 3km) following subway line 2. Smaller but more colourful arcades in the central area (Maps 4 & 5) include Chongno (at Chonggak subway station on line 1), Lotte (by the Lotte department store), Sogong (which connects to Lotte), Myŏng-dong (which connects to Sogong), Hoehyŏn (near the CPO) and Namdaemun (near Saerona department store).

The Samsung Underground Plaza is a new trendy subterranean mall which features cinemas, the Rodin Art Gallery and a cybercafe. It's beneath the Samsung building, which is about half way between City Hall and Namdaemun gate. It's open from 11 am to 8 pm.

Above-Ground One place little visited by tourists is an arcade running above ground for four blocks in a straight north-south line. The northern end of the arcade is across the street from Chongmyo Plaza (Map 3), just east of the Chongno 3-ga subway station on lines 1, 3 and 5. The southern end is close to Ch'ungmuro subway station on lines 3 and 4.

The arcade changes its name on each block, so from north to south it is known as the Seun, Taerim, Samp'ung and Shinsŏng arcades. The northernmost arcade, Seun, is the one that has the widest appeal – the specialty is electronics and home appliances. The remaining arcades specialise in hardware, everything from lawn mowers to jackhammers.

Unfortunately, the arcade is not aesthetically pleasing, and the items sold here make unlikely tourist souvenirs. However, if you're

an expat waging a do-it-yourself home repair war, this is the place to choose your weapons. Also note that a jackhammer can be a great tool for getting even with a noisy neighbour.

The arcade operates from around 9 am to 8 pm, though some shops close earlier. Everything is shut down on the 2nd and 4th Sunday of each month.

One other above-ground arcade that might be worth a quick look is the Nakwon Elevated Arcade (Map 4), just north of T'apkol Park. Musical instruments are a specialty here. On the east side of the arcade (but not in it) are a number of shops selling the most exotic-looking rice cakes you'll ever see. The nearest subway station is Chongno 3-ga.

Areas

It'aewon (Map 8) Although well known as the sleaze centre of Seoul, It'aewon is rather interesting for shopping. If there's a market for it among foreigners in Seoul, the shopkeepers of It'aewon will have thought of it. Prices here are also amazingly low, but bargaining is *de rigueur*. It's advisable to complete your shopping expedition during daylight hours – It'aewon is not the best place to be after dark.

Shopkeepers in It'aewon are happy to quote prices to you in either *won* or US dollars, and will usually also accept payment in either currency. Paying in US dollars won't make things any cheaper, though.

It's important to take your time and do a bit of careful sifting through the mountains of junk. There's an awful lot of detritus here that's cheap and could win bad-taste awards, particularly when it comes to souvenirs. Need a glow-in-the-dark Buddha with the words 'Seoul, Korea' emblazoned on his forehead? Or one of those nasty 'whoopie cushions' that emit foul noises when you sit on them? If so, It'aewon is the place to stock up.

It'aewon is effectively just one street of wall-to-wall shops, bars, restaurants and short-time hotels. Most of the side alleys also contain shops, and it's worth exploring some of these, but for the most part the best shopping is on the main drag.

Leather jackets are an It'aewon speciality. A perennial favourite among military services staff and tourists alike are the leather bomber jackets (bombs not included). Leather jackets, depending on the leather used and the quality of the work, average between US$60 and US$100. There are, of course, many other kinds of jackets and coats.

There is quite a range of prices for Nikes and Reeboks depending on the type of shoe. Prices start as low as US$30 for cross trainers and range up to US$100 for basketball boots. Beware of fakes.

It'aewon sells T-shirts, often with unusual slogans ('North Korea – where's the beef?'). Ditto for slogan-enhanced coffee mugs and sarcastic messages to hang over your desk or attach to the rear bumper of your car ('My take-home pay won't take me home', and so on).

South Korea is one place where the fur industry continues its operations uninterrupted by any public outcry, and It'aewon offers bargain prices for cuddly animal skins if you're game to take them home – though you wouldn't want to do that, would you?

Insa-dong (Map 4) Many of the arts and crafts in this area are outlandishly priced, but it pays to poke around for a while. It's usually possible to come up with some small, tasteful oddity without breaking your budget. Some of the speciality items in this neighbourhood include ceramics, calligraphy tools and paper, Korean-style storage chests (some of which are stunning), old herbal medicine cabinets studded with tiny labelled drawers, antiquated coins and hand-crafted masks.

For details on Insa-dong, see its entry in the Things to See & Do chapter.

Myŏng-dong (Map 5) Myŏng-dong is Seoul's trendiest central shopping district, reminiscent of Tokyo's Ginza. The narrow streets are lined with fashion boutiques, CD outlets, coffee shops and very tiny eateries. Rents are so high here that most shops cannot turn a profit – fast-food chains keep a small money-losing branch here simply for the sake of advertising their hamburgers and French fries.

Apkujŏng (Map 7) On the south side of the Han River is Apkujŏng, the trendy fashion district that rivals Myŏng-dong. Prices here tend to be quite high – Seoul's well heeled class doesn't seem to notice and business is booming.

To reach Apkujŏng, take subway line 3 to Apkujŏng station. To find the fashion boutiques, walk along Apkujŏngno.

Rodeo Shopping St (Map 2) Also on Han-gang's south side is the new Rodeo Shopping St (not to be confused with Rodeo St in Apkujŏng). Rodeo Shopping St is great for brand names (Nike, Adidas, Timberland, Fila, The North Face, Abercrombie & Fitch etc), and prices seem to be very good.

To find it, take subway line 8 to Munjŏng station (two stops after Songp'a station) and follow the signs in the subway for 'Rodeo'.

Markets

Namdaemun Market (Map 5) Namdaemun Market draws in large numbers of foreign tourists due to its central location near the CPO. As a result, there are some good souvenir items on sale (pottery, baskets, trinkets etc). Nevertheless, Namdaemun is primarily a local market catering for a Korean clientele, so much of what's on sale is geared towards household needs (eg you can stockpile ingredients for making kimch'i). If you fancy metal chopsticks, Namdaemun may well be the best place in the world to stock up.

If you've already been to It'aewon, it's a good idea to look out for things you've seen there and compare prices. This is particularly true of clothing. Many of the shops in It'aewon buy their goods here and resell them at inflated prices. If you do buy any clothes and need them altered, there are elderly ladies lurking in the alleyways who will do your alterations while you wait.

There is a good range of camping equipment available, mostly at the southern boundary of the market adjacent to Hoehyŏn station on subway line 4. There are also sections for touristy handicrafts, and locals claim the market is an excellent place to buy children's clothing.

Namdaemun Market can be photogenic, but be cautious about hot-tempered vendors who don't like to be models. One fellow we know was attacked with a basket and treated to a shower of verbal abuse for taking a photograph of a bowl of beans (very sensitive about their beans, the Koreans are).

How much you enjoy Namdaemun depends on how you feel about crowds. If you need lots of space while you leisurely try on jackets and sweaters, you'd better stick to It'aewon. On the other hand, Namdaemun is certainly one place where you can (literally) rub elbows with the masses.

Namdaemun Market is directly to the east of Namdaemun gate. The market is closed on Sunday, though a few shops stay open.

Tongdaemun Market (Map 3) Tongdaemun is the largest market in Korea. Unlike Namdaemun (which is an open-air market), Tongdaemun is enclosed and can be armpit to armpit with boisterous Korean shoppers. This gives you even less room to manoeuvre than at Namdaemun. You won't get a chance to indulge in the luxury of leisurely bargaining here, but prices are lower than in It'aewon. Indeed, most of the goods that end up in It'aewon shops started out at Tongdaemun.

Tongdaemun is more like a multi-level warehouse than a shopping centre. There are sections specialising in everything from gardening seeds to hazardous chemicals. There has just got to be something you need in this mega-size maze of stalls and hole-in-the-wall shops, provided that you've got the endurance to persevere. The main problem is dealing with the crowds.

Tongdaemun is one good place to pick up a new backpack or any other type of camping and hiking gear. Check out the standard 'uniform' of Korean hikers, a red vest worn with 'mountain shorts' and flashy knee-high socks.

One part of Tongdaemun is devoted entirely to displays of materials for making *hanbok*, the traditional Korean dress for women (and very rarely nowadays, men). Many shopkeepers set up searing lights to bring out the best in the brilliant colours of their cloths. It's fun wandering through this area and watching prospective brides measuring up lengths of material and haggling over prices.

Reaching Tongdaemun is easy – just hop on subway line 1 or 4 to Tongdaemun station. The market is closed on the 1st and 3rd Sunday of every month.

Kyŏngdong Market (Map 2) There are about 1000 stalls in this market. Its speciality is herbal medicines which include everything from ginseng to dried sea horses. One alley also specialises in spices – enthusiasts of Korean food may want to stock up on chilli powder and try their hand at creating homemade kimch'i.

Kyŏngdong Market is open from 7 am to 7 pm daily, except the 1st and 3rd Sunday of every month. It's very close to Chegidong station near the eastern end of subway line 1.

Hwanghak-dong Flea Market (Map 2) This market is perhaps the most important shopping area for newly arrived shoestring travellers interested in setting up in Seoul. Everything from second-hand furniture to used refrigerators can be bought here. You can even pick up a chic second-hand military uniform or army helmet (the bullet holes make for good ventilation).

Vendors here may also be willing to buy second-hand goods from you if you're departing Seoul for good. You might also think of this place as a budget antique market.

The market is east of Tongdaemun. Take subway line 2 to Shindang station and walk north. You will first encounter Chung'ang Market, which basically sells food (even live chickens and dogs). Continue north for another block and you'll find the flea market – if you've passed the elevated roadway then you've gone too far.

International Flea Market (Map 5) An 'international' flea market sets up outside of the popular Chŏngdong Theatre, which is behind Tŏksugung. The market operates only on Saturday and Sunday during the warmer months.

Changhanp'yŏng Antique Market (Map 2) Not everything sold here is in fact antique, but there are plenty of interesting wares that at least look like they could be antiques. Items for sale include calligraphy scrolls, paintings, chests, stone carvings, lacquerware, porcelain vases, tea sets and other ceramics.

Changhanp'yŏng Antique Market is spread out in about 150 shops in six different buildings. It's open from 10 am to 9 pm, closed Sunday. The market is in Tongdaemun-gu; take subway line 5 to Changhanp'yŏng station.

Yejidong Watch & Jewellery Alley (Map 3) If it hasn't occurred to you by now, Seoul has a number of markets which specialise in a particular line of goods. One is Yejidong Watch & Jewellery Alley, which is just west of Kwangjang Market. Take subway line 1 to Chongno 5-ga station.

Stores

Department Stores Seoul is well endowed with enormous multi-storey department stores which are tourist attractions in themselves. These cavernous high-rises are stocked to the skyline with every imaginable consumer item, not to mention restaurants, decorative water fountains and even the odd ice-skating rink. While department stores are not the place to pick up real bargains, they do have the advantage of bringing together a formidable range of goods under one roof. Prices are usually labelled, and this can give you a good indication of the prices you want to undercut when you do some bargaining in the street markets or the shops of It'aewon.

The densest assemblage of large department stores is clustered on the fringes of Myŏng-dong (Map 5). These include Lotte,

Metro Midopa, Shinsegae, Utoo Zone and Printemps department stores.

Opening hours for big department stores are usually from 10.30 am to 7.30 pm, and there is a kind of roster system for the days they are closed. However, more and more stores are switching to a system where they are open daily, so don't be surprised if some of the following information changes:

Galleria
(Map 7, ☎ 15 3131) Kangnam-gu, Apkujŏng station on subway line 2; closed the 1st and 3rd Monday
Grand Mart
(Map 9) Map'o-gu, opposite Shinch'on station on subway line 2
Hyundai
Branch 1 (Map 7, ☎ 320 3000) Kangnam-gu, next to Shinch'on station on subway line 2; Branch 2 (Map 7, ☎ 547 2233) Kangnam-gu, by Apkujŏng station on subway line 3; Branch 3 (Map 7, ☎ 552 2233) Kangnam-gu, next to Korea World Trade Centre by Samsŏng station on subway line 2; closed Monday
Lotte
(Map 5, ☎ 759 8114) Chung-gu, subway line 2 to Ŭlchiro 1-ga station; closed Monday
Lotte World
(Map 2, ☎ 411 2500) Songp'a-gu, Chamshil station on subway line 2; closed Monday
Metro Midopa
(Map 5, ☎ 754 2222) Chung-gu, subway line 2 to Ŭlchiro 1-ga station; open daily
New Core
(Map 7, ☎ 530 5000) Sŏch'o-gu, subway line 3 to the Seoul Express Bus Terminal station; open daily
Printemps
(Map 4, ☎ 773 2111) Chung-gu, between Ŭlchiro 1-ga and Ŭlchiro 3-ga stations; open daily
Saerona
(Map 5, ☎ 778 8171) Chung-gu, subway line 4 to Hoehyŏn station; closed Thursday
Shinsegae
(Map 5, ☎ 754 1234) Chung-gu, subway line 4 to Hoehyŏn station; closed Thursday
Utoo Zone
(Map 5) Chung-gu, subway line 4 to Myŏng-dong station

Mega-Stores Western-style mega-stores (also known as 'hypermarts') offer everyday goods at great prices, but they tend to be located out in the suburbs and are therefore not easily accessible to people who don't have a car. Some charge a membership fee, and much of what's on sale comes in large quantities (care for 10kg of kimch'i?). Mega-stores are normally open daily from 9.30 am to 10 pm.

E-Mart (Map 10, ☎ 901 1234) requires no membership fee and is open from 10.30 am to 10 pm. It's in Tobong-gu at the northern tip of Seoul. Take subway line 4 to Ch'angdong station.

West of Yŏŭido is Price Club (☎ 679 1234) – take subway line 2 or 5 to the Yŏngdŭngp'o-gu Office station (Map 2). Annual membership costs W30,000.

On the south side of the Han River is Kim's Club (Map 7, ☎ 530 5704) – take subway line 3 to the Express Bus Terminal station. The membership fee is W30,000.

Makro (☎ 0344-910 1114) is north-west of Seoul in the suburb of Koyang. It's a five minute walk from Chuyŏp station on subway line 3. Membership costs W15,000 annually.

Duty-Free Shops In most cases you're better off avoiding Seoul's duty-free shops. The items for sale are nearly identical to those available in almost any other duty-free shop around the world. Don't expect any great bargains either. However, it may be worth taking a quick look – possibly a camera without tax will be cheaper than one purchased on the heavily taxed local market. Ditto for pricey perfumes, macadamia nuts from Hawaii and various other prestige items with French-Italian names like Pierre Cardin, Nina Ricci, Gucci and Yves Saint Laurent. You can get a non-Korean tobacco and alcohol fix relatively cheaply, though. The duty-free shops also do ginseng products, though prices are significantly higher than in Seoul's plush department stores.

There are eight duty-free shops in town, plus another at the airport and at the international ferry pier in Inch'ŏn. The catch is that you don't get your hands on your duty-free goods until you are in the departure lounge of Kimp'o airport. In other words, it's pay now, receive later. So if you purchase a duty-free camera, you can't use it until after you've left Korea. That also means you won't be able to exchange the camera if it's not working properly. In fact, the duty-free shops offer little in the way of practical items (like cameras) – mostly, it's brand-label gift items with snob appeal.

The large Donghwa Duty-Free Shop (Map 4, ☎ 399 3100) is in the basement of the Donghwa building near the Koreana Hotel, and seems to do a thriving business. Hotels in town with duty-free shops include the Hotel Lotte, Hotel Lotte World, Poongjeon Hotel, Sheraton Walker Hill, Hotel Shilla and the Hilton Hotel (Hanjin Duty-Free Shop).

Electronics Shops Without a doubt, the premier place to go for computers and other electronic items is the Yongsan Electronics Arcade (Map 2). Part of this burgeoning market is in one enormous building (a former bus terminal), but the market now spills out into many side-streets as well. In total, there are over 5000 shops in 21 buildings. Take subway line 1 to Yongsan station and follow the elevated walkway over the tracks. You can also take subway line 4 to Shinyongsan station and walk through the underpass. Most shops operate from about 10 am to 8 pm. The market is closed on the 1st and 3rd Sunday of every month.

Similar to these is Techno Mart (Map 2), a 10 storey mall crammed with electronic shops. The 9th floor has a good food court and there is a cinema complex on the 10th floor (with good views of the Han River). Techno Mart is open from 10 am to 8 pm. Take subway line 2 to Kangbyŏn station.

The Kukje Electronics Shopping Centre (Map 2) is the largest multi-storey mall on the south side of the Han-gang. Take subway line 3 to the Nambu Bus Terminal station.

T-Zone (Map 4, ☎ 285 1235) is an international chain computer store. The main shop is halfway between Chonggak and Chongno 3-ga subway stations on line 1.

Excursions

After its palaces, Seoul's best sightseeing options are outside the city. Most of the major attractions are only an hour or so by public transport from central Seoul. If possible, try to avoid the weekend stampede, when all you're likely to see are long queues to get on board the buses and trains.

Note that telephone numbers given without an area code in this chapter are local Seoul (02) numbers.

P'ANMUNJŎM

Situated 56km north of Seoul, P'anmunjŏm is the only place in the Demilitarised Zone (DMZ) where people are permitted. This is the truce village on the ceasefire line established at the end of the Korean War in 1953. In a building there, the interminable 'peace' discussions continue.

There's nowhere else in South Korea where you can get quite so close to North Korea without being arrested or shot, and the tension is palpable. In 1968, the imprisoned crew of the American warship USS *Pueblo* (kidnapped at sea by the North Koreans 11 months earlier) were allowed to cross to the South from there. In 1976, two American servicemen were hacked to death with axes by North Koreans at P'anmunjŏm. It was also there that an American soldier peacefully defected to North Korea in 1983, and has never been heard from again. Just a year later, a Russian tourist defected to the South at P'anmunjŏm, triggering a gun battle that killed three North Koreans and one South Korean soldier.

P'anmunjŏm was also in the news in mid-1989. It was there that Lim Soo-kyong, a Hanguk University student, and the Reverend Moon Gyu-hyon, a Catholic priest, were finally allowed to return to South Korea after protracted negotiations following Lim's visit to the Youth Festival in P'yŏngyang earlier in the year. Both were promptly arrested, whisked off to Seoul by helicopter and charged with violating the national security laws.

It's perhaps overrated as a 'tourist attraction' but that doesn't seem to stop the hordes flocking here to gawk at this tense 'truce village', learn the history of the DMZ and come face to face with stern-looking North Korean soldiers.

Part of the ongoing cold war between North and South is the existence of two civilian villages at P'anmunjŏm. On the southern side is Taesŏng-dong ('Great Success Village'), but the Americans call it 'Freedom Village'. It isn't terribly free for the villagers, as they must be out of the fields after dark and in their homes with doors locked by 11 pm. By way of compensation, it's a very prosperous agricultural community by South Korean standards – the villagers have plentiful land (though they don't own it), large homes and they are exempt from taxes. On the northern side of the border is Kijong-dong, which the Americans call 'Propaganda Village'. It differs from its southern counterpart in that it's uninhabited. However, it would be fair to say that both villages exist mainly for no other purpose than propaganda. On the north side, you can clearly see what is claimed to be the largest flagpole and flag in the world.

While you are permitted to take photos and use binoculars, there are a number of restrictions that visitors must adhere to. You must bring your passport, children under 10 years of age are not allowed and Korean nationals are not allowed unless special permission is obtained (a formidable bureaucratic procedure). There is a strict dress code which civilians must follow, and many travellers run foul of this rule! Shaggy or 'unkempt' hair (especially on men) also disqualifies some travellers. The military lists the following items as examples of inappropriate clothing for this formal occasion.

EXCURSIONS

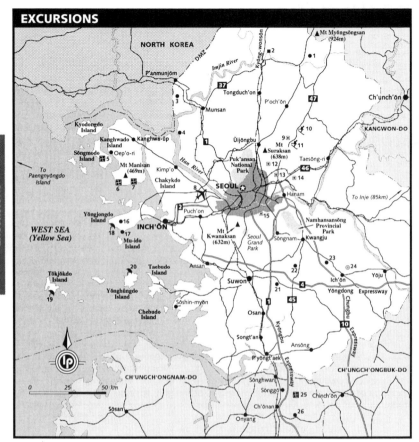

1) Shirts (top) without sleeves, T-shirts, tank tops and shirts of similar design

2) Dungarees or blue jeans of any kind, including 'designer jeans'

3) Shorts of any style, including hiking, bermuda, cut-offs, or 'short-shorts'

4) Miniskirts, halter tops, backless dresses and other abbreviated items of similar design

5) Any item of outer clothing of the 'sheer' variety

6) Shower shoes, thongs or 'flip-flops'

7) Items of military clothing not worn as an integral part of a prescribed uniform

8) Any form-fitting clothing including tight-knit tops, tight-knit pants and stretch pants

In addition, you are warned:

1) Visitors must remain in a group from the beginning to the end of the tour and will follow all instructions issued by their tour guide.

2) Any equipment, microphones or flags belonging to the communist side in the Military Armistice Commission (MAC) conference room are not to be touched.

3) Do not speak with, make any gesture towards or in any way approach or respond to personnel from the other side.

4) Firearms, knives or weapons of any type cannot be taken into the Joint Security Area.

EXCURSIONS

EXCURSIONS

Getting There & Away

Access to P'anmunjŏm is permitted for tour groups only – this is not a do-it-yourself trip. Your Korean tour guide will accompany you to Camp Bonifas on the southern side of the DMZ, where the group eats lunch and you'll have an opportunity to play slot machines (the military must really need the money). You are then given a slide show and briefing by an American soldier, who will then accompany your group on a military bus into the Joint Security Area of P'anmunjŏm. All things considered, it's a good party.

Commercial tours are available, but they're somewhat expensive at W48,000 (though lunch is thrown in free). Agencies offering these tours include Global Tour (☎ 335 0011), Grace Seoul Travel (☎ 332 8946), A-One Travel (☎ 701 0947), Star Travel (☎ 564 1232), Hanwha Travel (☎ 757 1232) and the Korea Travel Bureau (☎ 585 1191). You're expected to arrive at the pick-up point 20 minutes before departure time.

Not all the tours are the same. Most tours take in a visit to the 'Third Infiltration Tunnel', which the North Koreans presumably dug to attack the South. This side trip is worthwhile, and you should make sure the tunnel is included in the tour before handing over the cash.

The cheapest tours by far to P'anmunjŏm are offered by the USO (☎ 795 3028), the US Army's cultural and social centre opposite Gate 21 of the Yongsan Army Base in Seoul. The USO has at least one tour (usually two) weekly and it costs US$25 or the equivalent in *won*, but doesn't include lunch or a visit to the Third Infiltration Tunnel. However, there are separate USO tours to the tunnels, and Korean nationals may go on these. Because USO tours are cheap, they tend to be very heavily subscribed and you should book far in advance.

ODUSAN UNIFICATION OBSERVATORY

The Unification Observatory (T'ongil Chŏnmangdae) at Odusan is as close as most Korean civilians can get to the DMZ. P'anmunjŏm, north of Seoul, is actually inside the DMZ and can be visited by foreigners, but Koreans are not normally allowed there.

Since the Unification Observatory offers South Koreans a rare peak at the forbidden north, tourists by the busload turn up here daily throughout the summer months. It isn't quite the same as going to P'anmunjŏm – there's little of the palpable tension evident at P'anmunjŏm's 'Truce Village', since the Unification Observatory isn't in the DMZ. If you want to see anything at all (such as the UN post, the North Korean post and the North's propaganda signs), you have to use the telescopes – at W500 a pop for 2½ minutes viewing. It's essentially a non-event but it's a pleasant day out, there are no dress or age regulations, it's a little cheaper than going to P'anmunjŏm and the government lays on a free slide show.

Admission to the Unification Observatory is W1200 for adults and W700 for students and seniors. It's open from 9 am to 6.30 pm in summer, or until 5.30 pm in winter.

Take subway line 3 to Pulgwang station, where you'll find Seoul's Sŏbu bus terminal, and from there take a bus to Kŭmch'on. These buses run every 15 minutes and the ride takes 50 minutes. Or from Seoul station, take a train to Kŭmch'on – these depart hourly and take one hour. From Kŭmch'on bus station, take a local bus to the Unification Observatory (these buses are marked 'Songdong-ri'). The local buses depart once every 40 minutes and take 30 minutes for the ride.

PUK'ANSAN NATIONAL PARK

Just north of Seoul is Puk'ansan (Map 10). This national park *(kukrim kongwon)* boasts many massive white granite peaks, forests, temples, rock-cut Buddhist statues and tremendous views from various points.

Puk'ansan (836m) is the highest peak in the area, but there are at least 20 others within the park boundary. Puk'ansan in fact consists of three peaks connected to each other by a triangular-shaped ridge: Insubong (812m), Mangyongdae (800m) and Paekundae (836m). Other nearby peaks include Nojŏkbong (716m), Pohyŏnbong (705m), Pibong (560m) and Wonhyobong. Rock climbers are most enthralled with the

rugged granite face of Insubong, and you can expect them to be out in force whenever weather permits.

Insubong offers some of the best multi-pitch climbing in Asia for free-climbers. It has been referred to as Asia's 'Little Yosemite' and has routes of all grades. The local climbers are extremely friendly and enthusiastic, eager to introduce newcomers to their mountain. It is possible to hire a guide through one of the climbing shops in Seoul or through the mountaineering clubs. Information is available from KNTO – it's on the computer there too.

Darren DeRidder

At the northern end of the park is Tobongsan (740m), which is joined by ridges to Chaunbong, Manjangbong, Soninbong and Obongsan.

At the southern part of the park is Puk'ansansŏng (North Mountain Fortress). The fortress was originally built during the Paekche Dynasty but the present walls date from the time of the Yi king Sukchong, who rebuilt the battlements in the 16th century following invasions from China. Sections of the wall were destroyed during the Korean War but have since been restored.

As national parks go, it's fairly small (about 78 sq km) but still large enough to get lost in. There are a variety of trails which lead up into the park and along the ridges, and seven hikers' huts *(sanjang)* where simple accommodation is available for the night (bring your own bedding) as well as a limited selection of canned and packaged foodstuffs. There are 32 officially recognised campsites. Water is available at the huts as well as at many other points along the trails. There are free maps available at all the entrances to the park, but you have to ask for one. Purchasing a topographical map from the Chung'ang Atlas Map Service (Map 4) in Seoul is also advised. Entry to Puk'ansan National Park costs W1000.

Most of the trails are in good condition and well marked, but the climbing can be steep. Don't underestimate the difficulty – climbing any of the peaks in this park is

ROBERT STOREY

MARTIN MOOS

MARTIN MOOS

Seoul has consumed most of its trees, but Koreans still love wood. Among other offerings, you can find folk *t'al* (masks), and carefully retouched temple guardians, beams and symbolic figures brightly painted in *tanch'ŏng* (colours and patterns used to convey Buddhist principles, beauty and majesty).

Despite the ravages of history, the west gate and tower of Suwon's old city walls still stand.

One of Puk'ansan's three peaks peers out through autumn leaves.

fairly strenuous. Some recommended hiking routes include:

South Area

North-South Route 1 (9.1km) Ui-dong – U-i Hut – Paekundae – Taedongmun – Kugi-dong
North-South Route 2 (8.5km, 3.5 hours) Chŏngnŭng Resort – Pogukmun – Yongammun – Nojŏkbong – Paekundae
East-West Route 1 (6.5km) Ui-dong – Paekun Hut – Taesŏmun
East-West Route 2 (11km, 4.5 hours) Puk'ansansŏng Entrance – Taesŏmun, Paekundae – U-i Hut
Circular Route 1 (7.1km) Ui-dong – Paekundae – Puk'ansan Hut – Chŏngnŭng Resort
Circular Route 2 (8.1km) Ui-dong – Puk'ansan Hut – Paekundae – Ui-dong
Circular Route 3 (6.3km, 3.5 hours) Ui-dong – Tosŏnsa – Paekun Hut – Paekundae – Nojŏkbong – Yongammun – Ui-dong Resort
Circular Route 4 (5km) Kugi-dong – Taesŏmun – Taedongmun – 4.19 Memorial Tower
Circular Route 5 (7.5km, 4 hours) Kugi-dong – Munsusa – Taenammun – Pogukmun – Chŏngnŭng Resort

North Area (Tobongsan)

East-West Route 2 (8.5km) Tobong-dong – Podae Ridge – Obongsan – Ui-dong
East-West Route 3 (7.9km) Tobong-dong – Tobong Hut – Kwanumam Hermitage – Ui-dong
East-West Route 4 (8.3km) Tobong-dong – Kwanumam Hermitage – Obongsan – Ui-dong
Circular Route 6 (6.7km) Tobong-dong – Ch'ŏnch'uksa – Mangwolsa – Changsuwon

Getting There & Away

Getting to Puk'ansan by public transport is easy, and there are a number of entrances to the park. Some of the possibilities include:

City Hall – Ui-dong
  bus Nos 6, 8 and 23 (50 minutes)
Chongno 1-ga – Chŏngnŭng Resort
  bus No 5 (40 minutes)
Chongno 1-ga – Segŏmjŏng Resort
  bus No 59 (20 minutes)
Sejong Cultural Center – Puk'ansansŏng
  bus No 156 (40 minutes)
Sejong Cultural Center – Ui-dong
  bus No 8 (50 minutes)

Best of all, the recently opened subway line 7 is a boon to hikers. Its next-to-last stop is Tobongsan station, near the northern end of the national park.

Alternatively, you could take subway line 3 to Kup'abal station, then go the last 3km north-east towards the park by bus, taxi or on foot.

SURAKSAN

To the east of Puk'ansan National Park is Suraksan (638m), another attractive climbing area. It's not a national park, but it's still crowded with weekend Seoulites trying to get away from it all.

Suraksan is technically just north of the Seoul city limits, but it is connected by a ridge to **Pulamsan** (508m), which is in Seoul. Hiking along the ridge between the two peaks is recommended.

Access to Suraksan is possible from several angles, and it's not a bad idea to ascend and descend the mountain by different routes. An easy way to begin a hike would be to take subway line 4 to Sanggye station – Pulamsan is 2km to the east of this station. From Pulamsan you can follow the ridgeline north about 7km to Suraksan. Along the way you must cross a small highway, and just off to the east is **Hŭngguksa**, a temple worth the small detour. From here there are several obvious trails down – one leads north-west to Ŭijŏngbu, from where there are trains back to Seoul. Be warned that the route described is a long walk and will take a full day, so start early.

KWANAKSAN

Straddling the southern boundary of metropolitan Seoul and the surrounding province of Kyŏnggi-do, Kwanaksan is another fine hiking spot. The summit is a moderate 632m above sea level.

To reach the peak, start from the Seoul National University campus. To get there, take subway line 2 to Seoul National University station, and from there a bus southward for about 2km to the campus. From the campus, Kwanaksan is the large and obvious peak towards the south-east. There

Hiking

JUST GOING FOR A STROLL DEAR

Perhaps the biggest problem with hiking (*tŭngsan*) in Korea is escaping the crowds. Some areas are so popular that you sometimes have to stand in line to reach the summit of a peak. The problem with crowds can be formidable – at times it feels as if you're riding the Seoul subway rather than visiting the wilderness. Fortunately, this predicament can be bypassed if you simply avoid the most popular spots during weekends and holidays.

If you want to travel with a group, Korean friends can help you join a mountaineering club (*san ak hoi*). Don't expect hikers at the Korean clubs to be able to speak much English.

The USO in Seoul operates an English-speaking hiking club. Although geared towards US military personnel, civilians are welcome to participate.

Koreans are serious about the great outdoors; any excursion away from the concrete of Seoul is prepared for with a thoroughness worthy of an expedition primed to assault Everest. This includes ice axes (in summer) and ropes (for walking up a gentle slope). Koreans must also be the best-dressed hikers in the world – check out the red vests, yellow caps and multi-coloured knee-high socks.

While the Koreans no doubt overdo it, there are a few things which you should bring. Useful, if not fashionable, items include sun protection (sunglasses, sunscreen lotion and sunhat), rain gear, food, maps, compass, mosquito repellent and warm clothing. The most important item you can bring is water – no less than 2L per person per day in summer.

---

are a number of hiking trails, and students can easily point out the way.

NAMHANSANSŎNG PROVINCIAL PARK

Like Puk'ansan, Namhansan is topped by a fortress (Namhansansŏng). This park is about 25km south-east of Seoul. Although it doesn't offer the hiking trails that Puk'ansan does, Namhansansŏng does have a very impressive section of **walled fortifications** that date back to the 17th century. The wall, which winds sinuously over the Namhansan peak and foothills for around 5km, has been touted as Korea's answer to China's Great Wall. Of course, in terms of scale, there's no comparison, but at certain

points along the Namhansansŏng wall there's a definite similarity.

Historians maintain that there was an earthen fortress on the site of Namhansansŏng as long as 2000 years ago. The walls that remain today date from 1621. They were built as a line of defence against the Manchus. When the Manchus invaded Korea in 1635, the Korean king of the time retreated here, only to be forced to surrender shortly after the Manchus laid siege to the fortress. It was an act that led to the Chosŏn Dynasty being forced to accept the suzerainty of China.

The fortress area once accommodated nine temples, as well as various command posts and watch towers. Today a single command post, **Suŏjangdae**, and a single temple, **Chongyangsa**, remain. There are other more recent temples on the path up to the South Gate and fortress walls. The North, South and East gates have been restored. Not far from the East Gate is Chongyangsa.

Entry to the park costs W500, and don't forget to ask for a free map at the entrance station. In the park itself, a few places sell instant noodles, soft drinks and coffee.

Getting There & Away

The nearest town to Namhansansŏng is Sŏngnam, south-east of Seoul and to the west of Namhansansŏng. From the nearest subway station in Sŏngnam, taxis can drive you up the mountain into the fortress for about W7000. Subway line 8 has a Namhansansŏng station and Tandae station, both within a few kilometres of the fortress.

MORAN MARKET

The Moran Market in Sŏngnam is an ordinary rural market, but a very large and lively one. It's only open on the 4th, 9th, 14th, 19th, 24th and 29th day of each month.

Take subway line 3 to the south of Seoul and get off at Moran station which is in central Sŏngnam. Once you have seen the market, you can continue on to Namhansansŏng Provincial Park if you have sufficient time.

KOREAN FOLK VILLAGE

Along with the hiking at Puk'ansan, the Korean Folk Village (Han'guk Minsok Ch'on) rates as one of the best day outings from Seoul. Most people visit the village expecting large-scale tourist kitsch, but in fact the village is a surprisingly tasteful reconstruction of a traditional Korean village. The Koreans wandering around the village wearing traditional dress actually live here. Most of the buildings here are based on village life and have been constructed with authentic materials. There is a **Buddhist temple** and **Confucian shrine**, though perhaps most interesting are the **folk crafts** on display. It's possible to watch villagers making paper, weaving silk and working metal using traditional techniques. You'll be able to see

women playing some traditional games using devices such as a *nŏlttwigi* (Korean see-saw) and *kŭne-t'agi* (Korean swing).

Across the lake (and accessible by footbridge) is **Family Park**, a kiddie amusement zone complete with a small roller coaster and mini-train.

There are twice-daily performances of various sorts at the village. The farmers' dance, a riot of colour and movement to the sounds of gongs and drums, takes place at noon and 3 pm. At 12.30 and 3.30 pm is the acrobatics and tightrope dance. There is a traditional wedding in house No 9 at 1 and 4 pm. Over in the Family Park area, a traditional magic and acrobatic show is staged at 11.30 am, and 2 and 4 pm.

The Korean Folk Village is open daily from 9 am to 5.30 pm in winter, and until 6 pm in summer. In summer, the Family Park stays open until 9 pm.

Admission costs W7000 for adults, W4000 for students and W3000 for children.

Getting There & Away

To reach the folk village, the first thing to do is to get to Suwon, a suburb to the south of Seoul. Take subway line 1 south to the last stop (make sure the train says 'Suwon' on the front, not 'Inch'ŏn'). As you come out of Suwon station you'll see the ticket office and bus stop on the right-hand side on the same side of the street. Buses to the village go every hour on weekdays and every half hour on weekends from 9 am to 5 pm. The last free bus back from the village is at 5 pm on weekdays, and 6 pm on weekends and public holidays, but you can also take a regular local bus (bus No 37) and pay the fare. These regular buses run only once hourly until 8 pm. Of course, you can take a taxi between Suwon station and the folk village.

From the big Chamshil intersection in Seoul (next to Lotte World), you can catch bus Nos 100-2 or 1116 directly to the Korean Folk Village.

There are several bus companies in Seoul which offer tours of the village but they're pretty expensive. Lotte Travel (☎ 399 2300) offers a half-day tour for W38,000. Korea Travel Bureau (☎ 585 1191) has a full-day itinerary costing W62,000 (but at least you get a free lunch).

CHEBUDO

This is one of Korea's more surprising sights. The West Sea (Yellow Sea), which borders the west coast of Korea, is known for its exceptionally powerful tides. There is such an extreme variation between the high and low tides that many small islands are accessible by foot when the tide is out.

One such island is Chebudo. Not only can you walk to the island at low tide, but buses even make the journey (across a partially submerged concrete path). The tidal mudflats are a joy to walk on, with crabs and numerous other marine creatures scurrying about. Unfortunately, due to large land reclamation projects, many of Korea's tidal mudflats are rapidly disappearing.

The distance between Chebudo and the mainland is about 2km. It's possible to walk all the way across, but make sure you've allowed yourself enough time – it wouldn't be much fun to get caught in the middle when the tide rolls in.

There are two low tides daily, and therefore only two bus journeys per day to the island. You'll have to check the newspapers or make local inquiries to find out the exact times. To get to Chebudo, first go to Suwon. At the plaza in front of Suwon train station, take city bus No 450, 490 or 999 to Sŏshin-myŏn. From there you can catch the shuttle bus to Chebudo.

YONG-IN EVERLAND

North-east of Suwon is Yong-in Everland (☎ 759 1296), brought to you by the ever-enterprising *chaebŏl* Samsung. This is Korea's largest amusement park, divided into three subsections: Festival World, Caribbean Bay and the Everland Speedway.

Attractions include botanical gardens, a zoo, a safari park and a host of gut-gripping rides like the 'double loops and corkscrew'. You can ride a sled (in winter),

or go surfing in the 'big wave pool' during summer. Everland Speedway offers auto racing, motorcycle racing and mountain bike racing.

Somewhat surprising is the **Hoam Art Museum**, a private collection of Korean art that was owned by Lee Byung-chul, the now-deceased founder of Samsung. The museum is closed on Monday.

Everland even boasts large two-storey log cabins which can be rented for the night.

There are various kinds of admission tickets available. Basic admission to Festival World (no rides included) costs W11,000 for adults. An all-inclusive ticket for adults is W40,000 in summer, or W30,000 in winter. Teenagers get a 30% discount and children get 60% off.

The Everland complex is open daily from 9 am to 6 pm (10 pm during summer).

From Suwon station, there are frequent buses to Everland throughout the day. There are also buses every 10 minutes from the Seoul express bus terminal from 6.30 am to 9.30 pm. Buses also run every 20 minutes between Everland and Seoul's Nambu bus terminal from 6.40 am to 9.50 pm.

INCH'ŎN

East of Seoul, Inch'ŏn (population 2.2 million) is Seoul's major seaport and home to mega-corporations such as the Daewoo Motor Company. The city is most famous for General Douglas MacArthur's surprise landing here in the early weeks of the Korean War, a manoeuvre that enabled the recapture of Seoul and severed North Korea's supply lines.

The city is not blessed with numerous tourist sights, but it's a good change of scenery from Seoul. Most travellers come to Inch'ŏn only to catch one of the ferries that operate between here and China.

Information

The Inch'ŏn Tourist Association (☎ 032-884 4590) operates an information kiosk in the International Ferry Terminal. The Inch'ŏn city government also maintains a Web site (www.metro.inchon.kr).

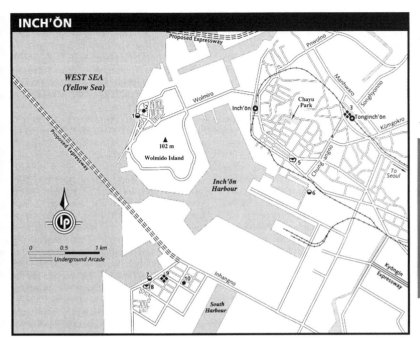

INCH'ŎN 인천

1 Tourist Ferries
  월미도선착장
2 Wolmido Cultural St
  월미도문화의거리
3 Inch'ŏn Department Store
  인천 백화점
4 Shinp'odong Underground Arcade
  신포동 지하상가
5 Post Office
  항도우체국
6 International Ferry Terminal
  국제여객터미널
7 Yŏn'an Pier (Island Ferries)
  연안부두
8 Post Office
  항도우체국
9 Life Shopping Centre
  라이프쇼핑센터
10 Inch'ŏn Market
  인천종합어시장

Chayu Park

Inch'ŏn's most famous sight is Chayu (Freedom) Park, which commemorates MacArthur's landing in 1950. There is a statue of MacArthur in the park, as well as a monument commemorating the 1982 centennial of US-Korean relations. Near the car park is what must be the biggest pigeon house in the world.

Chayu Park is next to Inch'ŏn station – it's a very steep walk uphill.

Shinp'odong Underground Arcade

If you exit Tonginchŏn station and descend through Inch'ŏn department store, you will find yourself in one of Korea's longest underground malls. You're likely to spot plenty of foreigners here, mostly sailors stocking up on electronics, chocoates, ginseng and other mementoes of Korea.

Wolmido

This was once an island, but land reclamation has turned it into a peninsula on the north-west side of Inch'ŏn harbour. Wolmido is a very trendy spot, boasting everything from raw fish restaurants to art galleries, and street opera on summer weekends. Along the waterfront is **Wolmido Cultural St**, where various cultural performances are scheduled during summer weekends and holidays. There is also a small booth here dishing out tourist information.

Two large sightseeing cruise ships *(Cosmos* and *Harmony)* dock at Wolmido and offer western buffet meals (not recommended if you're prone to sea sickness). The boat costs W7000 (half-price for children) for a one hour cruise. On weekdays, departures are once every 90 minutes between 8 am and 8 pm. On weekends and holidays, departures are every 50 minutes. This schedule gets cut back somewhat during the off season (winter).

The Inch'ŏn city government has plans to construct an Inch'ŏn Tower in this area to rival the one in Seoul, perhaps not the wisest idea given Wolmido's proximity to the new international airport.

Wolmido is a one hour walk or a five minute taxi ride from Inch'ŏn station. You can also catch bus No 2, 15, 23, 60, 101 or 550 from either Inch'ŏn station or Tonginchŏn station.

Islands

There are dozens of islands not far from Inch'ŏn, and some of them have decent beaches *(hesuyokjang)*. For the Koreans (and adventurous foreigners), the raw fish restaurants are a big attraction. Just be sure to ask the price first, as raw fish *(saengsŏn hoe)* often costs much more than cooked fish. Other delicacies include vinegared rice with raw fish *(saengsŏn ch'obap)*, broiled fish *(saengsŏn kui)* and spicy fish soup *(maeun t'ang)*.

On some nearby islands (especially on Kŏjedo) there are some unique smooth stone beaches. The stones are called *mŏngdol*, and it takes centuries of tidal action to produce

them. It is illegal to collect these stones, so don't try to take any home with you.

Chakyakdo This island is just 3km north of Wolmido. In summer the landscape is decked out with peonies *(chakyak)*, hence the island's name. The island is also heavily forested with pines.

You can reach Chakyakdo easily by taking a boat from Yŏn'an Pier. There is one *yŏgwan* (small hotel) on the island, plus 15 bungalows for rent.

Yŏngjongdo Sadly, the writing is on the wall for what has been a pleasant retreat from the concrete jungle. **Ŭrwangni Beach** on this island is one of the most accessible stretches of white sand in the Inch'ŏn area. Unfortunately, Yŏngjongdo is the site for the new Inch'ŏn international airport, due for completion in the year 2002. The noise from large jets will no doubt make the island less desirable for tourism. A bridge to the island is also being constructed, bringing in heavy traffic (which is blissfully absent at present). Yŏngjongdo is also known for its temple, **Yŏnggungsa**.

Boats depart from Inch'ŏn's pier at Wolmido hourly between 8 am and 9 pm and the sea journey takes 15 minutes. The boat drops you off at Yŏngjongdo pier, where there is a wonderful **fish market** (especially in the morning). From the pier you have to take a local bus (40 minutes) to Ŭrwangni Beach, which is on the opposite end of the island. There are no yŏgwan at Ŭrwangni, but *minbak* (homestays) are available.

Mu-ido This small island is off the southwest shore of Yŏngjongdo. **Hanakke Beach** is the big attraction, and boasts a small resort village.

There are two ways to get to the island. From the Tŏkkyo-dong pier on Yŏngjongdo (south of Ŭrwangni Beach) there are ferries to Kunmuri pier on Mu-ido (a 10 minute journey). Otherwise, catch a ferry from Yŏn'an Pier in Inch'ŏn, which drops you off at Saemkumi pier on Mu-ido (a 50 minute journey).

Yŏnghŭngdo The main attraction here is **Shimnip'o Beach** at the north-west corner of the island, and 30km from Inch'ŏn. The beach has a 4km-long pebbly stretch and a 1km-long sandy stretch.

Ferries to Yŏnghŭngdo depart Inch'ŏn about five or six times daily during summer, but it slows to two daily during winter. Ask a Korean speaker to call Wongwang Shipping Company (☎ 032-882 1316, 882 1714) for the current schedule. Ferries to Yŏnghŭngdo (and most other small islands) leave from Yŏn'an Pier on the south side of the harbour. Inch'ŏn city bus Nos 12, 14, 18 and 33 travel to the terminal.

Tŏkjŏkdo This is one of the most scenic islands reachable from Inch'ŏn, though it's a bit far for a day trip from Seoul. Fortunately, the new high speed ferries make a one day excursion possible.

The island is 77km from Inch'ŏn, and along its southern shore is **Sŏp'ori Beach**, which is 2km long and lined with a thick grove of pines. The beach is spectacular, and easily the most popular on the island. Much of the rest of the island has impressive rock formations, and it's worth climbing the highest peak, **Pijobong** (292m).

There are 11 yŏgwan at Sŏp'ori Beach and at least 40 minbak. There is an information phone number for minbak (☎ 032-886 7772, 888 0154). There is also a camping ground where tent rentals are W1000 to W2000.

The ferries to Tŏkjŏkdo depart from Inch'ŏn's Yŏn'an Pier. There are two kinds of boats: the fast ferries that make the trip in 50 minutes, or the slow ships that take two hours. In summer, the fast ferries sail five to seven times daily, but during winter it's cut back to three trips daily. The slow ships only run in summer three or four times daily.

No matter which boat you take, you will be dropped off at Jinri Pier on Tŏkjŏkdo. From there, it's a 20 minute bus ride to Sŏp'ori Beach.

Getting There & Away

Trains on subway line 1 leave Seoul for Inch'ŏn every four minutes from 5.10 am to 11.30 pm. The ride takes about 50 minutes, and costs W900.

KANGHWADO

To the west of Seoul and north of Inch'ŏn is Kanghwado, which has played a significant part in Korean history. It's where the Koryŏ court took refuge during the Mongol invasions of the 13th century, and where the Koreans resisted American and French troops in the late 19th century.

Being an island fortress, over the centuries Kanghwado has seen its fair share of fortifications, palaces and the like, but it's overrated as a tourist attraction. The tourist literature and some guidebooks to Korea rave about Kanghwado's attractions, giving the impression that the island is littered with fascinating relics and ruins. To a degree it is, but you have to be a real relic-and-ruin enthusiast to want to make the effort. However, there are some good **hikes** and beautiful views if you get away from the island's main town, Kanghwa-ŭp.

One thing you might want to keep your eye out for is *hwamunsok*, large rush mats with beautiful floral patterns. This is a Kanghwado specialty and makes a practical souvenir if you don't mind lugging it home. The island's other hot consumer product is Kanghwado *insam* (ginseng). There is a big **market** in Kanghwa-ŭp which only functions on the 2nd, 7th, 12th, 17th, 22nd and 27th day of each month.

Kanghwa-ŭp

The main town on the island, Kanghwa-ŭp is the gateway to the island. Despite the hype, the city is uninspiring. True, the city gates still stand, but the enclosing wall has disappeared. Likewise, the site of the Koryŏ court has a couple of traditional buildings of slight interest, but if your time is limited, you can skip it without a deep sense of loss. Fortunately, the island has better sights further afield.

Manisan

At the south-west tip of the island is Manisan (469m), 14km from Kanghwa-ŭp. On the mountain's summit is a 5m-tall altar called **Ch'amsŏngdan**. This is dedicated to Tan'gun, the mythical first Korean (born in 2333 BC).

It's a 3km walk one way from the bus stop to the summit, and the climb takes about one hour on the ascent and about 40 minutes back down. The concrete path with stone steps is easy enough to follow, but many people descend by a separate route which takes them past **Chŏngsusa**.

The entrance gate to the mountain (where you pay W800 admission) is 500m east of the bus stop in Hwado village. Buses between Hwado-ri and Kanghwa-ŭp (40 minutes) run every 20 minutes from 6.45 am to 8.50 pm and cost W1100.

Chŏndŭngsa

Originally constructed in the 4th century, this is one of the oldest temples in Korea. Needless to say, there have been numerous reconstructions and renovations since then.

The temple also has great historical significance, mainly because it was here that the second set of the **Koreana Tripitaka** was carved. The Koreana Tripitaka consists of 81,258 wooden blocks which spell out the Buddhist sutras. The blocks were carved at Chŏndŭngsa in the 13th century, but were later moved to the safer site of Haeinsa, a major temple near the city of Taegu in the south-eastern part of Korea. Only 120 of the blocks remain at Chŏndŭngsa.

The temple is found within the larger fortress complex of **Samnangsŏng**. The fortress is 1km south of Onsu-ri. Buses between Onsu-ri and Kanghwa-ŭp (25 minutes) run every 20 minutes from 6.30 am to 8.40 pm and cost W900.

Pomunsa

This important temple sits high up in the mountains on Sŏngmodo, off the western coast of Kanghwado. The compound is small, but there is some superb and very ornate painting on the eaves of the various buildings and especially those of the bell pavilion. The famous **grotto** here is quite plain and uninteresting, though it is cool on

a hot summer's day. One of Pomunsa's most interesting sights is the 10m-high **rock carving** of Kwansŭm Posal, the Goddess of Mercy, which stands below a granite overhang high above the temple compound.

It's a steep walk up to the temple from where the bus drops you, and there's a small tourist village with souvenir shops and restaurants at the bottom of the hill.

To get to Pomunsa from Kanghwa-ŭp, take a bus from the Kanghwa-ŭp bus station to Oep'o-ri (20 minutes). Buses depart every 20 minutes from 7.15 am to 6.40 pm and cost W900. The bus will drop you in front of the main ferry terminal, but this caters only for long-distance ferries and is not the terminal you want. Walk through to the front of the terminal, turn right and continue down the waterfront for about 100m. You'll see a concrete ramp going down to the water and another ferry terminal on the right. From there, ferries run daily to Sŏkmo-ri on Sŏngmodo approximately every hour from 7 am to 7 pm – ferries take both people and vehicles. It takes 10 minutes to cross the straits. On the opposite side there are buses to Pomunsa which take about half an hour. In order to take the ferry, you must fill out a silly form in which you state your name and passport number – the reasoning is that Kanghwado is close to North Korea. Keep your passport on hand in case anybody wearing a (South Korean) uniform wants to check it.

Getting There & Away

Regular buses to Kanghwado leave from the Shinch'on bus terminal in the western part of Seoul. Take subway line 2 to Shinch'on station and ask directions from there. It's a five minute walk.

The buses leave every 10 minutes from 5.40 am to 9.30 pm, take one hour and cost W3300. The buses drop you at Kanghwa-ŭp bus terminal.

SEOUL GRAND PARK

In the suburbs south of the megalopolis is Seoul Grand Park, a huge sprawling affair with a number of attractions. Although it's largely geared towards kids, there are also some sights for adults too. The park contains the National Museum of Contemporary Art, a major zoo with a botanical garden and Seoul Land, a hi-tech amusement park in the Disney tradition. If you don't want to be fighting crowds all day, it's best to visit on a weekday.

The **National Museum of Contemporary Art** (☎ 03-503 7744) has played hopscotch for a number of years. It was originally at Kyŏngbokkung, then Tŏksugung and currently resides in Seoul Grand Park. There's an extensive collection of Korean and western modern art in a variety of mediums, including video movies. Concerts, plays, traditional dance shows and films are on view, but the schedule varies. There are also a number of outdoor sculpture exhibits. One big annoyance – you can't bring your handbag into the museum and you'll need a stack of W100 coins for the too-small lockers (and of course no one has change). A shuttle bus runs every 20 minutes between the museum and the Seoul Grand Park subway station. The museum is open from 10 am to 6 pm, or until 5 pm during winter. It's closed on Monday.

The **zoo** has a good collection of animals, many of them in attractive roomy enclosures. There is even an ant ground. Dolphin shows take place three times daily at 11.30 am, 1.30 and 3.30 pm. Admission to the zoo is W1100 for adults. The zoo is open daily from 9 am to 7 pm from April to October, and until 6 pm from November to March.

Seoul Land (☎ 03-504 0011) is a full day out in itself. It has plenty of rides of the white-knuckle variety, as well as theme concepts like Tomorrow Land, Fantasy Land and Adventure Land. Admission costs W20,000 for adults, W16,000 for teenagers and W12,000 for children. There are some coupons floating around (ask at KNTO) which can net you a 20% discount.

Getting There & Away

You can reach Seoul Grand Park by taking subway line 4 south to the Seoul Grand Park station. From the city, the fare is W500 rather than the usual W450.

SEOUL HORSE RACE TRACK

In order to project a family image, the race track is officially called the Seoul Equestrian Park (☎ 03-509 1283). Horse racing is one of the very few legal gambling activities open to Koreans, but the race season is deliberately kept short. The track is open to the public during December and January on weekends only from 11 am to 6 pm. Admission costs W200 and bets range from a minimum of W100 to a maximum of W200,000. To impress even more of a family image to this activity, baby carriages and children's bicycles are available for hire at the track (but cannot be ridden on the track). The races can also be viewed on large-screen TVs at betting offices in central Seoul.

The race track is next door to Seoul Grand Park. Take subway line 4 to the Seoul Race Course station.

ICH'ŎN

Just 50km south-east of Seoul is the historic village of Ich'ŏn (not to be confused with Inch'ŏn). Though perhaps it won't be much longer before the Seoul megalopolis swallows it up, at present Ich'ŏn presents a semi-rural setting with several moderately interesting sights.

Ich'ŏn Ceramic Village

This is perhaps a specialised interest, but the Ich'ŏn Ceramic Village (Ich'ŏn Toye Ch'on), 10km north of Ich'ŏn, does attract a small but loyal following of pottery buffs. The Ich'on region – and nearby Kwangju – has been the centre of the Korean ceramics industry, going back at least to the Chosŏn dynasty (1392-1910). White porcelain is still an export item of Korea, though these days there is heavy competition from low-wage sweatshops in China. Nonetheless, the ceramic kilns of Ich'ŏn are still around and of great historical importance to Korea.

Ich'ŏn is also the home of the **Haegang Ceramics Museum** (☎ 0336-342226) – the admission cost is W1000.

Ich'ŏn Hot Springs

Though not the most spectacular hot springs in Korea, it's certainly one of the most accessible from Seoul. Water temperatures are a moderate 30°C. Ich'ŏn hot springs gained popularity during the (unpopular) Japanese colonial period from 1910 to 1945.

Perhaps that explains why hotels here charge Japanese prices – it's certainly not the cheapest hot springs resort around. However, you needn't be a hotel guest to use the facilities, though of course you have to buy an admission ticket.

Some of the cushy places where you can bathe or stay overnight include the *Solbong Hotel* (☎ *0336-635 5701)*, which costs a mere W133,000 to W164,000. Or you could go downmarket and stay at the *Miranda Ich'ŏn Hotel* (☎ *0336-332 001)*, where doubles are W38,000 to W96,800.

Getting There & Away

There are at least two options for getting to Ich'ŏn. Perhaps the easiest is from the Seoul express bus terminal – buses run once every 20 minutes from 6.30 am until 9.20 pm, taking just over an hour to make the journey. Buses are every 15 minutes from the Tong-Seoul bus terminal and take 50 minutes to do the trip. The fare is W2200.

You must tell the driver if you want to get off at the Ich'ŏn Ceramic Village rather than in Ich'ŏn itself, which is about 10km further down the highway. The Ceramic Village is about half way between Ich'ŏn and Kwangju. Some tours (not many) take in both Yong-in Everland and the Ich'ŏn Ceramic Village in one trip.

If going to the hot springs, take a taxi from central Ich'ŏn.

INDEPENDENCE HALL OF KOREA

About two hours south of Seoul near the city of Ch'ŏnan is the Independence Hall of Korea (☎ 0417-560 0114). It's possibly the best museum in the country – or rather it is if you can read Korean. Unfortunately, most of the explanations which accompany the exhibits are in Korean only.

Nonetheless, it's worth seeing. The Independence Hall is an architectural wonder, and by far the nation's largest feel-good project. When you see this place, it becomes apparent that all stops were pulled out to make this an uncompromising totem to national sovereignty.

The **main hall** is like something out of a science fiction movie. Built entirely out of concrete and tiles, it's a fine display of artistry and civil engineering skills.

At the back of this hall is a whole complex of seven air-conditioned exhibition halls cataloguing the course of Korean history from the earliest recorded times up to the present.

There's a high propaganda content to many of the exhibits, and the Japanese and North Koreans come in for some particularly virulent condemnation. On any weekday you will see busloads of school children being run through this place. Part of Korea's educational system includes a lengthy hate-mongering campaign against Japan – the **Japanese Aggression Hall** is the most prominent example. Intriguingly, there seems to be official amnesia about China's nasty behaviour during the Korean War.

Although Japanese travellers might be nonplussed by how they're portrayed in the history exhibits, travellers of other nationalities generally find this place enjoyable.

There is also the **Circle Vision Theatre**, which presents a 15 minute promotional film on Korea's scenic beauty, its traditions, customs and development.

The Independence Hall complex includes several *restaurants*, a bookshop, post office, souvenir shops and even a bank where you can change travellers cheques. Smoking, eating and drinking are prohibited inside the halls. Indoor photography is also prohibited, though plenty of film is on sale at kiosks throughout the site.

Entry to the Independence Hall costs W1600. Entry to the Circle Vision Theatre is an extra W1600. The Hall is open every day except Monday (unless Monday is a public holiday). Opening hours are 9 am to 5 pm from April to September, or to 4 pm from October to March. Admission ends one hour before closing times.

City buses shuttle between Ch'ŏnan and the Independence Hall every few minutes between 6 am and 8.50 pm. A convenient one to take is bus No 500, which stops opposite Ch'ŏnan train station. The ride takes 20 minutes and costs W700. There are also buses direct from the Seoul express bus terminal to the Independence Hall (1¾ hours) every 40 minutes from 6.30 am to 7.20 pm.

KAGWONSA

Some 7km north-east of Ch'ŏnan on the slopes of Taejosan stands Kagwonsa, a temple which has the largest bronze statue of Buddha in Asia (over 14m tall). It was erected in 1977 as a kind of plea for the re-unification of Korea.

You won't be likely to journey all the way from Seoul just to see Kagwonsa, but it is so close to Ch'ŏnan that it's easy to combine the trip with a visit to Independence Hall.

Local bus No 102 from the Ch'ŏnan station area will take you to Kagwonsa, or look for bus No 46. Both are rather infrequent, but taxis offer another possibility. It's a steep walk up more than 200 steps to the temple precincts from where the bus lefts you off.

TAESŎNG-RI RESORT

If you're a Seoul expat desperately looking for a day's escape from the city, Taesŏng-ri Resort (☎ 0356-840 088) is worth visiting. The resort town of Taesŏng-ri is on the Puk'an-gang (Puk'an River) and is a fine venue for boating, water-skiing, jet-skiing and windsurfing. Of course, these activities take place only during summer. The resort boasts a *camping ground*, but expect it to be packed out on weekends.

To get to Taesŏng-ri Resort, take line 1 to Ch'ŏngryangni subway station and walk over to the adjacent Ch'ŏngryangni train station. Catch any of the eastbound trains heading towards Ch'unch'ŏn, and get off at Taesŏng-ri (about a one hour ride from Seoul). The resort is across the river from Taesŏng-ri train station.

Language

Korean is a knotty problem for linguists. Various theories have been proposed to explain its origins, but the most widely accepted is that it is a member of the Ural-Altaic family of languages. Other members of the same linguistic branch are Turkish and Mongolian. In reality Korean grammar shares much more with Japanese than it does with either Turkish or Mongolian. Furthermore, the Koreans have borrowed nearly 70% of their vocabulary from neighbouring China, and now many English words have penetrated the Korean lexicon.

Chinese characters *(hanja)* are usually restricted to use in maps, and occasionally in newspapers and written names. For the most part Korean is written in *hangŭl*, the alphabet developed under King Sejong's reign in the 15th century.

Hangŭl consists of only 24 characters and isn't that difficult to learn. However, the formation of words using hangŭl is very different from the way that western alphabets are used to form words. The emphasis is on the formation of a syllable so that it resembles a Chinese character. Thus the first syllable of the word 'hangŭl' is formed by an 'h' in the top left corner, an 'a' in the top right corner and an 'n' at the bottom, the whole syllabic grouping forming a syllabic 'box'. These syllabic 'boxes' are strung together to form words.

In this book we have used the McCune-Reischauer Romanisation system which is the one officially adopted by the Korean government. As a Romanisation system, it has a number of fatal flaws and most Koreans don't understand it. As a result, all kinds of transliterations can be found in use in Korea. Many Koreans simply use English spellings of their own fancy, and this causes great confusion for foreigners.

An awkward feature of the McCune-Reischauer system is the use of apostrophes to indicate aspirated consonants (those accompanied by a puff of air), as in 'P'anmunjŏm'. Another ineffective feature of this system is the use of diacritics (marks above a letter) on the 'o' and 'u' to fully represent the sounds of Korean vowels. This is extremely troublesome, as there is a tendency for the diacritics to be omitted, and this undermines the whole system. For example, 'Seoul' should in fact be spelled 'Sŏul' under McCune-Reischauer, but the diacritic mark is such a nuisance that even the Korean government dispenses with it. Ironically, at one time Korea used a better system (the Ministry of Education system) which had no problem with accent marks and diacritics. Much of the current confusion stems from the fact that many Koreans tend to mix the two official systems together.

Another important feature of Korean which causes confusion is that, unlike English, there is no distinction between voiced and unvoiced consonants. For example, in the English words 'cot' and 'got', the only difference in pronunciation is that the vocal chords are made to vibrate when we say the 'g' – everything else about the pronunciation of the two words is identical. In Korean the voicing or non-voicing of consonants has no effect on the meaning of a word – as a result the same words can be spelt very differently. For example, the ever-popular Korean dish *pulgogi* is also popularly spelled 'bulgogi'. Generally this won't be a problem but it can be quite perplexing when trying to decipher place names if you're not aware of it.

The language is further complicated by Korea's complex social hierarchy – varying degrees of politeness are codified into the grammar according to one's social rank. Young Koreans tend to use the very polite forms a lot less than the older generations, but for safety's sake the sentences in this section employ polite forms.

Pronunciation
Vowels

ㅏ	a	as the 'a' in 'are'
ㅑ	ya	as in 'yard'
ㅓ	ŏ	as in 'of'
ㅕ	yŏ	as in 'young'
ㅗ	o	as in 'go'
ㅛ	yo	as in 'yoke'
ㅜ	u	as in 'flute'
ㅠ	yu	as the word 'you'
ㅡ	ŭ	as the 'oo' in 'look'
ㅣ	i	as the 'ee' in 'beet'

Combination Vowels

ㅐ	ae	as the 'a' in 'hat'
ㅒ	yae	as the 'ya' in 'yam'
ㅔ	e	as in 'ten'
ㅖ	ye	as in 'yes'
ㅘ	wa	as in 'waffle'
ㅙ	wae	as the 'wa' in 'wax'
ㅚ	oe	as the 'wa' in 'way'
ㅝ	wo	as in 'won'
ㅞ	we	as in 'wet'
ㅟ	wi	as the word 'we'
ㅢ	ŭi	as 'u' plus 'i'

Consonants

Apostrophes are used to indicate consonant sounds that are aspirated (accompanied by a puff of air). Consonants that aren't marked with an apostrophe are unaspirated and are generally difficult for English speakers to render. To those unfamiliar with Korean, an unaspirated 'k' will sound like 'g', an unaspirated 't' like 'd', and an unaspirated 'p' like 'b'.

Whether consonants in Korean are voiced or unvoiced depends in part on where they fall within a word – at the beginning, in the middle or at the end. The rules governing this are too complex to cover here – the following tables show the various ways you may see the Korean letter rendered into roman script.

Single Consonants

ㅅ is pronounced 'sh' if followed by the vowel ㅣ. In the middle of a word, ㄹ is pronounced 'n' if it follows ㅁ (m) or ㅇ (ng), but when it follows ㄴ (n) it becomes a double 'l' sound (ll).

ㄱ	k/g
ㄴ	n
ㄷ	t/d
ㄹ	r/n
ㅁ	m
ㅂ	p/b
ㅅ	s/sh/t
ㅇ	ng
ㅈ	ch/j/t
ㅊ	ch'/t
ㅋ	k'/k
ㅌ	t'/t
ㅍ	p'/p
ㅎ	h/ng

Double Consonants

Double consonants are said with more stress than single consonants.

ㄲ	kk/gg/k
ㄸ	tt/dd
ㅃ	pp/bb
ㅆ	ss/t
ㅉ	tch

Complex Consonants

These occur only in the middle or at the end of a word.

ㄱㅅ	ks/k
ㄴㅈ	nj/n
ㄴㅎ	nh/n
ㄹㄱ	lg/k
ㄹㅁ	lm/m
ㄹㅂ	lb/p
ㄹㅅ	ls/l
ㄹㅌ	lt'/l
ㄹㅍ	lp'/p
ㄹㅎ	lh/l
ㅂㅅ	ps/p

Greetings & Civilities

Hello.
annyŏng hashimnigga (formal)
안녕하십니까
annyŏng haseyo (less formal)
안녕하세요
Goodbye. (to person leaving)
annyŏnghi kaseyo
안녕히가세요
Goodbye. (to person staying)
annyŏnghi kyeseyo
안녕히계세요

LANGUAGE

Please.
put'ak hamnida 부탁합니다
Thank you.
kamsa hamnida 감사합니다
You're welcome.
gwaench'ansŭmnida 괜찮습니다
Yes.
ye/ne 예/네
No.
aniyo 아니요
Excuse me.
shillye hamnida 실례합니다
I'm sorry.
mianhamnida 미안합니다
My name is ...
che irŭmŭn ... 제 이름은 ...
imnida 입니다
I come from ...
ch'ŏnŭn ... e sŏ 저는 ... 에서
watsŭmnida 왔습니다

Getting Around
I want to get off here.
yŏgiyae naeryŏ juseyo
여기에 내려 주세요
I want to go to ...
... e kago shipsŭmnida
에 가고싶습니다
Where can I catch the bus to ...?
... haeng bŏsŭnŭn ŏtiesŏ t'apnigga?
... 행 버스는 어디에서 탑니까?

airport
konghang 공항
express bus terminal
kosok bŏsŭ t'ŏminŏl 고속버스 터미널
bus stop
bŏsŭ chŏngnyujang 버스 정류장
inter-city bus terminal
shi'oe bŏsŭ t'ŏminŏl 시여버스 터미널
ferry crossing
naru 나루
ferry pier
pudu 부두
subway station
chihach'ŏl yŏk 지하철역
train station
kich'a yŏk 기차역
airport bus
konghang bŏsŭ 공항버스
bus
bŏsŭ 버스

ferry boat
yogaeksŏn 여객선
taxi
t'aekshi 택시
train
kich'a 기차
timetable
shigakp'yo 시각표
bus card
bŏsŭ k'adŭ 버스카드
one-way (ticket)
p'yŏndo 편도
return (ticket)
wangbok 왕복
refund ticket
hwanbul 환불
multiple-use
subway ticket
chŏngaeksŭng 정액승차권
ch'agwon
lockers
boguanham 보갑함
lost & found office
punshilmulpo 분실물보갑센타
kwansaent'a
immigration office
ch'ulibkuk kwaliso 출입국 관리소
passport
yŏgwon 여권

Around Town
post office
uch'eguk 우체국
stamp
u'p'yo 우표
airmail letter
hanggong sŏgan 항공 서간
aerogramme
hanggong 항공 봉함엽서
ponghamnyŏpsŏ
International Express Mail
kukje t'ŭkgŭp up'yŏn 국제 특급우편
public phone
gongjung chŏnhwa 공중전화
telephone office
chŏnhwaguk 전화국
telephone card
chŏnhwa k'adŭ 전화카드

I'd like to know the phone number here.
yŏgi chŏnhwapŏnho jom
karŭch'yŏ juseyo
여기 전화번호 좀 가르쳐 주세요

bank
ŭnhaeng 은행
May I have change, please?
chandonŭro pakkwo juseyo 잔돈으로 바꿔 주세요?
How much does it cost?
ŏlmayeyo? 얼마예요?
That's too expensive.
nŏmu pissayo 너무 비싸요
Can I have a discount?
chom ssage hae juseyo 좀 싸게 해 주세요?
May I use a credit card?
k'adŭrŭl ssŭlsu issŭmnikka? 카드를 쓸수 웻습니까?

Accommodation

hotel
hot'el 호텔
guesthouse
yŏgwan 여관
cheap guesthouse
yŏinsuk 여인숙
home stay
minbak 민박
single room
shinggŭl lum 싱글룸
double room
tŏbŭl lum 더블룸
with shared bath
yokshil ŏmnŭn bang 욕실 없는 방
with private bath
yokshil innŭn bang 욕실 웻는 방
bathhouse
mogyokt'ang 목욕탕
towel
sugŏn 수건

Is there a room vacant?
bin bang issŭmnikka? 빈 방 있습니까?
May I see the room?
pang'ŭl polsu issŏyo? 방을 볼수 있어요?
Do you have anything cheaper?
tŏ ssan kot sun ŏpsŭmnigga? 더 싼 것은 없습니까?
May I have a name card?
myŏngham jom ŏtŭl su issŭlkkayo? 명함 좀 얻을 수 있을까요?

I'll pay you now.
chigŭm chibulhago ship'ŭn teyo 지금 지불하고 싶은 데요
Please give me a receipt.
yŏngsujŭng jom juseyo. 영수증 좀 갖다 주세요
I want to stay one more night.
haru tŏ mukgo ship'sŭmnida 하루 더 묵고 싶습니다
Please give me my key.
yŏlsoe jom juseyo 열쇠 좀 주세요
Could you clean my room, please?
bangchyŏngso jom hae juseyo 방청소 좀 해 주세요?
Can you have my clothes washed?
Set'ak ssobisŭ toemnikka? 세탁 써비스 됩니까?

Health

anti-diarrhoeal
sŏlsa yak 설사약
condoms
kondom 콘돔
mosquito coil
mogihyang 모기향
laxative
pyŏnbi yak 변비약
pain killer
chint'ongche 진통제
pharmacy
yakkuk 약국
sanitary pads
saengnidae 생리대
tampons
t'emp'o 템포
toilet
hwajangshil 화장실
toilet paper
hwajangji 화장지

Emergencies

Help!
saram sallyŏ! 사람살려!
Thief!
todugiya! 도둑이야!
Fire!
puriya! 불이야!
hospital
pyŏngwon 병원
Call a doctor!
ŭisarul pullŏ juseyo! 의사를 불러 주세요!

Call an ambulance!
*kugŭpch'a chom
pullŏ juseyo!*
구급차 좀 불러
주세요!
Call the police!
*kyŏngch'alŭl pullŏ
juseyo!*
경찰을 불러
주세요!
I'm allergic to penicillin.
*P'enishillin
allerugiga issŏyo*
페니실린 알레
르기가 있어요
I'm allergic to antibiotics.
*hangsaengche
allerugiga issŏyo*
항생제 알레
르기가 있어요
I'm diabetic.
*tangnyopyŏngi
issŏyo*
당뇨병이 있어요

Numbers

Korean has two counting systems. One is of Chinese origin and the other a native Korean system. Korean numbers only go up to 99. Either Chinese or Korean numbers can be used to count days. Chinese numbers are used for minutes and kilometres. Korean numbers are used for hours. The Chinese system is used to count money, not surprising since the smallest Korean banknote is W1000.

Number	Chinese		Korean	
0	–	–	*yŏng/kong*	영/공
1	*il*	일	*hana*	하나
2	*I*	이	*tul*	둘
3	*sam*	삼	*set*	셋
4	*sa*	사	*net*	넷
5	*o*	오	*tasŏt*	다섯
6	*yuk*	육	*yŏsŏt*	여섯
7	*ch'il*	칠	*ilgop*	일곱
8	*p'al*	팔	*yŏdŏl*	여덟
9	*ku*	구	*ahop*	아홉
10	*ship*	십	*yŏl*	열

Number	Combination	
11	*ship'il*	십일
20	*i'ship*	이십
30	*sam'ship*	삼십
40	*sa'ship*	사십
48	*sa'shipp'al*	사십팔
50	*o'ship*	오십
100	*paek*	백
200	*i'paek*	이백
300	*sampaek*	삼백
846	*p'alpaek
saship'yuk*	팔백사십육

| 1000 | *ch'ŏn* | 천 |
| 2000 | *i'ch'ŏn* | 이천 |
| 5729 | *o'ch'ŏn
ch'ilpaek
i'shipku* | 오천칠백이십구 |
| 10,000 | *man* | 만 |

FOOD
Useful Phrases

restaurant
shikdang
식당
I'm a vegetarian.
ch'aeshik juwi imnida
채식 주의 입니다.
I want to eat spicy food.
maepke hae juseyo
맵게 해 주세요.
I can't eat spicy food.
mae'un ŭmshikun mŏkji motamnida
매운 음식은 먹지 못합니다.
The menu, please.
menyurŭl poyŏ juseyo
메뉴를 보여 주세요
The bill/check, please.
kyesansŏ juseyo
계산서 주세요

| noodles | *myŏn/kuksu* | 면/국수 |
| rice (cooked) | *bap* | 밥 |

Seafood 생선요리

clam	*taehap*	대합
crab	*ke*	게
cuttlefish	*ojingŏ*	오징어
eel	*paemjangŏ*	뱀장어
fish	*saengsŏn*	생선
oyster	*kul*	굴
shrimp	*saeu*	새우

Meat 육류

beef	*sogogi*	소고기
chicken	*takkogi*	닭고기
mutton	*yanggogi*	양고기
pork	*taejigogi*	돼지고기

Vegetables 야채요리

beans	*k'ong*	콩
cucumber	*oi*	오이
dried seaweed	*kim*	김
garlic	*manŭl*	마늘
green or
red pepper	*goch'u*	고추

lotus root	yŏn'gŭn	연근
mushroom	pŏsŏt	버섯
onion	yangp'a	양파
potato	kamja	감자
radish	muu	무우
soybean sprouts	k'ongnamul	콩나물
spinach	shigumch'i	시금치

Condiments 양념

black pepper	huch'u	후추
butter	pŏt'ŏ	버터
hot chilli pepper	koch'u karu	고추가루
hot sauce	koch'ujang	고추장
jam	chaem	잼
ketchup	k'ech'ŏp	케찹
mayonnaise	mayonejŭ	마요네즈
mustard	kyŏja	겨자
salt	sogŭm	소금
soy sauce	kanjang	간장
soybean paste	toenjang	된장
sugar	sŏlt'ang	설탕
vinegar	shikch'o	식초

Drinks

hot water		
tŏun mul		더운물
cold water		
ch'an mul		찬물
mineral water		
sengsu/kwangch'ŏnsu		생수/광천수
tea		
ch'a		차
arrowroot tea		
ch'ik ch'a		칡차
barley tea		
bori ch'a		보리차
black tea		
hong ch'a		홍차
Chinese matrimony vine tea		
kugija ch'a		구기자차
citron tea		
yuja ch'a		유자차
five flavours tea		
omija ch'a		오미자차
ginger tea		
saengkang ch'a		생강차
ginseng tea		
insam ch'a		인삼차
green tea		
nok ch'a		녹차

herb tonic tea		
ssanghwa ch'a		쌍화차
honey tea		
kkul ch'a		꿀차
honey-ginseng tea		
kkul sam ch'a		꿀삼차
jujube tea		
taech'u ch'a		대추차
lemon tea		
remon ch'a		레몬차
mugwort tea		
ssuk ch'a		쑥차
pine nuts, walnuts & adlay tea		
yulmu ch'a		율무차
coffee		
kŏp'i		커피
hot cocoa		
k'ok'oa		코코아
juice		
chyusŭ		쥬스
orange juice		
orenji chyusŭ		오렌지쥬스
milk		
uyu		우유
Coca-Cola		
k'ok'a k'olra		코카콜라
beer		
maekchu		맥주
wine		
p'odoju		포도주
Kyŏngju Beobjoo (wine)		
Kyŏngju pŏbju		경주법주
milky white rice brew		
makkŏli		막걸리
yam or tapioca 'vodka'		
soju		소주
ginseng wine		
insamju		인삼주

Korean Dishes 한국음식

omelette with rice		
omŭ raisŭ		오므라이스
pork cutlet with rice & vegetables		
tonggasŭ		돈까스
barbecued beef & vegetables grill		
pulgogi		불고기
marinated beef/pork ribs grill		
pulgalbi		불갈비
barbecued beef ribs grill		
kalbi kui		갈비구이

barbecued pork ribs grill
taeji kalbi 돼지갈비
beef ribs soup
kalbi t'ang 갈비탕
salted beef ribs
sogŭm kui 소금구이
stew
tchigae 찌개
barbecued beef ribs stew
kalbi tchim 갈비찜
tofu stew
tubu tchigae 두부 찌개
tofu & clam stew
sundubu tchigae 순두부 찌개
chicken stew
talgtchim 닭찜
kimch'i stew
kimch'i tchigae 김치찌개
soybean paste stew
toenjang tchigae 된장찌개
cow intestine stew
kopch'ang chŏnggol 곱창전골
roasted chicken
t'ongdalggui 통닭구이
diced grilled chicken
tak kalbi 닭갈비
fried kimch'i rice
kimch'i bogŭmbap 김치볶음밥
steamed rice
konggibap 공기밥
rice, egg, meat &
vegetables in hot sauce
pibimbap 비빔밥
rice & vegetable pot
tolsot pibimbap 돌솥비빔밥
meat, fish & vegetables
broth cooked at table
shinsŏllo 신선로
cold noodle soup
mul naengmyŏn 물냉면
cold noodle kimch'i soup
yŏlmu naengmyŏn 열무냉면
spicy cold noodles
without soup
pibim naengmyŏn 비빔 냉면
noodle dish & soy
milk broth
k'ong kuksu 콩국수
thick hand-made noodles
k'al kuksu 칼국수
fried ramen noodles
ramyŏn boggi 라면볶이

soup ramen noodles
ramyŏn 라면
mixed vegetables & beef
with soybean noodles
chapch'ae 잡채
vegetables, meat, noodles
& chicken broth
mak kuksu 막국수
octopus hotpot
nakchi chŏn-gol 낙지전골
tripe hotpot
kopch'ang chŏn-gol 곱창전골
soup
kuk or *t'ang* 국 / 탕
ginseng chicken soup
samgye t'ang 삼계탕
soft boiled stuffed chicken
tak paeksuk 닭백숙
beef & rice soup
sŏllŏng t'ang 설렁탕
beef soup
kom t'ang 곰탕
ox tail soup
kkorikom t'ang 꼬리곰탕
ox leg soup
togani t'ang 도가니탕
spicy beef soup
yukkaejang 육개장
spicy fish soup
maeun t'ang 매운탕
spicy assorted seafood soup
haemul t'ang 해물탕
mudfish soup
ch'uŏ t'ang 추어탕
brown seaweed soup
miyŏk kuk 미역국
pollack (seafood) soup
pugŏ kuk 북어국
boiled silkworm snack
ppŏndaegi 뻔대기
dumplings
mandu 만두
soup with meat-filled
dumplings
mandu guk 만두국
seafood & vegetables
fried in batter
t'wigim 튀김
spicy rice bean sprout
porridge
k'ongnamul kukpap 콩나물국밥
abalone porridge
chŏnbokchuk 전복죽

pickled vegetables,
garlic & chilli
  kimch'i   김치
corn on the cob
  oksusu   옥수수
green onion pancake
  p'ajŏn   파전
mung bean pancake
  pindaettŏk   빈대떡
spicy rice rolls
  ttŏkpokki   떡볶이
pickled daikon radish
  tongchimi   동치미
seasoned raw beef
  yukhoe   육회
dog meat soup
  poshin t'ang   보신탕
pork sausage
  sundae   순대
steamed pork hocks
  chokpal   족발
steamed pork & cabbage
  possam   보쌈
steamed spicy angler fish
  agutchim   아구찜
grilled eel
  chang-i kui   장이구이
jellied acorn puree
  mug much'im   묵무침
live octopus tentacles
  munŏbal   문어발
banquet
  hanjŏngshik   한정식
laver-wrapped sushi
  kimbap   김밥
beef sushi
  soegogi kimbap 쇠고기김밥
cheese sushi
  ch'iju kimbap   치즈 김밥
tuna sushi
  ch'amch'i kimbap 참치 김밥
kimch'i sushi
  kimch'i kimbap   김치 김밥
assorted sushi
  modŭm kimbap   모듬 김밥

Desserts 디저트
cake   *k'eik'ŭ*   케이크
ice cream *aisŭk'ŭrim* 아이스크림
pie   *p'ai*   파이
pastry   *kwaja*   과자
red bean *p'atbingsu*   팥빙삭
  parfait

waffles   *wap'ŭl/*   와플/
           p'ulbbang 풀빵

Chinese Food 중국음식
Chinese restaurant
  chungkuk chip   중국집
noodles with hot beef sauce
  tchajang myŏn 짜장면
thick noodles with sauce
  udong   우동
spicy seafood noodle soup
  tchambbong   짬뽕
vegetables with noodles &
hot beef sauce
  kan tchajang myŏn 간짜장면
soupy noodles
  ul myŏn   울면
noodles & spicy sauce
  samsŏn tchajang 삼선짜장
noodles & flavoured sauces
  samsŏn ganjajang 삼선간짜장
spicy noodles with
vegetables
  samsŏn tchambbong 삼선짬뽕
seafood noodles
  samsŏn udong   삼선우동
seafood soupy noodles
  samsŏn ul myŏn 삼선울면
fried rice
  poggŭm bap   볶음밥
fried rice with noodles
  chapch'ae bap   잡채밥
assorted seafood, meat,
vegetables & rice
  chapt'ang bap   잡탕밥
rice with mushroom sauce
  song'idŏp bap   송이덮밥
shrimp fried rice
  sae'u poggŭm bap 새우볶음밥
fried dumplings
  kun mandu   군만두
fried vermicelli, meat &
vegetables
  chapch'ae   잡채
sweet & sour pork
  t'angsu yuk   탕수육
pork & green pepper rice
  goch'u chapch'ae 고추잡채
pork & scallions rice
  puch'u chapch'ae 부추잡채
seafood & vegetables
  p'albo ch'ae   팔보채

chicken dish
　kkanp'unggi　깐풍기
spicy chicken dish
　rajogi　라조기
spicy pork & beef dish
　rajoyuk　라조육
minced pork or beef balls
　nanjawansŭ　난자완스
shrimp dish
　saeut'wikim　새우튀김
prawns
　k'ŭnsaeut'wikim　큰새우튀김
Sichuan dish
　sach'ŏn t'angyuk　사천탕육
cold Chinese salad
　samp'um naengch'ae　삼품냉채
sliced meats
　ohyang jangyuk　오향장육
egg soup
　kyeran t'ang　계란탕
assorted soup
　chap t'ang　잡탕

Japanese Food　일식

Japanese restaurant
　ilshikchib　일식집
shrimp tempura with
vegetables
　saeu t'wigim　새우튀김
fish tempura
　saengsŏn t'wigim　생선튀김
vegetable tempura
　yach'ae t'wigim　야채튀김
sashimi (raw fish)
　saengsŏn hoe　생선회
sushi
　ch'obap　초밥
tofu-wrapped sushi
　yubu ch'obap　유부초밥

Glossary

agashi – an unmarried or young woman
ajashi – a married or older man, a term of respect
ajimma – a married or older woman, a term of respect
am – hermitage
anju – snacks (peanuts, dried cuttlefish etc) to accompany drinking

bang – a room, eg in a hotel
bong – peak

ch'a – tea
chaebol – huge corporate conglomerate
changgi – Korean chess, played much the same way it once was in China; a forerunner of western-style chess
chihach'ŏl yŏk – subway station
ch'ŏnhwa – telephone

dae – great, large
daehakkyo – university (also spelled tae-hakkyo); often shortened, eg 'Yonsei-dae' (Yonsei University)
do – island, eg Kanghwado
-do – province, eg Kyŏnggi-do
dong – administrative 'neighbourhood', eg Apkujŏng-dong
dong-dongju – a slightly more refined version of *makkŏlli*

-ga – section of a long street
gak, **nu** or **ru** – pavilion
gang – river, eg Han-gang
gil – street
-gu – urban district
guk – country, eg Hanguk (Korea)
gun – county
gung or **kung** – palace

hae – sea, eg Tong-hae (East Sea, called Sea of Japan in English)
hagwon – private language school often employing foreign teachers
haksuljip – boarding house

halmŏni – respectful term for an elderly woman
hanbok – traditional loose-fitting dress
han'gŭl – Korean phonetic alphabet
hanja or **hancha** – Chinese-character based writing system
harabŏji – respectful term for an elderly man
hesuyokjang – beach
ho – lake
hof – (from German, pronounced 'hopu') pub

insam – ginseng

jŏng – hall of a temple

kibun – an ethic of sensing and maintaining a harmonious atmosphere
kich'a – train
kimch'i – spicy fermented cabbage, Korea's 'national dish'
kŏbuksŏn – 'turtle ship', the iron-clad warships made famous by Admiral Yi
konghang – airport
kongwon – park

maekchu – beer
makkŏlli – a milky-white rice 'wine', traditionally a farmer's drink
minbak – homestay, a private home with rooms for rent
mogyokt'ang – bathhouse
mun – gate
myo – shrine
myŏn – township

nam – south
-nim – an honorific suffix, eg *songsaeng-nim* ('respected teacher')
no or **ro** – large street, boulevard
nŭng or **rŭng** – tomb

ondol – unique and efficient form of ducted underfloor heating

paduk – the Korean version of an old Chinese game of strategy, known as *go* in Japan
puk – north
pulgogi or **bulgogi** – barbecued beef and vegetables (especially garlic) grilled at the table, the most popular dish with carnivorous foreigners
p'yŏng – a unit of measure, one p'yŏng equals 3.3 sq metres

ri or **ni** – village

sa – temple, eg Chogyesa
san – mountain, eg Namsan
sanjang – mountain hut
sansŏng – fortress built on a mountaintop, eg Namhansansŏng
shi – city
shich'ŏng – city hall
shijang – market
sŏ – west
soju – a cheap 'n' nasty version of Japanese *shochu*; a *sake*-like product, soju is sold by the millions in small bottles, which are recycled as Molotov cocktails by ecologically oriented student radicals
songsaeng – teacher
sŏwon – former Confucian academies, which are preserved as national treasures
ssirŭm – Korean wrestling

tabang – tearoom
tae – see *myo*
t'aekkyŏn – original form of *t'aekwondo*

t'aekwondo – Korea's most well known martial art
taepiso – mountain shelter
t'ap – pagoda
tchimjilbang – sauna, usually only for women
tong – east
t'ongil – unification

ŭp – town

weiguksaram – foreigner (literally 'outside country person')
wonch'ŏn – hot spring

yak – medicine; pharmacy
yŏgwan – small family-run inn, usually with private bath
yŏinsuk – cheaper but increasingly rare version of a *yŏgwan*, with closet-sized rooms and shared bath
yŏk – station, eg *kich'a yŏk* (train station)

ACRONYMS
CPO – Central Post Office
DMZ – Demilitaised Zone
DPRK – Democratic People's Republic of Korea (commonly known as North Korea)
KAL – Korean Air
KNR – Korean National Railroad
KNTO – Korean National Tourism Organisation
ROK – Republic of Korea (in other words, South Korea)
USO – United Service Organisation

Acknowledgments

Many thanks to the following travellers who used the last edition and wrote to us with helpful hints, useful advice and interesting anecdotes:

David Benner, Peter Caruana, Eric van Dort, Richard Ewen, Robin Fletcher, Joan Giblin, Michelle Grott, Chua Siaw Hui, Todd Jackson, Steven James, Sheldon Johnston, Baylor Lancaster, Rosario Lapus, Claire Lessard, Claudia Li, Gregory McElwain, Gary Mink, Veronica Munk, Heather J Sharkey, Vinod Vijayakumar, Jane Willdigg, Sean D Williams, Bo Young Yoon, R Zellingen

LONELY PLANET

Phrasebooks

Lonely Planet phrasebooks are packed with essential words and phrases to help travellers communicate with the locals. With colour tabs for quick reference, an extensive vocabulary and use of script, these handy pocket-sized language guides cover day-to-day travel situations.

- handy pocket-sized books
- easy to understand Pronunciation chapter
- clear & comprehensive Grammar chapter
- romanisation alongside script to allow ease of pronunciation
- script throughout so users can point to phrases for every situation
- full of cultural information and tips for the traveller

'... vital for a real DIY spirit and attitude in language learning'
— *Backpacker*

'the phrasebooks have good cultural backgrounders and offer solid advice for challenging situations in remote locations'
— *San Francisco Examiner*

Arabic (Egyptian) ● Arabic (Moroccan) ● Australian *(Australian English, Aboriginal and Torres Strait languages)* ● Baltic States *(Estonian, Latvian, Lithuanian)* ● Bengali ● Brazilian ● Burmese ● British *(English, dialects, Scottish Gaelic, Welsh)* ● Cantonese ● Central Asia *(Kazakh, Kyrgyz, Pashto, Tajik, Tashkorghani, Turkmen, Uyghur, Uzbek & others)* ● Central Europe *(Czech, German, Hungarian, Polish, Slovak, Slovene)* ● Costa Rica Spanish ● Eastern Europe *(Albanian, Bulgarian, Croatian, Czech, Hungarian, Macedonian, Polish, Romanian, Serbian, Slovak, Slovene)* ● East Timor *(Tetun, Portuguese)* ● Egyptian Arabic ● Ethiopian (Amharic) ● Europe *(Basque, Catalan, Dutch, French, German, Greek, Irish, Italian, Maltese, Portuguese, Scottish Gaelic, Spanish, Turkish, Welsh)* ● Farsi (Persian*)* ● Fijian ● French ● German ● Greek ● Hebrew ● Hill Tribes *(Lahu, Akha, Lisu, Mong, Mien & others)* ● Hindi/Urdu ● Indonesian ● Italian ● Japanese ● Korean ● Lao ● Latin American Spanish ● Malay ● Mandarin ● Mongolian ● Moroccan Arabic ● Nepali ● Papua New Guinea ● Pidgin ● Pilipino (Tagalog) ● Polish ● Portuguese ● Quechua ● Russian ● Scandinavian *(Danish, Faroese, Finnish, Icelandic, Norwegian, Swedish)* ● South-East Asia *(Burmese, Indonesian, Khmer, Lao, Malay, Tagalog Pilipino, Thai, Vietnamese)* ● South Pacific *(Fijian, Hawaiian, Kanak languages, Maori, Niuean, Rapanui, Rarotongan Maori, Samoan, Tahitian, Tongan & others)* ● Spanish *(Castilian, also includes Catalan, Galician & Basque)* ● Sri Lanka ● Swahili ● Thai ● Tibetan ● Turkish ● Ukrainian ● USA *(US English, Vernacular, Native American, Hawaiian)* ● Vietnamese

LONELY PLANET

Lonely Planet Travel Atlases

L onely Planet has long been famous for the number and quality of its guidebook maps. Now we've gone one step further and produced a handy companion series: Lonely Planet travel atlases – maps of a country produced in book form.

Unlike other maps, which look good but lead travellers astray, our travel atlases have been researched on the road by Lonely Planet's experienced team of writers. All details are carefully checked to ensure the atlas corresponds with the equivalent Lonely Planet guidebook.

- full-colour throughout
- maps researched and checked by Lonely Planet authors
- place names correspond with Lonely Planet guidebooks
- no confusing spelling differences
- legend and travelling information in English, French, German, Japanese and Spanish
- size: 230 x 160 mm

Available now: Chile & Easter Island • Egypt • India & Bangladesh • Israel & the Palestinian Territories • Jordan, Syria & Lebanon • Kenya • Laos • Portugal • South Africa, Lesotho & Swaziland • Thailand • Turkey • Vietnam • Zimbabwe, Botswana & Namibia

---

Lonely Planet TV Series & Videos

L onely Planet travel guides have been brought to life on television screens around the world. Like our guides, the programs are based on the joy of independent travel, and look honestly at some of the most exciting, picturesque and frustrating places in the world. Each show is presented by one of three travellers from Australia, England or the USA and combines an innovative mixture of video, Super-8 film, atmospheric soundscapes and original music.

Videos of each episode – containing additional footage not shown on television – are available from good book and video shops, but the availability of individual videos varies with regional screening schedules.

Video destinations include: Alaska • American Rockies • Australia – The South-East • Baja California & the Copper Canyon • Brazil • Central Asia • Chile & Easter Island • Corsica, Sicily & Sardinia – The Mediterranean Islands • East Africa (Tanzania & Zanzibar) • Ecuador & the Galapagos Islands • Greenland & Iceland • Indonesia • Israel & the Sinai Desert • Jamaica • Japan • La Ruta Maya • Morocco • New York • North India • Pacific Islands (Fiji, Solomon Islands & Vanuatu) • South India • South West China • Turkey • Vietnam • West Africa • Zimbabwe, Botswana & Namibia

The Lonely Planet TV series is produced by: Pilot Productions
The Old Studio
18 Middle Row
London W10 5AT, UK

LONELY PLANET

Guides by Region

Lonely Planet is known worldwide for publishing practical, reliable and no-nonsense travel information in our guides and on our Web site. The Lonely Planet list covers just about every accessible part of the world. Currently there are sixteen series: Travel guides, Shoestring guides, Condensed guides, Phrasebooks, Read This First, Healthy Travel, Walking guides, Cycling guides, Watching Wildlife guides, Pisces Diving & Snorkelling guides, City Maps, Road Atlases, Out to Eat, World Food, Journeys travel literature, Traveller's Advice titles and Illustrated pictorials.

AFRICA Africa on a shoestring • Cairo • Cairo Map • Cape Town • Cape Town Map • East Africa • Egypt • Egyptian Arabic phrasebook • Ethiopia, Eritrea & Djibouti • Ethiopian (Amharic) phrasebook • The Gambia & Senegal • Healthy Travel Africa • Kenya • Malawi • Morocco • Moroccan Arabic phrasebook • Mozambique • Read This First: Africa • South Africa, Lesotho & Swaziland • Southern Africa • Southern Africa Road Atlas • Swahili phrasebook • Tanzania, Zanzibar & Pemba • Trekking in East Africa • Tunisia • Watching Wildlife East Africa • Watching Wildlife Southern Africa • West Africa • World Food Morocco • Zimbabwe, Botswana & Namibia
Travel Literature: Mali Blues: Traveling to an African Beat • The Rainbird: A Central African Journey • Songs to an African Sunset: A Zimbabwean Story

AUSTRALIA & THE PACIFIC Aboriginal Australia & Torres Strait Islands • Auckland • Australia • Australian phrasebook • Australia Road Atlas • Bushwalking in Australia • Cycling Australia • Cycling New Zealand • Fiji • Fijian phrasebook • Healthy Travel Australia, NZ and the Pacific • Islands of Australia's Great Barrier Reef • Melbourne • Melbourne Map • Micronesia • New Caledonia • New South Wales & the ACT • New Zealand • Northern Territory • Outback Australia • Out to Eat – Melbourne • Out to Eat – Sydney • Papua New Guinea • Papua New Guinea Phrasebook • Pidgin phrasebook • Queensland • Rarotonga & the Cook Islands • Samoa • Solomon Islands • South Australia • South Pacific • South Pacific phrasebook • Sydney • Sydney Map • Sydney Condensed • Tahiti & French Polynesia • Tasmania • Tonga • Tramping in New Zealand • Vanuatu • Victoria • Walking in Australia • Watching Wildlife Australia • Western Australia
Travel Literature: Islands in the Clouds: Travels in the Highlands of New Guinea • Kiwi Tracks: A New Zealand Journey • Sean & David's Long Drive

CENTRAL AMERICA & THE CARIBBEAN Bahamas, Turks & Caicos • Baja California • Bermuda • Central America on a shoestring • Costa Rica • Costa Rica Spanish phrasebook • Cuba • Dominican Republic & Haiti • Eastern Caribbean • Guatemala • Guatemala, Belize & Yucatán: La Ruta Maya • Havana • Healthy Travel Central & South America • San Diego & Tijuana • Jamaica • Mexico • Mexico City • Panama • Puerto Rico • Read This First: Central & South America • World Food Mexico • World Food Caribbean • Yucatán
Travel Literature: Green Dreams: Travels in Central America

EUROPE Amsterdam • Amsterdam Map • Amsterdam Condensed • Andalucía • Austria • Baltic States phrasebook • Barcelona • Barcelona Map • Belgium & Luxembourg • Berlin • Berlin Map • Britain • British phrasebook • Brussels, Bruges & Antwerp • Brussels Map • Budapest • Budapest Map • Canary Islands • Central Europe • Central Europe phrasebook • Copenhagen • Corfu & the Ionians • Corsica • Crete • Crete Condensed • Croatia • Cycling Britain • Cycling France • Cyprus • Czech & Slovak Republics • Denmark • Dublin • Dublin Map • Eastern Europe • Eastern Europe phrasebook • Edinburgh • England • Estonia, Latvia & Lithuania • Europe on a shoestring • Europe Phrasebook • Finland • Florence • France • Frankfurt Condensed • French phrasebook • Georgia, Armenia & Azerbaijan • Germany • German phrasebook • Greece • Greek Islands • Greek phrasebook • Hungary • Iceland, Greenland & the Faroe Islands • Ireland • Istanbul • Italian phrasebook • Italy • Krakow • Lisbon • The Loire • London • London Map • London Condensed • Madrid • Malta • Mediterranean Europe • Milan, Turin & Genoa • Moscow • Mozambique • Munich • The Netherlands • Normandy • Norway • Out to Eat – London • Paris • Paris Map • Paris Condensed • Poland • Polish Phrasebook • Portugal • Portuguese phrasebook • Prague • Prague Map • Provence & the Côte d'Azur • Read This First: Europe • Rhodes & the Dodecanese • Romania & Moldova • Rome • Rome Condensed • Rome Map • Russia, Ukraine & Belarus • Russian phrasebook • Scandinavian & Baltic Europe • Scandinavian phrasebook • Scotland • Sicily • Slovenia • South-West France • Spain • Spanish phrasebook • St Petersburg • St Petersburg Map • Sweden • Switzerland • Trekking in Spain • Tuscany • Ukrainian phrasebook • Venice • Vienna • Walking in Britain • Walking in France • Walking in Ireland • Walking in Italy • Walking in Spain • Walking in Switzerland • Western Europe • World Food France • World Food Ireland • World Food Italy • World Food Spain
Travel Literature: A Small Place in Italy • After Yugoslavia • Love and War in the Apennines • On the Shores of the Mediterranean The Olive Grove: Travels in Greece • Round Ireland in Low Gear

LONELY PLANET

Mail Order

Lonely Planet products are distributed worldwide. They are also available by mail order from Lonely Planet, so if you have difficulty finding a title please write to us. North and South American residents should write to 150 Linden St, Oakland, CA 94607, USA; European and African residents should write to 10a Spring Place, London NW5 3BH, UK; and residents of other countries to Locked Bag 1, Footscray, Victoria 3011, Australia.

INDIAN SUBCONTINENT Bangladesh • Bengali phrasebook • Bhutan • Delhi • Goa • Healthy Travel Asia & India • Hindi & Urdu phrasebook • India • Indian Himalaya • Karakoram Highway • Kerala • Mumbai (Bombay) • Nepal • Nepali phrasebook • Pakistan • Rajasthan • Read This First: Asia & India • South India • Sri Lanka • Sri Lanka phrasebook • Tibet • Tibetan phrasebook • Trekking in the Indian Himalaya • Trekking in the Karakoram & Hindukush • Trekking in the Nepal Himalaya
Travel Literature: The Age of Kali: Indian Travels and Encounters • Hello Goodnight: A Life of Goa • In Rajasthan • A Season in Heaven: True Tales from the Road to Kathmandu • Shopping for Buddhas • A Short Walk in the Hindu Kush • Slowly Down the Ganges

ISLANDS OF THE INDIAN OCEAN Madagascar & Comoros • Maldives • Mauritius, Réunion & Seychelles
Travel Literature: Maverick in Madagascar·

MIDDLE EAST & CENTRAL ASIA Bahrain, Kuwait & Qatar • Central Asia • Central Asia phrasebook • Dubai • Farsi (Persian) phrasebook • Hebrew phrasebook • Iran • Israel & the Palestinian Territories • Istanbul • Istanbul Map • Istanbul to Cairo on a shoestring • Istanbul to Kathmandu • Jerusalem • Jerusalem Map • Jordan • Lebanon • Middle East • Oman & the United Arab Emirates • Syria • Turkey • Turkish phrasebook • World Food Turkey • Yemen
Travel Literature: Black on Black: Iran Revisited • The Gates of Damascus • Kingdom of the Film Stars: Journey into Jordan

NORTH AMERICA Alaska • Boston • Boston Map • Boston Condensed • British Colombia • California & Nevada • California Condensed • Canada • Chicago • Chicago Map • Deep South • Florida • Great Lakes • Hawaii • Hiking in Alaska • Hiking in the USA • Honolulu • Las Vegas • Los Angeles • Los Angeles Map • Louisiana & The Deep South • Miami • Miami Map • Montreal • New England • New Orleans • New York City • New York City Map • New York City Condensed • New York, New Jersey & Pennsylvania • Oahu • Out to Eat – San Francisco • Pacific Northwest • Puerto Rico • Rocky Mountains • San Francisco • San Francisco Map • San Diego & Tijuana • Seattle • Southwest • Texas • Toronto • USA • USA phrasebook • Vancouver • Virginia & the Capital Region • Washington DC • Washington DC Map • World Food Deep South, USA • World Food New Orleans
Travel Literature: Caught Inside: A Surfer's Year on the California Coast • Drive Thru America

NORTH-EAST ASIA Beijing • Beijing Map • Cantonese phrasebook • China • Hiking in Japan • Hong Kong • Hong Kong Map • Hong Kong Condensed • Hong Kong, Macau & Guangzhou • Japan • Japanese phrasebook • Korea • Korean phrasebook • Kyoto • Mandarin phrasebook • Mongolia • Mongolian phrasebook • Seoul • Shanghai • South-West China • Taiwan • Tokyo • World Food – Hong Kong
Travel Literature: In Xanadu: A Quest • Lost Japan

SOUTH AMERICA Argentina, Uruguay & Paraguay • Bolivia • Brazil • Brazilian phrasebook • Buenos Aires • Chile & Easter Island • Colombia • Ecuador & the Galapagos Islands • Healthy Travel Central & South America • Latin American Spanish phrasebook • Peru • Quechua phrasebook • Read This First: Central & South America • Rio de Janeiro • Rio de Janeiro Map • Santiago • South America on a shoestring • Santiago • Trekking in the Patagonian Andes • Venezuela
Travel Literature: Full Circle: A South American Journey

SOUTH-EAST ASIA Bali & Lombok • Bangkok • Bangkok Map • Burmese phrasebook • Cambodia • East Timor Phrasebook • Hanoi • Healthy Travel Asia & India • Hill Tribes phrasebook • Ho Chi Minh City • Indonesia • Indonesian phrasebook • Indonesia's Eastern Islands • Jakarta • Java • Lao phrasebook • Laos • Malay phrasebook • Malaysia, Singapore & Brunei • Myanmar (Burma) • Philippines • Pilipino (Tagalog) phrasebook • Read This First: Asia & India • Singapore • Singapore Map • South-East Asia on a shoestring • South-East Asia phrasebook • Thailand • Thailand's Islands & Beaches • Thailand, Vietnam, Laos & Cambodia Road Atlas • Thai phrasebook • Vietnam • Vietnamese phrasebook • World Food Thailand • World Food Vietnam

ALSO AVAILABLE: Antarctica • The Arctic • The Blue Man: Tales of Travel, Love and Coffee • Brief Encounters: Stories of Love, Sex & Travel • Chasing Rickshaws • The Last Grain Race • Lonely Planet Unpacked • Not the Only Planet: Science Fiction Travel Stories • Lonely Planet On the Edge • Sacred India • Travel with Children • Travel Photography: A Guide to Taking Better Pictures

FREE Lonely Planet Newsletters

We love hearing from you and think you'd like to hear from us.

Planet Talk

Our FREE quarterly printed newsletter is full of tips from travellers and anecdotes from Lonely Planet guidebook authors. Every issue is packed with up-to-date travel news and advice, and includes:

- a postcard from Lonely Planet co-founder Tony Wheeler
- a swag of mail from travellers
- a look at life on the road through the eyes of a Lonely Planet author
- topical health advice
- prizes for the best travel yarn
- news about forthcoming Lonely Planet events
- a complete list of Lonely Planet books and other titles

To join our mailing list, residents of the UK, Europe and Africa can email us at go@lonelyplanet.co.uk; residents of North and South America can email us at info@lonelyplanet.com; the rest of the world can email us at talk2us@lonelyplanet.com.au, or contact any Lonely Planet office.

Comet

Our FREE monthly email newsletter brings you all the latest travel news, features, interviews, competitions, destination ideas, travellers' tips & tales, Q&As, raging debates and related links. Find out what's new on the Lonely Planet Web site and which books are about to hit the shelves.

Subscribe from your desktop: www.lonelyplanet.com/comet

Index

Text

Boxed Text

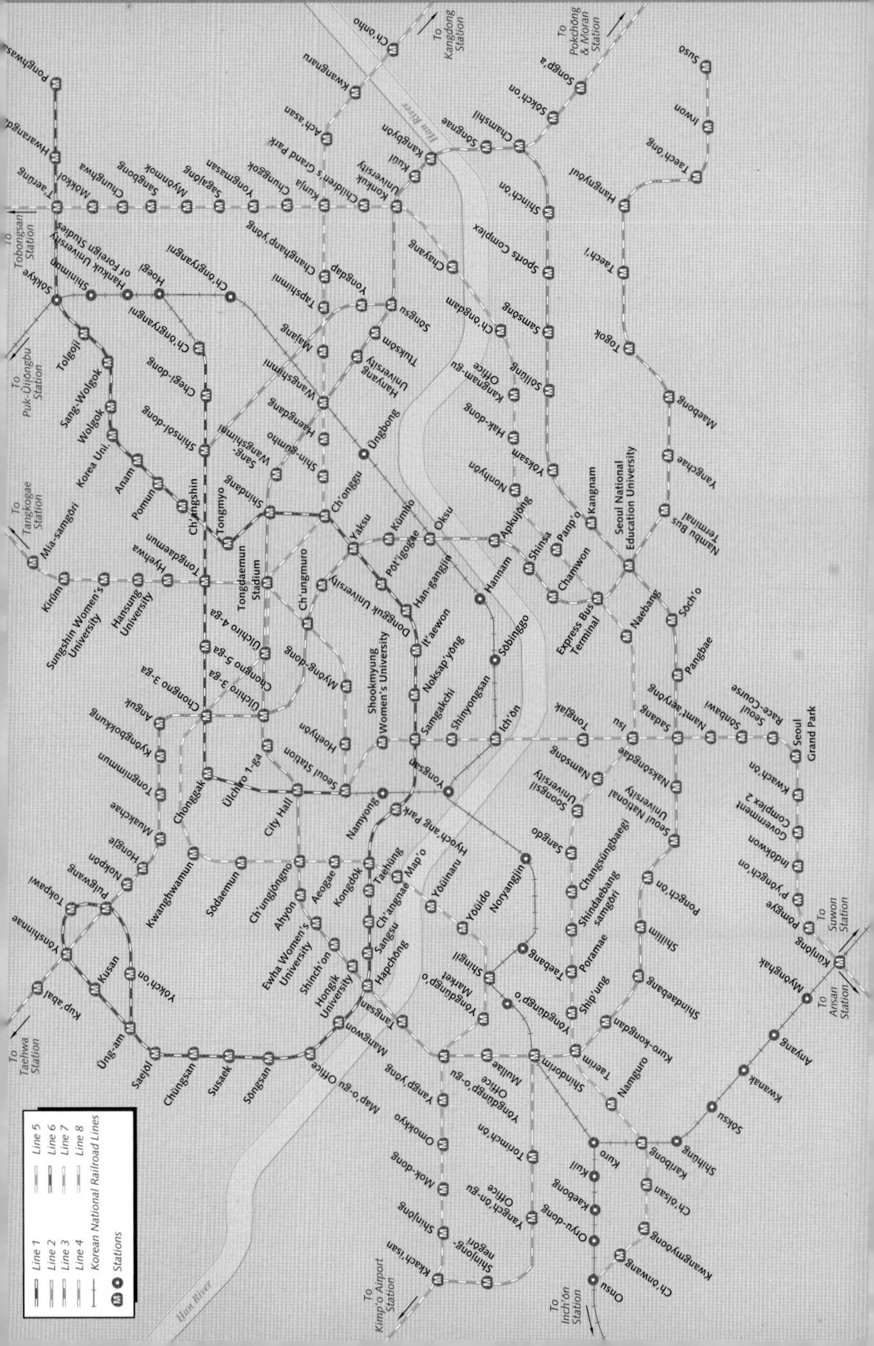
Line 1
Line 2
Line 3
Line 4
Line 5
Line 6
Line 7
Line 8
Korean National Railroad Lines
Stations
Han River
To Kangdong Station
To Pokchŏng & Moran Station
To Tobongsan Station
To Puk-Ŭijŏngbu Station
To Tangkogae Station
To Taehwa Station
To Kimp'o Airport Station
To Inch'ŏn Station
To Ansan Station
To Suwon Station
Ch'ŏnho
Kwangnaru
Ach'asan
Children's Grand Park
Kangbyŏn
Kuui
Konkuk University
Chamshil
Sŏngnae
Songp'a
Sŏkch'on
Suso
Irwon
Taech'ŏng
Hangnyŏul
Taech'i
Togok
Maebong
Yangjae
Nambu Bus Terminal
Seoul National Education University
Kangnam
Yŏksam
Sŏnnŭng
Samsŏng
Sports Complex
Shinch'ŏn
Chayang
Ch'ŏngdam
Kangnam-gu Office
Hak-dong
Nonhyŏn
Sinsa
Apkujŏng
Panp'o
Chamwon
Express Bus Terminal
Naebang
Sŏch'o
Pangbae
Sadang
Isu
Namt'aeryŏng
Sŏnbawi
Seoul Race-Course
Seoul Grand Park
Kwach'ŏn
Government Complex 2
Indŏkwon
P'yŏngch'on
Pŏmgye
Kŭmjŏng
Myŏnghak
Anyang
Kwanak
Sŏksu
Shihŭng
Kwangmyŏng
Ch'ŏlsan
Karibong
Kuro
Kuil
Kaebong
Oryu-dong
Onsu
Ch'ŏnwang
Namguro
Kuro-kongdan
Taerim
Shindaebang
Shillim
Pongch'ŏn
Seoul National University
Naksŏngdae
Namsŏng
Tongjak
Soongsil University
Sangdo
Changsŭngbaegi
Shindaebang samgŏri
Poramae
Ship'ung
Shindorim
Mullae
Yŏngdŭngp'o-gu Office
Yangp'yŏng
Omokkyo
Mok-dong
Shinjŏng
Kkach'isan
Shinjŏng-negŏri
Yangch'ŏn-gu Office
Torimch'ŏn
Yŏngdŭngp'o
Yŏngdŭngp'o Market
Shingil
Taebang
Noryangjin
Yŏŭido
Yŏŭinaru
Map'o
Kongdŏk
Hyoch'ang Park
Namyŏng
Yongsan
Ich'ŏn
Shinyongsan
Samgakchi
Noksap'yŏng
It'aewon
Han-gangjin
Hannam
Sŏbinggo
Oksu
Kŭmho
Yaksu
Pot'igogae
Tongguk University
Ch'ungmuro
Myŏng-dong
Hoehyŏn
Seoul Station
Shookmyung Women's University
Ŭlchiro 1-ga
City Hall
Chonggak
Chongno 3-ga
Ŭlchiro 3-ga
Chongno 5-ga
Ŭlchiro 4-ga
Tongdaemun Stadium
Tongdaemun
Hyehwa
Hansung University
Sungshin Women's University
Kirŭm
Mia-samgŏri
Anguk
Kyŏngbokkung
Tongnimmun
Muakchae
Hongje
Nokpŏn
Pulgwang
Tokpawi
Yŏnshinnae
Kusan
Kup'abal
Yŏkch'on
Ŭng-am
Saejŏl
Chŭngsan
Susaek
Sŏngsan
Map'o-gu Office
Mangwon
Hapchŏng
Tangsan
Sangsu
Ch'angnae
Kwangheungch'ang
Taehŭng
Hongik University
Shinch'on
Ewha Women's University
Ahyŏn
Aeogae
Ch'ungjŏngno
Sŏdaemun
Kwanghwamun
Ch'ŏnggu
Shindang
Tongmyo
Ch'angshin
Sang-Wangshimni
Shinsŏl-dong
Chegi-dong
Ch'ŏngnyangni
Hoegi
Hankuk University of Foreign Studies
Shinimun
Sŏkkye
Tolgoji
Sang-Wolgok
Wolgok
Korea Uni.
Anam
Pomun
Haengdang
Shin-gŭmho
Wangshimni
Hanyang University
Ŭngbong
Tuksŏm
Sŏngsu
Yongdap
Tapshimni
Majang
Changhanp'yŏng
Kunja
Chunggok
Yongmasan
Sagajŏng
Myŏnmok
Sangbong
Chunghwa
Mokkol
T'aerŭng
Hwarangdae
Ponghwasan

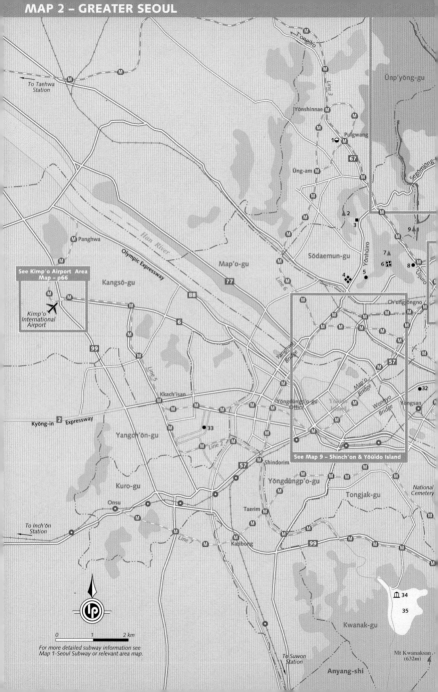

MAP 2 – GREATER SEOUL

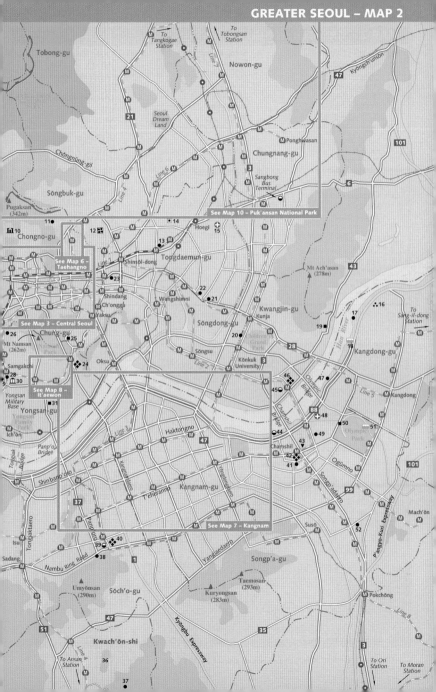

MAP 2 – GREATER SEOUL 서울

The War Memorial is in fact a museum, one of Seoul's best.

Guardian poles watch over visitors at Namsan.

Fresh chilli peppers *(goch'u)* dry in a back-street lane, central Seoul

An 'Astro Boy jungle gym' art piece punctuates Seoul's ambition to become a 'global city'.

MAP 3 – CENTRAL SEOUL

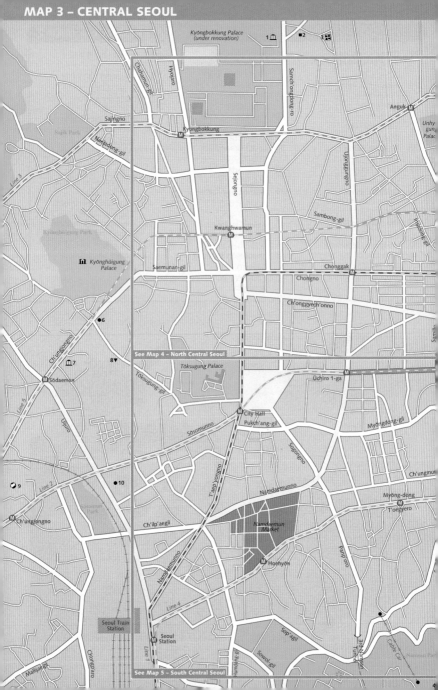

Kyŏngbokkung Palace
(under renovation)

1 ▥ ■2 3 ⊞

Samch'ongdong-ro

Chibanun-gil

Hyoja-ro

Anguk Ⓜ

Unhyŏ
gun
Palac

Sajngno

Naejadong-gil

M Kyŏngbokkung

Ujŏngguknno

Sajik Park

Sejongno

Line 3

Sambong-gil

Kwanghwamun Ⓜ

Kyŏnghŭigung Park

Insadong-gil

Kyŏnghŭigung
Palace

Saemunan-gil

Chonggak Ⓜ

Chongno

Ch'onggyech'onno

●6

Ch'ungjŏngno

Samill

See Map 4 – North Central Seoul

7

8▼

Tŏksugung Palace

Sŏdaemun Ⓜ

Tŏksugung-gil

Ⓜ

Ŭchiro 1-ga

Line 5

Ŭiro

Sŏsomunno

Myŏngdong-gil

Ⓜ City Hall

Pukch'ang-gil

Sogongno

●9

Line 2

●10

Saemun Park

T'aep'yŏngno

Ch'ilp'aegil

Namdaemunno

Myŏng-dong Ⓜ

Ch'ungmul

Myŏng-dong

T'oegyero

Namdaemun
Market

Namdaemunno

Ⓜ Ch'ungjŏngno

Namdaemunno

Ⓜ Hoehyŏn

P'anp'aro

Line 4

Sop'agil

Seoul Train
Station

Seoul
Station Ⓜ

3rd Namsan
Tunnel

Cable Car

Namsan Pa

Malli jae-gil

Ch'ŏngp'aro

Line 1

Sowol-gil

See Map 5 – South Central Seoul

Piwon
(Secret Garden)

Ch'angdŏkkung
Palace

Ch'anggyŏnggung
Palace

Line 4

aehwagwan-gil

Yulgongno

Chongmyo
(Royal Shrine)

Ch'angdŏkkung-ro

See Map 6 – Taehangno

4 ●

Taehangno

Yulgongno

M Chongno 3-ga

5

P

Chongno 5-ga   ● 15   Tongdaemun

Line 1   M   16 ■

17 ■

Tongdaemun
Market

14   i

Tongdaemun Chain
Store

M Chongno 3-ga

Chongno   12 ●   13

● 18

Hung-in
Market

11   22 ●   21 ●

24 ■

Hunginmuno

19
Tongdaemun
Stadium

Tonghwamuno

25

20
Tongdaemun
Stadium

Ŭlchiro   Ŭlchiro 4-ga   23

M Ŭlchiro 3-ga   M   M Tongdaemun
Stadium

Sup'yogak-gil   Marŏnnaegil   Chungbu
Market   Line 2

26

27 ■   Marunnaegil   Tongdaemun Stadium   M

Paegogaegil

28   Hunjŏngmuno   Ch'ŏnggyech'ŏngno-gil   Line 5

T'oegyero

M   Tonghoro

Ch'ŏnggyesye   Ch'ŏngmuro   Tonghoro

29

30 ▼   33

31   Dongguk University   M

32 ■

Changch'ung
Park

Dongguk University   34   Line 3

40

39   35

1st Namsan
Tunnel

Namsan'gongwŏn-gil

Tunnel   38 ●   LP   Yaksu M

37 ●   ■ 36   0   150   300 m   Tasanno

2nd Namsan
Tunnel   Underground Arcade

MAP 3 – CENTRAL SEOUL 서울중심부

PLACES TO STAY
- 2 The Nest
  네스트
- 17 Eastern Hotel
  이스턴호텔
- 24 Traveller's A Motel
  A모텔
- 27 Poongjeon Hotel
  풍전호텔
- 32 Sofitel Ambassador Hotel; Kŭmsujang
  소피텔앰배서더호텔
- 35 Shilla Hotel
  호텔신라
- 36 Tower Hotel
  타워호텔

PLACES TO EAT
- 8 Ipanema Brazilian Restaurant
  브라질 식당
- 30 Korea House
  한국의집

OTHER
- 1 National Folk Museum
  국립민속박물관
- 3 Lotus Lantern Buddhist Centre
  연등 회관
- 4 Royal Asiatic Society (RAS)
  로얄아시아협회
- 5 Chongmyo Plaza
  종묘시민광장
- 6 Munhwa Ilbo Hall
  문화체육관
- 7 Agricultural Museum
  농업박물관
- 9 French Embassy
  불란서대사관
- 10 Hoam Art Hall
  호암미술관
- 11 Seun Arcade
  세운상가
- 12 Yejidong Watch & Jewellery Alley
  예지동 금 은
  시계도매상가

It may not look like much from down here, but the view from Seoul Tower is worth the ascent.

Kim Ku fought for Korean independence from Japanese colonialism and US postwar tutelage.

King Sejong is best remembered for creating *han'gŭl*, the ingenious Korean alphabet.

A monument to infinite industrial expansion –
or to getting screwed by high commerce?

MAP 4 – NORTH CENTRAL SEOUL

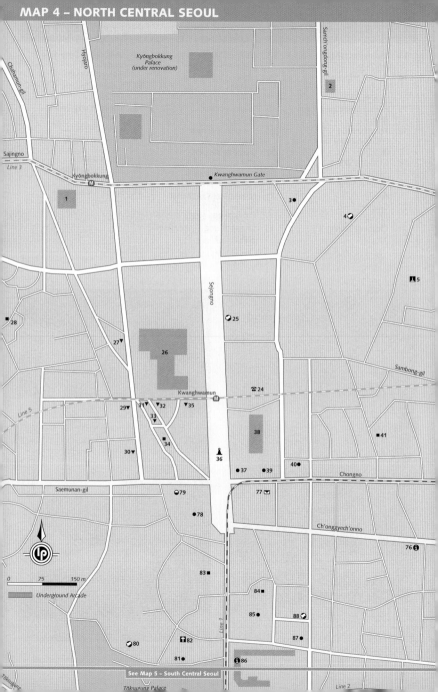

Chaŏmun-gil

Hyoja-ro

Kyŏngbokkung
Palace
(under renovation)

Samch'ŏngdong-gil

2

Sajingno

Line 3

Kyŏngbokkung Ⓜ

● Kwanghwamun Gate

1

3 ●

4 ↺

Sejongno

⚿ 5

● 28

25 ↺

Sambong-gil

27 ▼

26

Line 5

Kwanghwamun Ⓜ

☎ 24

29 ▼ 31 ▼ ▼ 32   **▼ 35**

33 ▼

38

30 ▼

34 ■

41 ■

36 ⚑

● 37   ● 39

40 ●

Chongno

Saemunan-gil

79 ↺

77 ☒

● 78

Ch'onggyech'ŏnno

76 ⓘ

0   75   150 m

83 ■

84 ■

85 ●

88 ↺

80 ↺

82 🏳

87 ●

81 ●

ⓘ 86

Line 1

Tŏksugung
Palace

See Map 5 – South Central Seoul

Tŏksugung Palace

Line 2

To Ch'angdŏkkung
Palace

To Ch'anggyŏnggung
Palace

Yulgongno

Tonhwamunno

Anguk
●12

11

Unhyŏn-gung
Palace

13 ■

14 ■

15 ■

Chongmyo
(Royal Shrine)

16 ■

Ujonggungno

10 ■   ■ 9   ■ 8

▼ 6   ▼ 7

22 ▼

▼ 21

Insadong-gil

23 ▼

T'aehwagwan-gil

19 ■ 18 ■

■ 17

20

Line 5

Chongno 3-ga

52 ●

42 ▶

▼ 53

44 ■

54 ■

58 ●

To
Chongmyo
Plaza

60 ●

■ 49

■ 48   ■ 50

▼ 47   ▼ 51

55

56 ▼ 57 ▼   59 ▼

Line 1

Chongno 3-ga

Chonggak

▼ 43

45 ■

46

●74   ▼73   ●71   68   67 ▼   ▼65   ■64

69 ▼

72 ▼

●70

●66

63 ●

●61

62 ■

5

Tonhwamunno

89 ✦

Samilno

Supyodanggil

Line 3

90 ▼

Line 2

See Map 5 – South Central Seoul

Ŭlchiro 1-ga

Ŭlchiro 3-ga

MAP 4 – NORTH CENTRAL SEOUL

PLACES TO STAY

8 Shingung-jang Yŏgwan
신궁장여관

9 Kwanhun-jang Yŏgwan
관훈장여관

10 Hanhŭng-jang Yŏgwan
한흥장여관

13 Munhwa Yŏgwan
문화여관

14 Motel Jongrowon
종로원여관

15 Seahwa-jang Hotel
세화장여관

16 Sun Ch'ang Yŏgwan
순창여관

17 Hwasŏng-jang Yŏgwan
화성장여관

18 Yong Jin Yŏgwan
용진여관

19 Emerald Hotel
애머랄드호텔

28 Inn Sung Do
성도여관

34 Inn Daewon
대원여관

41 Seoul Hotel
서울관광호텔

44 Taewon Yŏgwan
대원여관

45 YMCA
와이엠씨에이

48 Chongno Yŏgwan
종로여관

49 Wongap Yŏgwan
원갑여관

50 Insŏng Yŏgwan
인성여관

62 Central Hotel
쎈츄럴호텔

83 Koreana Hotel
코리아나호텔

84 New Kukje & New Seoul Hotels
뉴국제호텔,
뉴서울관광호텔

PLACES TO EAT

6 Youngbin Garden
영빈가든

7 Coffee Gallery Restaurant
커피갤러리

21 Arirang Restaurant; The Old Teahouse
옛찻집다실

22 Sanch'on
산촌식당

23 Cafe Little India; Paris Baguette
각은인디아, 파리바게뜨

27 Tonghwaru Chinese Restaurant
동화루반점

29 Venezia Italian Spaghetti
베네치아

30 Koryŏ Supermarket
고려쇼핑

31 Paris Baguette
파리바게뜨

32 Sapporo Restaurant
삿뽀로우동

33 Tongsŏnggak Chinese Restaurant
동성각반점

35 Kabongru Chinese Restaurant
가봉루반점

43 Pizza Hut
피자헛

47 Subway Sandwiches
써브웨이

51 Baskin Robbins; Dunkin' Donuts
배스킨라빈스

53 Doutor Coffee Shop
도토루

56 Seoul Kimbap
서울김밥

57 Chongno Kimbap
종로김밥

59 Pizza Hut
피자헛

65 Burger King; Tower Records
버거킹, 타워레코드

67 Hardee's; KFC
하디스, 케이에프씨

68 Shinp'ouri Shikp'um Korean Fastfood
신포우리식품

69 Chongno Kimbap
종로김밥

72 TGI Friday's Restaurant
야! 금요일이다

73 Popeye's Chicken
파파이스

90 Pan Korea
판코리아

OTHER

1 Immigration Office; KYHA
적선현대빌딩

2 French Cultural Centre
불란서문화원

3 Net House
네트하우스

4 Japanese Embassy
일본대사관

5 Chogyesa Temple
조계사

11 Anguk Post Office
안국우체국

12 Japanese Cultural Centre
일본문화원

20 Nakwon Elevated Arcade
낙원상가

24 Kwanghwamun Telephone Office
광화문전화국

25 US Embassy
미국대사관

26 Sejong Cultural Centre
세종문화회관

36 Yi Sun-shin Statue
이순신장군동상

37 Pigak Pavilion
비각

38 Kyobo Building
교보빌딩

39 Kyobo Book Centre
교보문고

40 Net Cyber Cafe
넷카페

42 Chung-ang Map & Atlas
중앙지

46 Chonggak Underground Arcade
종각지하상가

52 Hollywood Cinema
허리우드극장

54 Pagoda Cinema
파고다극장

55 T'apkol Post Office
탑골우체국

58 Picadilly Cinema
피카디리극장

60 Dansŏngsa Cinema
단성사극장

61 Seoul Cinema Town
서울시네마타운

63 Cine Plaza Cinema
시네프라자극장

64 Musicland
뮤직랜드

66 T-Zone
티존

70 Core Art Hall Cinema
코아아트홀

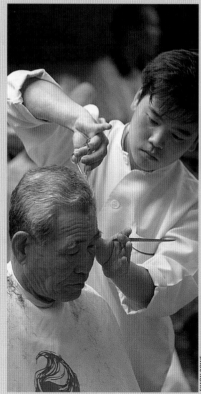

A senior enjoys a free Sunday clipping at T'apkol Park.

Korea's older citizens are living archives of the country's turbulent transformations.

MAP 5 – SOUTH CENTRAL SEOUL

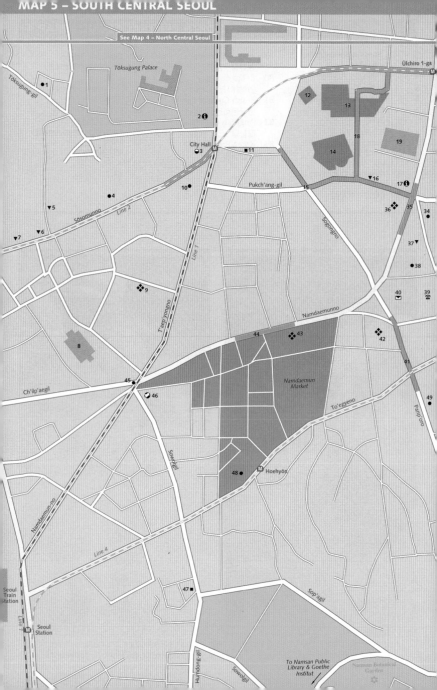

See Map 4 – North Central Seoul

Tŏksugung Palace

Ülchiro 1-ga

Tŏksugung-gil

● 1

2 ●

City Hall
● 3

■ 11

12 ◆

13

18

14

19

Pukch'ang-gil

15

▼ 16

17

36

35

34 ●

10 ●

4 ●

Sŏsomunno

Line 2

▼ 5

Sŏgongno

37 ▼

38 ●

▼ 7

▼ 6

Line 1

40

39

9

T'aep'yŏngno

Namdaemunno

8

44

43

42

41

45

Namdaemun
Market

49

Ch'ilp'aegil

46

To'egyeno

Pamp'oro

Sowŏlgil

Namdaemunno

48 ●

Hoehyŏn

Line 4

Seoul
Train
Station

Seoul
Station

47 ■

Sop'agil

Hunhdong-gil

Sowŏlgil

To Namsan Public
Library & Goethe
Institut

Namsan Botanical
Garden

See Map 4 – North Central Seoul

Samilio

Line 2

Ŭlchiro 3-ga

● 20

Ŭlchiro

25

Sup'yodangil

Marŏnnaegil

21 ■   22 ▼

24 ●

● 26

23

27 ●

Myŏngdong-gil

Ch'ŏnggye (Elevated Road)

Tonhwamunno

Line 3

● 32

⊘ 33

✦ 31

✝ 28

■ 30

Ch'ungmuro

29 ■

Line 4

T'oegyero

Myŏng-dong
Ⓜ

52 ■

■ 53

■ 50

51 ■

Underground Arcade

Sop'a-gil

54 ●

55 ●

0   75   150 m

3rd Namsan Tunnel

Cable Car

Namsan Park

1st Namsan Tunnel

MAP 5 – SOUTH CENTRAL SEOUL

PLACES TO STAY

11 Plaza Hotel; Deli Plaza
서울프라자호텔
12 President Hotel
프레지던트호텔
13 Lotte Hotel
호텔롯데
14 Westin Chosun Hotel;
O'Kim's;
Compass Rose
조선호텔
21 Metro Hotel
메트로호텔
23 Royal Hotel
서울로얄호텔
29 King Sejong Hotel;
Firenze
세종호텔
30 Savoy Hotel
사보이호텔
47 Hilton Hotel; Pharaoh's
힐튼호텔
50 New Oriental Hotel
뉴오리엔탈호텔

51 Pacific Hotel
퍼시픽호텔
52 Prince Hotel
프린스호텔
53 Astoria Hotel
아스토리아호텔

PLACES TO EAT

5 Paejae Chinese
Restaurant
배재반점
6 Koryŏ Ginseng Chicken
고려삼계탕
7 Kukil Chinese Restaurant
극일반점
16 Tony Roma's Restaurant
토니로맑
22 TGI Friday's Restaurant;
OK Corral;
금요일이다
37 Shillawon Chinese
Restaurant
신라원

OTHER

1 Chŏngdong Theatre
정동극장
2 Tourist Information Booth
관광안내소
3 Airport Bus Stop
정류장 (공항)
4 Korean Air (KAL)
대한항공
8 Chamber of Commerce &
Industry
대한상공회의소
9 Samsung Underground
Plaza
삼성프라자
10 International Union
Travel Service
국제연합여행사
15 Sogong Underground
Arcade
소공 지하상가
17 Tourist Information Booth
관광안내소

SIMON ROWE

Herbs displayed outside a Korean medicine (hanyak) shop – at least here you can be sure the pharmaceuticals you're ingesting were once organic ...

18 Lotte Underground
    Arcade
    롯데 지하상가
19 Lotte Department Store
    롯데백화점
20 Ŭlchi Book Centre
    을지서적
24 Chung-ang Cinema
    중앙극장
25 Ŭlchiro Underground
    Arcade
    을지로 지하상가
26 Myŏngbo Plaza Cinema
    명보극장
27 Scala Cinema
    스카라극장
28 Myŏng-dong Cathedral
    명동성당
31 Utoo Zone Department
    Store
    유투존
32 Korea Cinema
    코리아극장

33 Chinese Embassy
    중국 대사관
34 Myŏng-dong Cinema
    명동극장
35 Myŏng-dong
    Underground Arcade
    명동 지하상가
36 Metro Midopa
    Department Store
    미도파 백화점
38 Chinese Book Store
    중국문고
39 Central Telephone Office
    중앙전화국
40 Central Post Office (CPO)
    중앙우체국
41 Hoehyŏn Underground
    Arcade
    회현 지하상가
42 Shinsegae Department
    Store
    신세계 백화점

43 Saerona Department
    Store
    새로나 백화점
44 Namdaemun
    Underground Arcade
    남대문 지하상가
45 Namdaemun
    (Sungnyemun) Gate
    남대문 (숭례문)
46 German & Irish Embassies
    독일대사관,
    아일랜드대사관
48 Backpacking Equipment
    Shops
    등산 장비상가
49 Asiana Airlines
    아시아나항공
54 Diplomatic Club
    외교구락부
55 Namsan Cable Car
    Station
    케이블카

Another shop displays its extensive range of *paem sul*, or snake wines.

MAP 6 – TAEHANGNO

Uamgil

To Seoul Dream Land

Tongsomunno

Line 4

■ 1

2

3 ✉

4 ▼

8 ⟨⟩

17

16

5 ●

6 🏨

7

9 ▼

● 15

Ch'anggyŏnggungno

21

10 ▼

▼ 14

▼ 13

12 ▼

▼ 11

To Ch'anggyŏn-gung Palace

▼ 18

🏨 19

▼ 20

🏨 21

P

🅿

▼ 23

Hyehwa M

● 24

▼ 22

🏨 26

● 25

▼ 27

▼ 28

Marronnier Park

29

✚ 30

● 31

Taehangno (Culture & Art Street)

32

☎ 33

20

To Chongmyo

To Tongdaemun (East Gate)

Line 4

0   50   100 m

Suwon is now basically a suburb of Seoul, but its well preserved city walls and gates are a reminder of the town's former autonomy and importance.

MAP 7 – KANGNAM

Kangbyŏn Expressway

47

Line 7

Tuksŏmgil

77

Tuksŏm
Riverside Park

14

Han River

Yŏngdong Bridge

13

12

15

Olympic Expressway

Tosandaero

Ch'ŏngdam
Park

Ch'ŏngdam

Haktongno

Ch'ongdam Bridge

88

36   37

Seoul Sports
Complex

38

Pŏngŭng
Park

35

41

40   39

Line 2

Pangnunsaro

54

42

43

Samsong Bridge

Sports Complex

Asian Park

Samsung
Park

44

47

45   46   Samsŏng

49

52

48

53

Teheranno

Sŏllŭng

50

51

Yongdongdaero

Yoksamno

Samsŏngno

T'anch'on 2 Bridge

47

72

Hangnyŏul

Taech'i

Yŏngdong 5gyo

Togoktong-gil

Togok

99

Nambusunhwanno   Yŏngdong 5gyo

Line 3

Taech'ŏng

Line 3

0   250   500 m

MAP 7 – KANGNAM 강남

PLACES TO STAY

13 Elle Lui Hotel
엘루이호텔

15 Riviera Hotel
호텔리베라

18 Sunshine Hotel; Tony Roma's
선샤인호텔, 토니로마스

20 Youngdong Hotel
영동호텔

21 Samhwa Hotel
삼화호텔

29 Dynasty Hotel
호텔다이너스티

30 New Hilltop Hotel
뉴힐탑호텔

32 YMCA Kangnam Branch
와이엠씨에이 강남지회

33 Amiga Hotel
호텔아미가

46 Inter-Continental Hotel
호텔인터컨티넨탈

53 Green Grass Hotel
그린그래스호텔

54 New World Hotel
뉴월드호텔

55 Seoul Renaissance Hotel
서울르네상스호텔

56 Samjung Hotel; OK Corral
삼정호텔

57 Novotel Ambassador Hotel
노보텔앰배서더호텔

58 Ritz-Carlton Hotel
리츠칼튼서울호텔

PLACES TO EAT

4 Chili's Grill & Bar
칠리

5 Uno Chicago Bar & Grill
우노

7 McDonald's
맥도날드

9 Bennigan's Chicago
베니간스

10 Coco's California Restaurant
코코스

12 Hard Rock Cafe
하드 락 까페

16 TGI Friday's
아! 금요일이다

27 Outback Steak House
아웃백

47 Bennigan's Seattle & Food Court
베니간스

49 Ponderosa Steak House
판다로사

50 Coco's California Restaurant
코코스

51 Hanmiri Restaurant
한미리

52 Carne Station
까르네스테이션

61 Paris Baguette
파리바게뜨

65 TGI Friday's
금요일이다

66 Carne Station
까르네스테이션

OTHER

1 UN Village
유엔 단지

2 Hyundai Department Store
현대백화점

3 Shinsa Telephone Office
신사전화국

6 Nightlife Area
유흥가

8 Galleria Department Store
갤러리아백화점(서관)

11 Kinema Cinema
키네마극장

14 Ttuksŏm Ferry Terminal
뚝섬선착장

17 Cine House Cinema
씨네하우스극장

A woodworker preserves his craft at the Korean Folk Village.

Given the abundance (and variety) of fruit piled up for sale everywhere, scurvy is clearly not a problem in contemporary Korea.

SIMON ROWE

MAP 8 – IT'AEWON

MAP 8 – IT'AEWON 이태원

PLACES TO STAY

1 Ihwa-jang Yŏgwan
이화장여관
15 Grand Hyatt Hotel
그랜드하얏트호텔
19 Hamilton Hotel; Chohung Bank
해밀턴호텔, 조흥은행
26 It'aewon Hotel
이태원호텔
31 Mido Hotel; Domino's Pizza
미도여관, 도미노피자
32 Hannam Yŏgwan
한남여관
34 Hilltop Motel
힐탑모텔
44 Kwangsŏn-jang Yŏgwan
광선장여관
49 Crown Hotel
크라운호텔

PLACES TO EAT

2 McDonald's
맥도날드
3 Pizza Hut
피자 헛
5 Churchills Restaurant
처칠즈 레스토랑
9 Paris Baguette; Baskin Robbins
파리바게뜨, 배스킨라빈스
11 Moghul Restaurant
파키스탄 전문 음식점
12 La Cucina
라쿠지나
14 Jeil Deli
제일 델리

16 Le Petite France
라 쁘띠 프랑스
17 Chalet Swiss Restaurant
스위스식 산장
18 It'aewon Restaurant
이태원 갈비
27 Thai Orchid Restaurant; Funky Mega Night Club
타이오키드
29 New York Pizza
뉴욕 피자
30 Deutches Haus
독일 호프
38 Manhattan Hof
맨하탄 호프
39 Inca Restaurant
잉카
41 Burger King
버거킹
46 Taj Mahal
타지마할

OTHER

4 Post Office
이태원1동우체국
6 Korea Exchange Bank
외환은행
7 All That Jazz
댓 재즈
8 Cyberia Cafe; Fox'N Goose Pub
사이베리아
10 Tourist Information Booth
관광안내소
13 Argentine Embassy
아르헨티나 대사관
20 Casablanca & Black Jack Club
카사블랑카, 블랙잭 클럽

21 Ruby's Club
루비즈 클럽
22 Hollywood Club
허리우드 클럽
23 Woodstock; Mug Club & Prohibition
우드스탁
24 International Clinic
국제의원
25 NASA Disco
나사 디스코
28 Commercial Bank of Korea
한국상업은행
33 Club Viagra
클럽 비아그라
35 Gulliver Disco
걸리버
36 Stomper Bar
스톰퍼 바
37 Grand Ole Opry
그랜드 올 오프리
40 Cowboy Club
카우보이 클럽
42 Nashville Bar & Restaurant
내슈빌 클럽
43 Giorgio's Club
죠지오즈 클`
45 Bus Stop (Nos 23 & 401)
정류장 (23 & 401)
47 King Club
킹 클럽
48 Korean Islam Mosque
이슬람교중앙서원

Ginseng *(insam)* is so abundant, it's virtually a weed at Namdaemun Market stalls.

RICHARD I'ANSON

MAP 9 – SHINCH'ON & YŎUIDO ISLAND

MAP 9 – SHINCH'ON & YŎUIDO ISLAND 신촌,여의도

PLACES TO STAY

2 Seokyo Hotel
서교호텔
31 Mirabeau Hotel
미라보호텔
33 Yŏgwan Area
숙박 지역
47 Cheil Hotel
제일호텔
56 Holiday Inn
홀리데이인서울
59 Manhattan Hotel
맨하탄호텔
62 Yŏuido Hotel
여의도호텔

PLACES TO EAT

1 TGI Friday's
야! 금요일이다
3 Pizza Hut
피자헛
4 Ponderosa Steak House
판다로사
6 Popeye's Chicken; Burger King
파파이, 버거킹
7 Khan Antique Pub
칸
10 Coco's California Restaurant
코코스
19 Ch'unch'on Chicken; Rolling Stone Bar
춘천집, 롤링스톤
21 Kenny Roger's Roasters Restaurant
케니로저스
22 La Vecchia Stazione
스타찌오네
24 Subway Sandwiches
써브웨이
25 Jessica's Pizzeria
제시카 피자리아
26 Burger King
버거킹
27 Pizza Hut
피자헛
28 Amato Pizza Buffet
피자부페
29 Bennigan's New York
베니간스
34 McDonald's
맥도날드
36 KFC
캔터키 프라이 치킨
44 Subway Sandwiches
써브웨이
50 Solomon Chinese Restaurant
솔로몬반점

OTHER

5 Be Bop Jazz Club
비밥
8 Saab Disco I
싸브 디스코
9 Bonanza Hole
보낸자호을
11 Macondo Bar
마콘도
12 Shinch'on Telephone Office
신촌전화국
13 First Saint Jesus Church
말일성도예수교회
14 Bar 33
바삼십삼
15 Club Savage; The Doors
사베지 앤, 도어스 클럽
16 Woodstock
우드스탁
17 Twenty Something
투웨니썸씽

Traditional village life is beautifully recreated in the Korean Folk Village.

RICHARD I'ANSON

A lattice-work window lights up a stroll through an old Seoul neighbourhood.

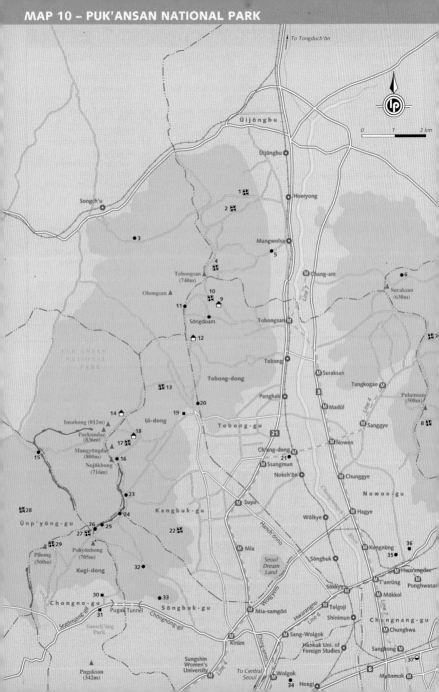

MAP 10 – PUK'ANSAN NATIONAL PARK

To Tongduch'ŏn

Ûijŏngbu

Ûijŏngbu

Hoeryong

Songch'u

1

2

Mangwolsa

3

5

Chang-am

Suraksan
(638m)

4

6

Tobongsan
(740m)

Obongsan

10 9

11

Sŏngdoam

Tobongsan

12

Tobong

PUK'ANSAN
NATIONAL
PARK

13

Tobong-dong

Suraksan

Tangkogae

Pulamsan
(508m)

14

20

19

Insubong (812m)

Ui-dong

Paekundae
(836m)

18

Tobong-gu

Panghak

Madul

8

17

Mangyŏngdae
(800m)

15

16

Ch'ang-dong

Sanggye

Nojŏkbong
(716m)

21

Ssangmun

Nowon

Nokch'ŏn

Chunggye

Nowon-gu

23

28

Suyu

Hagye

Ûnp'yŏng-gu

24

Kangbuk-gu

Wŏlgye

26 25

29

27

22

Kongnŭng

36

Pibong
(560m)

Pohyŏnbong
(705m)

Mia

Songbuk

35

Hwarangdae

Kugi-dong

32

Seoul
Dream
Land

T'aerŭng

Ponghwasan

30

33

Sŏngbuk-gu

Sŏkkye

Mŏkkol

Chungnang-gu

31

Pugak Tunnel

Chŏngnŭng-gil

Mia-samgŏri

Tolgoji

Chunghwa

Samch'ŏng
Park

Segŏmjŏng-gil

Shinimun

Hwarango

Sang-Wolgok

Sanggong

Pugaksan
(342m)

Kirŭm

Hankuk Uni. of
Foreign Studies

37

Sungshin
Women's
University

To Central
Seoul

Wolgok

Myŏnmok

34

Hoegi

MAP 10 – PUK'ANSAN NATIONAL PARK 북한산국립공원

PLACES TO STAY

9 Tobong Hut
도봉산장
12 Pomun Hut
보문산장
14 Insu Hut
인수산장
18 U-i Hut
우이산장
19 Green Park Hotel
그린파크호텔
30 Pugak Park Hotel
북악파크호텔
31 Olympia Hotel
올림피아호텔

OTHER

1 Sŏkch'ŏnsa Temple
석천사
2 Hoeryongsa Temple
호룡사
3 Songch'u Resort
송추유원지
4 Mangwolsa Temple
망월사
5 Changsuwon
장수원
6 Naewonam Hermitage
내원암
7 Hŭngguksa Temple
흥국사
8 Pulamsa Temple
불암사
10 Ch'ŏnch'uksa Temple
천축사
11 Kwanŭmam Hermitage
관음암
13 Yongdŏksa Temple
용덕사
15 Taesŏmun Gate
대서문
16 Yongammun Gate
용암문
17 Tosŏnsa Temple
도선사
20 U-i-dong Resort
우이동유원지
21 E-Mart
이마트
22 Hwagyesa Temple
화계사
23 Taedongmun Gate
대동문
24 Pogukmun Gate
보국문
25 Taesŏngmun Gate
대성문
26 Taenammun Gate
대남문
27 Munsusa Temple
문수사
28 Chingwansa Temple
진관사
29 Sŭnggasa Temple
승가사
32 Chŏngnŭng Resort
정릉유원지
33 Kukmin University
국민대학교
34 Hongnŭng Arboretum
산림청 수목원
35 Military Academy;
Museum
륙군사관학교
36 Seoul Women's
University
서울여자대학교
37 Sangbong Bus Terminal
상봉시외버스터미널
38 Yongma Land
용마자연공원

Puk'ansan shines in early evening.

MARTIN MOOS

MAP LEGEND

BOUNDARIES

- ━ ━ ━ ━ International
- ━ ━ ━ ━ Provincial
- ━ ━ ━ Disputed

HYDROGRAPHY

- Coastline
- River, Creek
- Lake
- Intermittent Lake
- Salt Lake
- Canal
- Spring, Rapids
- Waterfalls
- Swamp

ROUTES & TRANSPORT

- Expressway
- Highway
- Major Road
- Minor Road
- Unsealed Road
- City Expressway
- City Highway
- City Road
- City Street, Lane
- Arcade
- Tunnel
- Train Route & Station
- Subway & Station
- Tramway
- Cable Car or Chairlift
- Walking Track
- Walking Tour
- Ferry Route

AREA FEATURES

- Building
- Park, Gardens
- Cemetery
- Market
- Hotel
- Urban Area

MAP SYMBOLS

✪	**CAPITAL**	National Capital		✈	Airport	
◉	**CAPITAL**	Provincial Capital		✇	Bank	
●	**CITY**	City		⚲	Beach	
●	**Town**	Town		⚲	Bird Sanctuary	
●	**Village**	Village			Buddhist Temple	
○		Point of Interest			Church	
					Cliff or Escarpment	
■		Place to Stay		⊘	Embassy	
⚠		Camping Ground			Fortress or City Wall	
		Caravan Park		⊕	Hospital	
⌂		Hut or Chalet		▮	Monument or Statue	
				☾	Mosque	
▼		Place to Eat		▲	Mountain or Hill	
▮		Pub or Bar		⛫	Museum	
				‡	Pagoda	
				▣	Parking	
				)(	Pass	
				⚑	Petrol Station	
				✉	Post Office	
				∴	Ruins	
				❖	Shopping Centre	
				⚡	Ski Field	
				血	Stately Home	
				⊟	Swimming Pool	
				☎	Telephone	
				▫	Tomb	
				❶	Tourist Information	
				●	Transport	

Note: not all symbols displayed above appear in this book

LONELY PLANET OFFICES

Australia
Locked Bag 1, Footscray, Victoria 3011
☎ 03 8379 8000 fax 03 8379 8111
email: talk2us@lonelyplanet.com.au

UK
10a Spring Place, London NW5 3BH
☎ 020 7428 4800 fax 020 7428 4828
email: go@lonelyplanet.co.uk

USA
150 Linden St, Oakland, CA 94607
☎ 510 893 8555 TOLL FREE: 800 275 8555
fax 510 893 8572
email: info@lonelyplanet.com

France
1 rue du Dahomey, 75011 Paris
☎ 01 55 25 33 00 fax 01 55 25 33 01
email: bip@lonelyplanet.fr
www.lonelyplanet.fr

World Wide Web: www.lonelyplanet.com *or* AOL keyword: lp
Lonely Planet Images: lpi@lonelyplanet.com.au